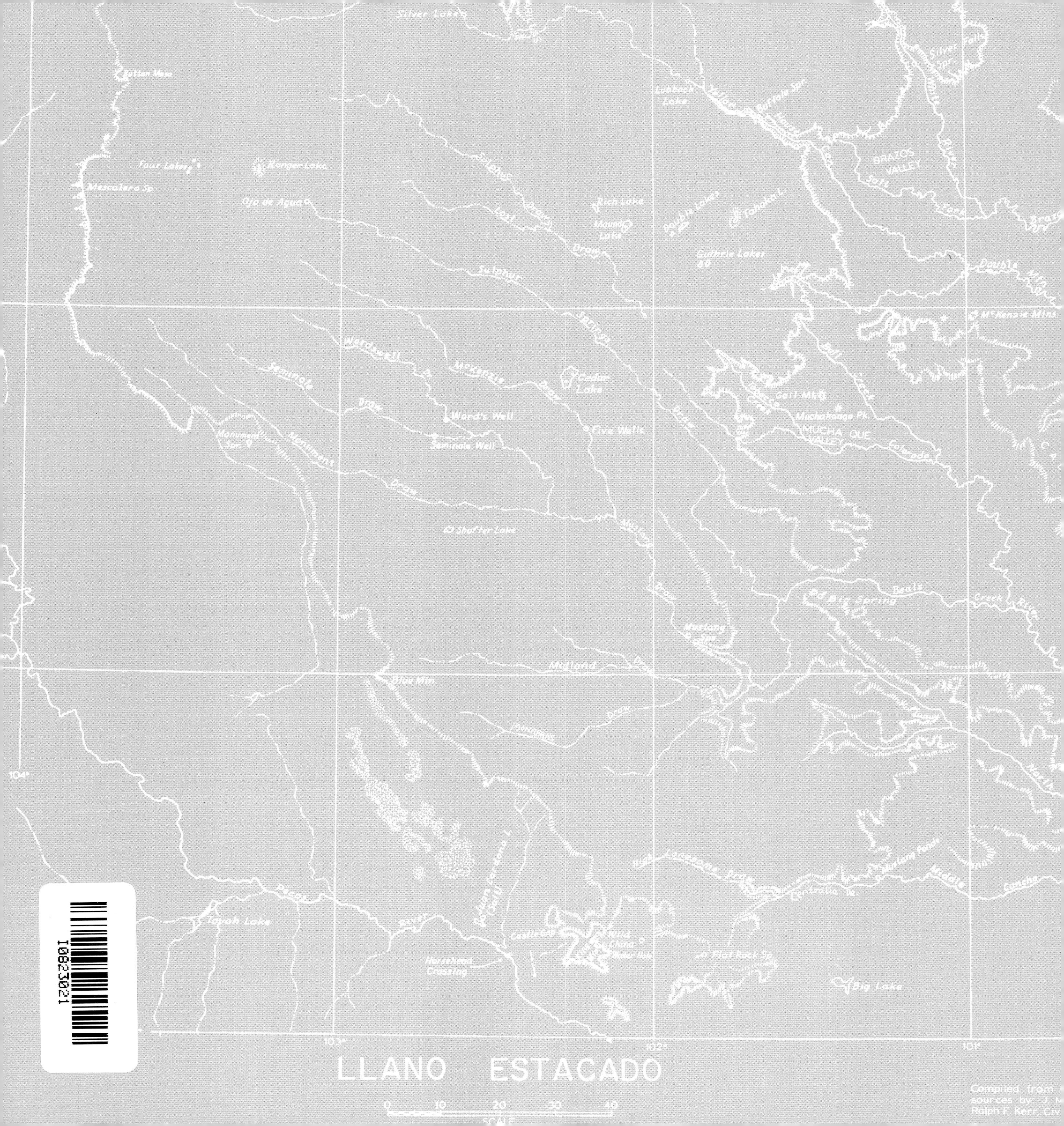

LLANO ESTACADO
0
10
20
30
40
SCALE
Compiled from
sources by: J. N
Ralph F. Kerr, Civ
101°
102°
103°
104°
Silver Lake
Button Mesa
Four Lakes
Ranger Lake
Mescalero Sp.
Ojo de Agua
Sulphur Draw
Lost Draw
Rich Lake
Mound Lake
Double Lakes
Tahoka L.
Guthrie Lakes
Lubbock Lake
Yellow House Can.
Buffalo Spr.
Silver Falls Spr.
White River
BRAZOS VALLEY
Salt Fork
Double Mtn
McKenzie Mtns.
Sulphur Springs
Wardswell Dr.
Seminole Draw
McKenzie Draw
Cedar Lake
Ward's Well
Five Wells
Seminole Well
Monument Spr.
Monument Draw
Shafter Lake
Mustang Draw
Bull Creek
Tobacco Creek
Gall Mt.
Muchakooga Pk.
MUCHA QUE VALLEY
Colorado
Big Spring
Beals Creek
River
Mustang Sps.
Midland Draw
Blue Mtn.
Monahans Draw
North
Juan Cordona L. (Salt)
High Lonesome Draw
Mustang Ponds
Middle Concho
Centralia Dr.
Pecos River
Toyah Lake
Castle Gap
Wild China Water Hole
Flat Rock Sp.
Horsehead Crossing
Big Lake
I0823021

VOICE IN THE AMERICAN WEST

Andy Wilkinson, Series Editor

ALSO IN THE SERIES

Cowboy's Lament: A Life on the Open Range
Frank Maynard; edited by Jim Hoy

In My Father's House: A Memoir of Polygamy
Dorothy Allred Solomon

Rightful Place
Amy Hale Auker

A Sweet Separate Intimacy: Women Writers of the American Frontier, 1800–1922
Susan Cummins Miller, editor

Texas Dance Halls: A Two-Step Circuit
Gail Folkins and J. Marcus Weekley

LLANO ★ ESTACADO

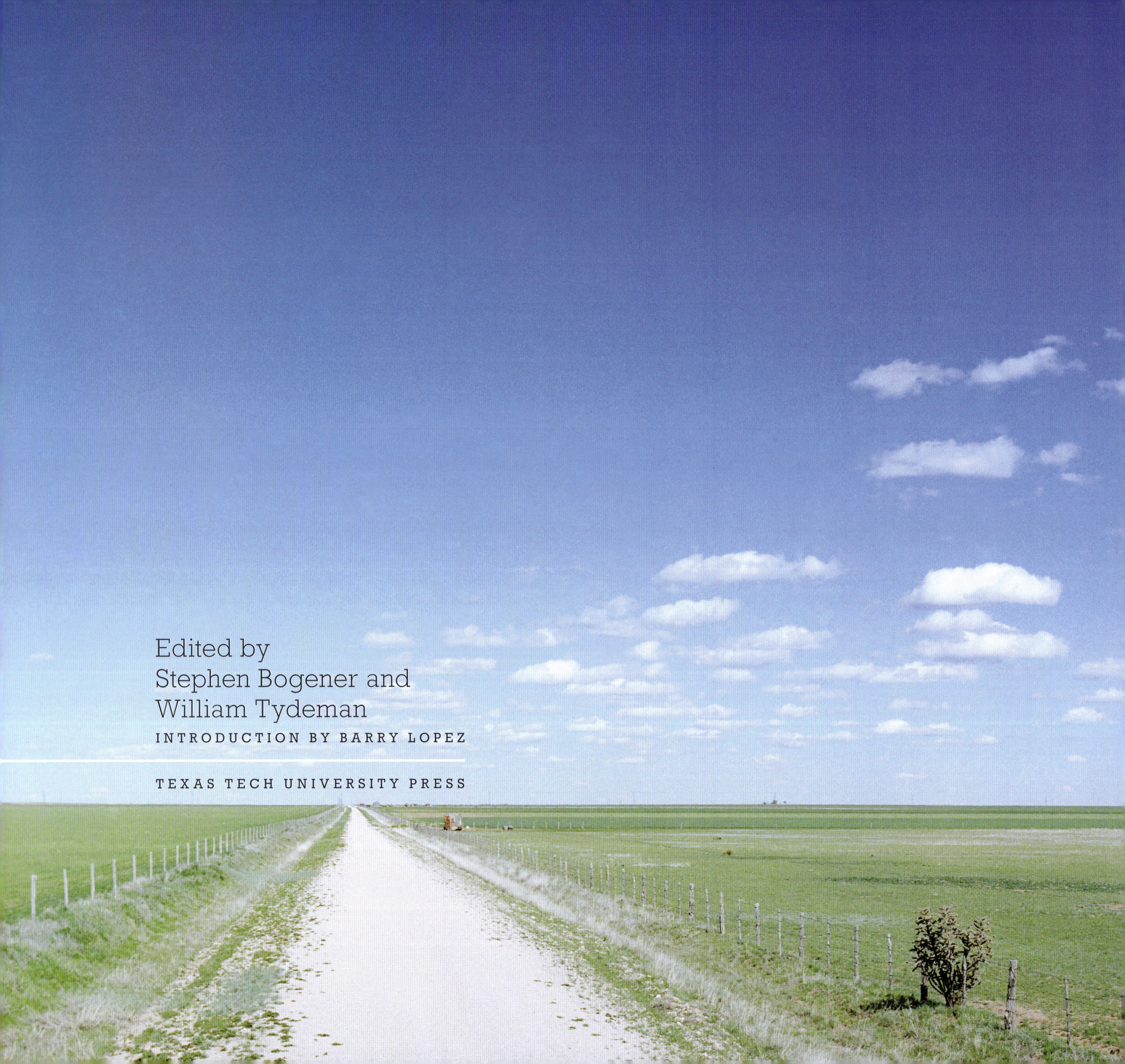

Edited by
Stephen Bogener and
William Tydeman
INTRODUCTION BY BARRY LOPEZ

TEXAS TECH UNIVERSITY PRESS

An Island in the Sky

Llano Estacado

This book is typeset in Monotype Haarlemmer. The paper used in this book meets the minimum requirements of ANSI/NISO Z39.48-1992 (R1997). ♾

Designed by Lindsay Starr

Title page image from "Horse, Wheatland, New Mexico"
by Rick Dingus

LIBRARY OF CONGRESS CATALOGING-IN-PUBLICATION DATA
Llano Estacado : an island in the sky / edited by Stephen Bogener and William Tydeman.
p. cm. — (Voice in the American West)
Includes index.
Summary: "Essays and photography on the nature and culture of the Llano Estacado. Demonstrates multiple visions of the region and serves as a much-needed corrective to characterizations of the Llano Estacado as featureless, flat, and uninteresting"—Provided by publisher.
ISBN 978-0-89672-682-6 (hardcover : alk. paper)
1. Llano Estacado—History. 2. Llano Estacado—Pictorial works. 3. Landscape—Llano Estacado—Pictorial works. 4. Natural history—Llano Estacado—Pictorial works. I. Bogener, Steve. II. Tydeman, William E., 1942–
F392.L62L53 2011
976.4'8—dc22 2010040586

PRINTED IN KOREA
11 12 13 14 15 16 17 18 19 / 9 8 7 6 5 4 3 2 1

TEXAS TECH UNIVERSITY PRESS
Box 41037, Lubbock, Texas 79409-1037 USA
800.832.4042 | ttup@ttu.edu | www.ttupress.org

CONTENTS

Looking for the Llano: A Personal View

WILLIAM TYDEMAN

★

I.

In my family there were no stories. Oh, there were stories to be told, but my father, mother, aunts, and uncles never shared a remembrance or offered a cautionary tale. Secrets were kept and stories locked away. I didn't learn until my parents' silver anniversary that I was born seven months after my parents' wedding. Only long after their death did I hear of an uncle arrested as a Peeping Tom, another uncle "shellshocked" and wounded as an ambulance driver in World War II. My father, now eighty-seven and a little more willing to talk, told me last Christmas that my grandmother and all her four brothers and sisters spoke fluent German. They were second-generation German immigrants from Würzburg, and I knew that, but speak German? I never heard a word. I knew nothing of their youth, their parents, or their childhood growing up in a brownstone in Brooklyn at the beginning of a new century. Another set of uncles spent their entire working lives as salesmen in New York's garment district, but never said a word about life on the job.

I have a snapshot of me at age two sitting in an Adirondack chair in the lap of my great-grandmother. The chair sits surrounded only by an expanse of front lawn. Great-Grandma sits uneasily, hair pulled back in a bun, spectacles on, unsmiling, a long flower-print dress tucked around her ankles. It's my only photo and only memento of my father's mother's mother.

Now I don't mean to suggest that I had a deprived childhood. My parents were loving, and we lived comfortably in what was described in the 1950s as the fastest-growing county in the U.S.A.: Nassau County, Long Island, New York. Thirty-five miles from New York City, there was still open space. We frequented the vacant lots, built forts in the corner woods, trapped birds, played softball in the streets, and lived outdoors. And, thank goodness, we had Momma, who saw to it that every family activity was recorded in photos. The snapshot tradition was alive and well in our family; a Brownie Hawkeye or Instamatic camera always at the ready. My sister now possesses twenty albums devoted to our family history; close to half have my name on the brown and black imitation leather cover. Every birthday through age twenty-one is documented with a photo of me sitting on my mother's lap (much to my embarrassment as a teenager). Awash in snapshots, we hardly missed the stories.

Mother was also a reader. She read fiction exclusively, but voraciously, from romance historical fiction (I can still see the hundreds of distinctive 1950s book jackets that graced our living-room bookshelves) to Gene Stratton-Porter and Steinbeck. In my memory, she sits on the couch next to white colonial-style bookcases built by Father, a floor lamp cascading light on the book she holds in her hand. When Mother wasn't cooking, she was reading. I can't say as a teen I had very sophisticated reading habits : I read Action Comics, the Hardy Boys, all of L. Frank Baum, Claire Bee's Chip Hilton series. I read indiscriminately, but somehow found time for Jules Verne, Stevenson, and Hemingway's Nick Adams stories. So-called serious literature came later.

II.

Now in my late middle age, I'm fond of asking my Honors students, what sticks? What have we read in seminar that will stay with you? How has the play of emotion and memory and text created stories you will never forget? When I left home to attend college, it was only the Latin-American writers—Enrique Anderson Imbert, Borges, and Paz—that ignited my imagination. Only a few courses in geography stayed with me—the geography of Anglo America and Donald Meinig's brilliant lectures in world political geography.

It wasn't until graduate school that I broadened my interests: I discovered the writing of J. B. Jackson, studied the history of photography with Beaumont Newhall, and explored the connections between literary criticism and photo analysis with photographer Tom Barrow. Then, in typical academic fashion, I rambled, chasing jobs from the mountains of North Carolina, to New Mexico and the Rio Grande Valley, up to the Pacific Northwest to Boise, and then back to the Llano Estacado and West Texas. Maybe it was a longing for the plains of my Long Island home, but I found the Llano Estacado agreeable, comfortable, and somewhat mysterious. As I settled into my life in Lubbock, I saw the grounded observation others practiced, and discovered relationship and connection that helped explain the distinctive geography of the shortgrass prairie. I saw, too, that my familiarity with photography, literature, and geography might provide a deeper, more variegated understanding of the region. I wanted to find the stories and the storytellers; I had learned not to allow the stories to go untold. I felt in my bones the power of the landscape. I was stumbling my way to a subject.

Many of the faculty at Texas Tech University knew more than they said about the Llano Estacado's problems: the disastrous land management practices, the perils of monoculture, the declining water table, to name only three. They understood that geographical intimacy requires a lifelong residency and local expertise. Willing to embrace the community beyond the ivory tower, they helped extend the conversation to non-university people; we talked, planned, and built a modest agenda. We wanted to better our understanding of our home place and use the tools at our disposal to shatter the misconceptions of the High Staked Plains.

Rick Dingus, professor of art, taught classes in documentary photography and had long experience in the field. He was a member of the much admired re-photography project of the late 1970s. He brought into the conversation his student Andrew John Liccardo, with a just completed MFA in photography. Dr. Stephen Bogener, working in the Exhibits and Outreach Department at TTU's Southwest Collection, had just completed a dissertation on the irrigation projects of the southeast New Mexico plains. I brought along my interests in photography, landscape, and literature. In 1999, Rick had launched the Millennial Collection Project, where his documentary students explored semester-long projects in response to their experiences on the Llano Estacado. Their portfolios were reviewed annually by the photography faculty during the next ten years, and the best became part of the Southwest Collections. The Millennial Collection, as Dingus conceived it, is an open time capsule. It serves as a catalyst for communication within and beyond the university community. Here all sides of the photographer-audience-subject triangle can be investigated. Exhibits and educational activities are built around an engagement with the complexities of a changing sense of place. As Dingus put it, "Unlike a lot of projects that happened at the turn of the Millennium, this project looks to the last fifty years and the next fifty years . . . collecting materials that . . . will be of use to us here and now as we think about the changes we're going through." This theme of ongoing change propelled further investigations and a conference, titled "Shifting Landscapes," devoted to the nature and uses of the documentary tradition. There we held up for examination many of the shibboleths of the straight and documentary photographic traditions.

From the beginning we recognized that the projects, conferences, and discussions revealed multiple truths and ways of seeing. Casting a photographic eye on the land and people of the High Staked Plains didn't result in a uniform vision. A happy conjunction with these photographic initiatives was, at the same time, the creation and growth of the James Sowell Family Collection in Literature, Community and the Natural World. It was fast becoming the most important collection in the U.S. on the literature of place. While many of the Sowell Collection writers wrote about other geographies, their stories and narratives guided us in our deliberations. Why not combine these perspectives for a study of the Llano Estacado? I knew we had thousands of snapshots, just like my mother's family albums, in the collection. What if we made a pointed effort to add the work of full-time photographers? What if, later on, we added perspectives of place-based writers? We were tired of complaining in our meetings of the endless characterizations of the flat, featureless plains, the homogeneous descriptions of local culture; the failure of writers and chroniclers to invite attention and discover natural beauty. Why couldn't others see how light played against an endless sky and how the wind rippled the grass? These writers, this work, would help us see the multiple truths of landscape and life on the Llano. The Llano and its geography would be properly placed in the foreground. The subject would be geography and the subtle ways it shaped culture. The flow of ideas would not be about writers or photographers but about the geographic forces that create place.

We started with photography. We were fortunate to secure a grant from the CH Foundation to pay six photographers to photograph the Llano from a variety of startling perspectives during the one-year grant period of 2005. We extended an invitation to a diversity of master photographers. The six featured here were those who responded passionately, those who already claimed, or who came eagerly to, the Staked Plains.

Rick Dingus and Andrew John Liccardo were obvious choices. Steve Fitch photographed the region for his highly regarded book, *Gone: Photographs of Abandonment on the High Plains.* Miguel Gandert had worked in Eastern New Mexico and West Texas. His book, *New Mexico Profundo,* was a work we all admired. Peter Brown's *On the Plains* was, to our way of thinking, a demonstration of a passion for place brave enough to embrace the decline as well as the hope of Llano communities. Tony Gleaton spent three years at Texas Tech University as a visiting professor and artist-in-residence at the Southwest Collection. His current project centers on the Black Route West (also the title of a forthcoming book). We knew that, collectively, the photographs of these gifted photographers revealed a history of diversity and difference unseen by most nonresidents.

We brought the photographers together for a collaborative discussion in January 2005. We hoped to stimulate and intensify the imaginative possibilities in a regional survey, bringing together Texas Tech faculty and community people to share their views on unexplored and important themes in the culture and nature of the Llano. In a stimulating daylong meeting, ideas flowed; the tone of the discussion was rich with meaning and possibility. Geographers, historians, agricultural economists, water-rights specialists, and creative writers had accepted our invitation to a conversation. The geographer Kevin Mulligan stirred the group with his unveiling of a GIS map on the Llano. His work revealed connections and relationships, from water wells and pumping stations to traditional springs and Indian trails. He gave us, as well, a precise delineation of the Llano's southern terminus. The map seemed to symbolize the rich layers of meaning awaiting visual documentation, suggesting pathways to a more variegated understanding of our region. We had cast a wide net to snare diverse participants and perspectives. I recall talking to community people like Darryl Birkenfeld from Ogallala Commons and writer Barry Lopez. They felt the energy, the focus, and the commitment. "Let's get after it," was the advice.

Not long before, Steve Bogener came up with the phrase we used in the title, *Island in the Sky*. Steve later said the notion of an island brought to mind the nearly eight-hundred-foot dropoff from the Caprock to the bottom of Palo Duro Canyon. While we knew the Llano Estacado to be a mesa or a plateau, the island concept to us seemed to suggest the isolation, the distinctive biogeography that characterizes island ecosystems. For me, a recent visit to the Davis Mountains in far west Texas yielded an enduring image of mountain tops as fertile islands for distinctive plant and animal communities. I imagined wind-borne seeds floating from one mountain peak to another. Steve pointed out that the Llano elevation rises from 3,000 to 5,000 feet, moving southeast to northwest; it is one of the highest elevations in Texas. Later he recalled that the Colorado Plateau was occasionally referred to as an island. We pictured an island in the sky that rises from a plain below, isolated, distinctive, surrounded by a sea of grass with an ocean of wind. The phrase fired our imagination.

III.

As I reflected on the day's events, I allowed myself to think back to earlier photo projects in those dark days of the Depression—when Roy Stryker gathered, under the banner of the Farm Security Administration, a talented assemblage of photographers to document the Depression and New Deal recovery. Unlike Stryker and the F.S.A., we had no complex shooting scripts, no list of places and objects to be photographed. We promoted no methodology and provided none of the supporting apparatus of social science surveys. Rather, we trusted everything would be enriched by the lessons of art. Photographers would find beauty in the everyday. I felt certain their work would command attention. These photographers loved this land, and their photographs would reveal the Llano's hidden splendor. I knew, too, that words like *beauty* and *splendor* came with the weight of ponderous tones and endless aesthetic critical theories. As traditional as it sounds, I shared Robert Adams's view that "[T]he Beauty that concerns me is that of form. Beauty is . . . a synonym for the coherence and structure underlying life . . . Beauty is the overriding demonstration of the pattern that one observes."

As the year progressed, those of us residing in the Hub City had ample opportunity to plan how we might use literature to extend and broaden the photographic documentation. Context seemed all-important for expanding the connections. We saw the accumulating parallels between photographs and words revealing not indisputable fact but patterns and coherence. I thought back, as well, to my graduate-school days when photographer Tom Barrow and I sought to apply the literary criticism of Owen Barfield and Northrop Frye to photographic explication. The work of the novelist George P. Elliot on Dorothea Lange had stuck with me as well: Elliot reported the quotation from Francis Bacon that Lange had tacked on her darkroom door from 1923 to her death in 1965: "The contemplation of things as they are/ Without error or confusion/ Without substitution or imposture/ Is in itself a nobler thing than a whole harvest of invention." The relationship between the choices of subject, authority, the contemplation of things as they are, acknowledged the importance of context. All seemed to suggest the interrelationship of photos and words. Words . . . Why not invite writers into the conversation?

Project photographers were enthusiastic about the idea. Perhaps the combined perspectives could help break the aura of mystery and simplicity that characterized so much of the documentation on the plains. Essays by prominent writers would provide additional demonstration of the multiple ways of seeing the Llano.

When we exhibited the work at the Houston Center for Photography during FotoFest in March and April of 2006, over 400 people attended the opening. With help again from the CH Foundation; we reassembled the photographers at the Southwest Collection at Texas Tech in March of 2007 to explore adding essays to the photographs. We debated the form and content of a book. We wanted at least one essay to provide an historical background, a context for the photos and essays that followed. We selected writers from the James Sowell Family Collection in Literature, Community and the Natural World. Bill Kittredge and Annick Smith had written on and worked in photography and film. Rick Bass grew up in Texas and knew the territory. So did Sandra Scofield and her daughter Jessica Scofield. Sandra Scofield's growing-up years were at the edge of the Llano in Wichita Falls and later in Odessa. Stephen Graham Jones was a faculty member in creative writing at Texas Tech.

Once again, we provided no elaborate set of instructions. Writers could comment on the photographs, write about their experiences living in or traveling through the Llano, or tell about other facets of Llano life and culture. We made no attempt to combine and find an exact fit between the photos and the essays. In so doing, I believe we reaffirmed the relationship between art and nature. We called on the lessons of our pasts: Tell the stories. Take the pictures. More conceptually, our hope was not to complete nature and define its boundaries but to reveal the connections. Or as Robert Adams once put it, "[A]rt and its practice are of a piece with life." The result you have in hand suggests our additional hope that these stories and photos light the way to understanding while nourishing our imagination. I believe they succeed in demonstrating the beauty of everyday life. They summon us to a human, literate, and loving recovery of the region we call *An Island in the Sky*.

ACKNOWLEDGMENTS

We recognize that this book caps more than a decade-long conversation at Texas Tech University on American regionalism and meaning of place. Its roots rest on initial conversations with Rick Dingus on documentary photography and its utility in demonstrating the subtle geographic and cultural variations of the Llano Estacado. With Rick's leadership, the Southwest Collection/Special Collections Library launched the Millennial Photograph Collection documenting the High Staked Plains at the beginning of the new century. As students in his documentary class began to photograph the region, Rick helped us acquire the photographic portfolios of professional photographers whose landscape and documentary work centered on the Llano and the American Southwest. When our planning turned to a conference on the meaning of documentary photography as both art and fact, Rick led the charge, suggesting and contacting speakers as well as helping to structure the conference logistics. When we moved from a conference to seeking grant monies for a photo project on the Llano, Rick assisted with every step. When we decided on a book, Rick was there for advice and counsel in every phase of the publication process. For all this and more, we owe him a special debt of gratitude. This book would not have happened without his efforts.

We also owe an immeasurable debt to Emily Nash Long for her unstinting labors and administrative support. She provided computer support and logistical planning, as well as serving as a sounding board and consultant on the book. I feel inadequate in expressing our thanks and gratitude for the hundreds of behind-the-scenes tasks she took on without complaint.

This book also grows out of conversations with faculty and academics with a long-standing interest in the Llano. Kevin Mulligan, Paul Carlson, Shelley Armitage, and Darryl Birkenfeld of the Ogallala Commons all helped formulate our thinking. Robin Dru Germany provided key help in early conference planning. Series editor Andy Wilkinson was never too busy to sit down and share ideas. The contributors to this volume, both the photographers and writers, couldn't have been more cooperative and understanding. Andrew Liccardo deserves special thanks for his work in organizing the Millennial Collection, assisting with conference planning, and helping to get the Llano Project started. Jim Brink, as director of the Southwest Collection/Special Collections Library, was constantly supportive.

In addition, we all continue to learn and expand our thinking in conversations (now over a decade long) with Barry Lopez.

Finally, this book would never have come to publication without the generous support of The CH Foundation. They supported our fieldwork and conferences and provided a subvention grant to offset publication costs of this book. For decades The CH Foundation has been central to the culture and education of the Southern Plains.

To all, our deepest gratitude and appreciation.

LLANO ★ ESTACADO

Introduction

BARRY LOPEZ

The physical reaches of the Earth—deserts, river valleys, glaciated mountains, marshes, oceans, and grasslands—are bounded as much by politics, agriculture, urbanization, fences, and energy transmission and travel corridors as they are by nature's own lines of demarcation. (Biologists call such natural borders ecotones, the quavering edges where a forest abuts a clearing or a braided creek meets the banks of a shortgrass prairie.)

At least a human observer is prone to see it this way.

History and myth—the Canadian poet and translator Robert Bringhurst calls myth "history edited by the imagination"—place a temporal grid over this pattern of man-made and natural lines, framing each locale with names both historical and geographical. If our first inquiry about a *place* concerns its where, its latitude and longitude, the next might be about its when, as in, "When did this *where* become a place to someone?" Or, "What is the specific *when* of this place you wish to draw my attention to?"

The Earth, even in its most remote quarters, is subject these days to a kind of constriction, a final parceling-out of fresh water, ore, fish, petroleum, and arable land. Whatever the actual case might be, many of the Earth's warier and more informed inhabitants are conferencing and writing and lecturing about an impending apocalypse, some with an irritating fervor. The climate in every region, we are told, is shifting, repositioning itself; and the buildup of synthetic chemicals—of pesticides and hormones and the catalysts that smooth the skids of industry—is notable, and noticed in every corner of the world, from the icefields of the Transantarctic Mountains to your spleen.

The Llano Estacado is one of this Earth's places, a sky-domed and once undemarcated landscape, given a generalized geographic perimeter by a striking layer of pale hardpan, a scribing from which hang the ocherous curtains of various escarpments, the Mescalero and the eponymous Caprock among them. Perhaps it was once too vast, too intimidating a space for Clovis hunters to enter at the beginning of the local Holocene, a place too stingy with surface water for hunters to chance an *entrada* far from a dependable, quenching drink. Or maybe we need to reimagine the early Holocene, and see the progeny of the Clovis hunters at Blackwater Draw the way we have come to reimagine pre-contact Polynesians at sea in double-hulled, ocean-going catamarans, guided by navigators who knew that the Hawaiian Islands (fresh water, food, an opportunity for stable habitation) were *there*, long before any human eye caught hold of them.

Clovis hunters gave the Llano a name, we can reasonably assume, a word now unfetchable but a name packed with meaning, standing for a region since stripped of most of its wetlands and large mammals. The Holocene Llano gave way two hundred years ago to the Anthropocene Llano. The twentieth-century horseman found no footprint of a short-faced bear on the dry bank of a Llano creek, but instead the pawprint of a feral dog. The great reservoir of silence suspended above the plain, through which birdsong, wind-washed grass, and thunder once flowed, outlining and intensifying the silence, today carries the ceaseless wheezing of the pump jack, the *whump-whump-whump* of the wind charger, the hammer of diesels. The snowflake Appaloosa of a Comanche youth is now the blooded equine of suburban backyards. The crazy quilt of migrating shovelers and pintails overhead is now an invisible web of electromagnetic radiation, anchored to cell-phone towers like a monofilament net, and where open vistas once provoked an endless replication of possibility (or boredom for some), there are now fences and property lines for the once-upon-a-time hunter-gatherer to negotiate.

The modern Llano, fashioned from the raw earth and history of the Llano's past, and shaped as much by politics and economics as by rain and wind, is the meditation point for the photographers and writers brought before us here. Their translations alert us to the complexity, the idiosyncrasy, the passion, the forlorn hopes, the sublimity of the place, and sound across these pages one of the clarion calls of the twenty-first century: *We've reached the horizon.* Now we are asking, "Where are we?" And also a more difficult, more polarizing question, "Where do we go from here?"

A starting place might be to hold everything dear. The vanished enclaves of the Clovis hunters, whose pressure-flaked spearpoints are symbolic of our long human effort. The flutter of blue and side-oats grama grass in an untended cemetery. The coyote strung up on a fence wire for his ignorance about private property. A preacher fearful his parishioners will lose the knowledge of God's munificence and grace. A woman painting in Blanco Canyon on a November afternoon, experimenting at her easel with hues of magenta and celadon, while ice crystals begin to spread through her watercolors.

In reevaluating the impact humanity has had on the Earth, we might come together as ordinary people and ask each other what matters. Some of what we love, or profess to have loved, is gone and not to be recovered. Some of the change that is upon us, according to a gathering of scientists large enough to matter, is dangerous. Before we can decide what is to be done on the Llano—or anywhere else—we must develop a shared vision of where we are. To do that, we must assemble relevant information about the history and biology of the place, its human architecture and the trending of its trails and roadways, the strains of its spirituality and profanity; assemble it all, guided by an image of our grandchildren stepping out tomorrow on a mythic Llano, able to believe in the possibility of rich and fully imagined lives. The time to act solely in our own interest is gone.

Here, on these pages devoted to the Llano Estacado and its life, human and wild, is the beginning of a reconsideration of a single place, the first sentence of a story never before told. It is a story people in every oasis in the world are now convening to draft, about their own revered and cherished places, a story written according to their own particular insights. A blueprint.

Peter Brown

I've photographed on the Llano Estacado for the past twenty years or so, first as a part of a long-term study of the western High Plains that culminated in a book called *On the Plains*, and then more recently in a more geographically circumscribed way—work I did for *Llano Estacado: Island in the Sky*, and also for *West of Last Chance*, a collaboration with the novelist Kent Haruf.

Technically, I use a 4 × 5 camera and color negative film, and generally make my own prints. For the most part, I have photographed as a wanderer, picking and choosing with an eye for images that describe both what is there (my sense of the visual truth of the place) and moments that resonate in ways that are more personal: my own response to color, space, light, the natural world, and the cultural life of the Plains.

I normally photograph with a mix of intuition and planning and then link the photographs together in narrative ways. For this book, ten photographs have been selected that represent a cross-section of my interests. They range from open untouched landscape, to environmental portraits, to small buildings. I am often struck by conjunctions of word and image and have photographed a number of signs—so interpretive reading may go along with the viewing.

Apricot tree, Lingo, New Mexico, 2004

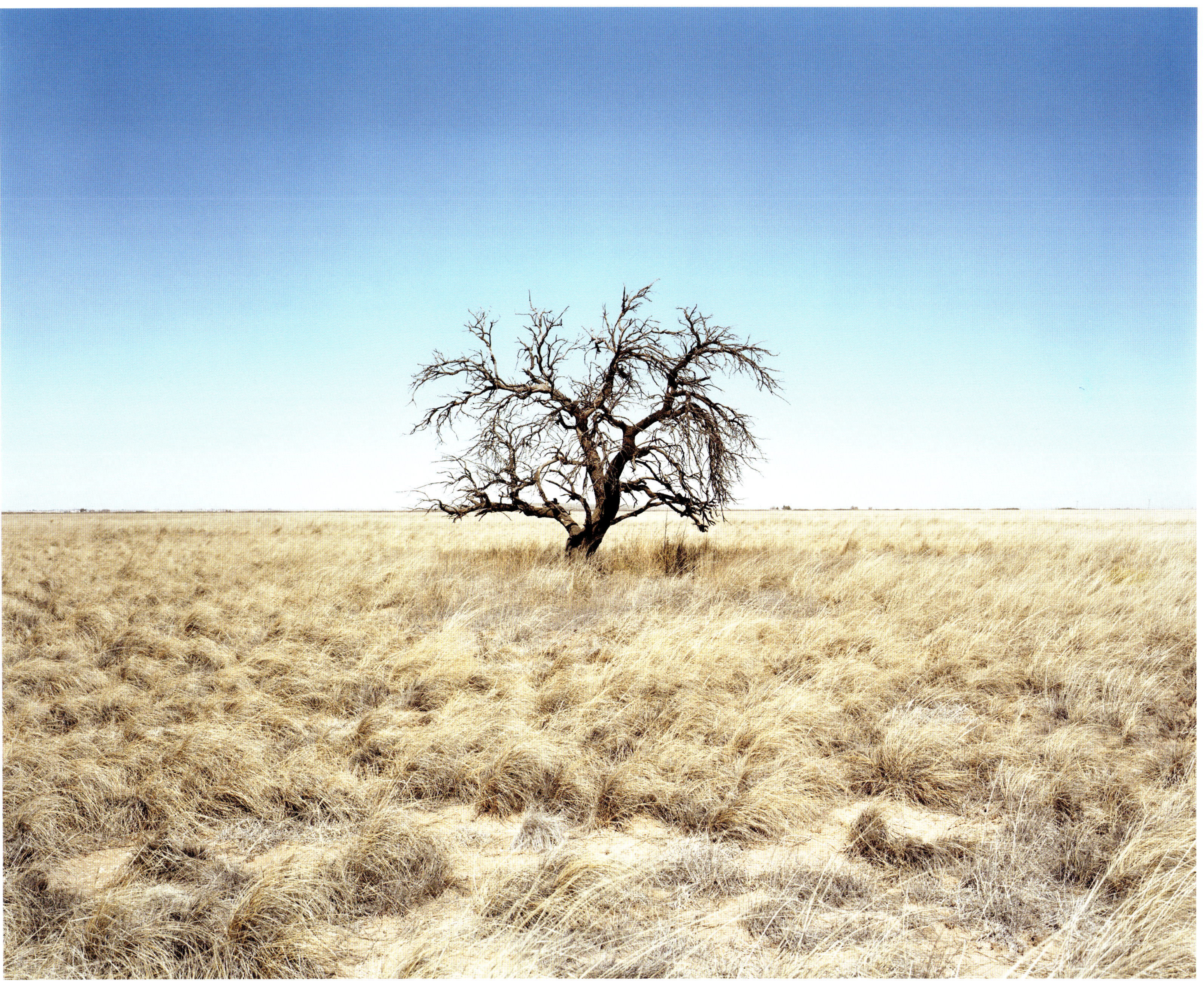

David's Garage, Olton, Texas, 2001

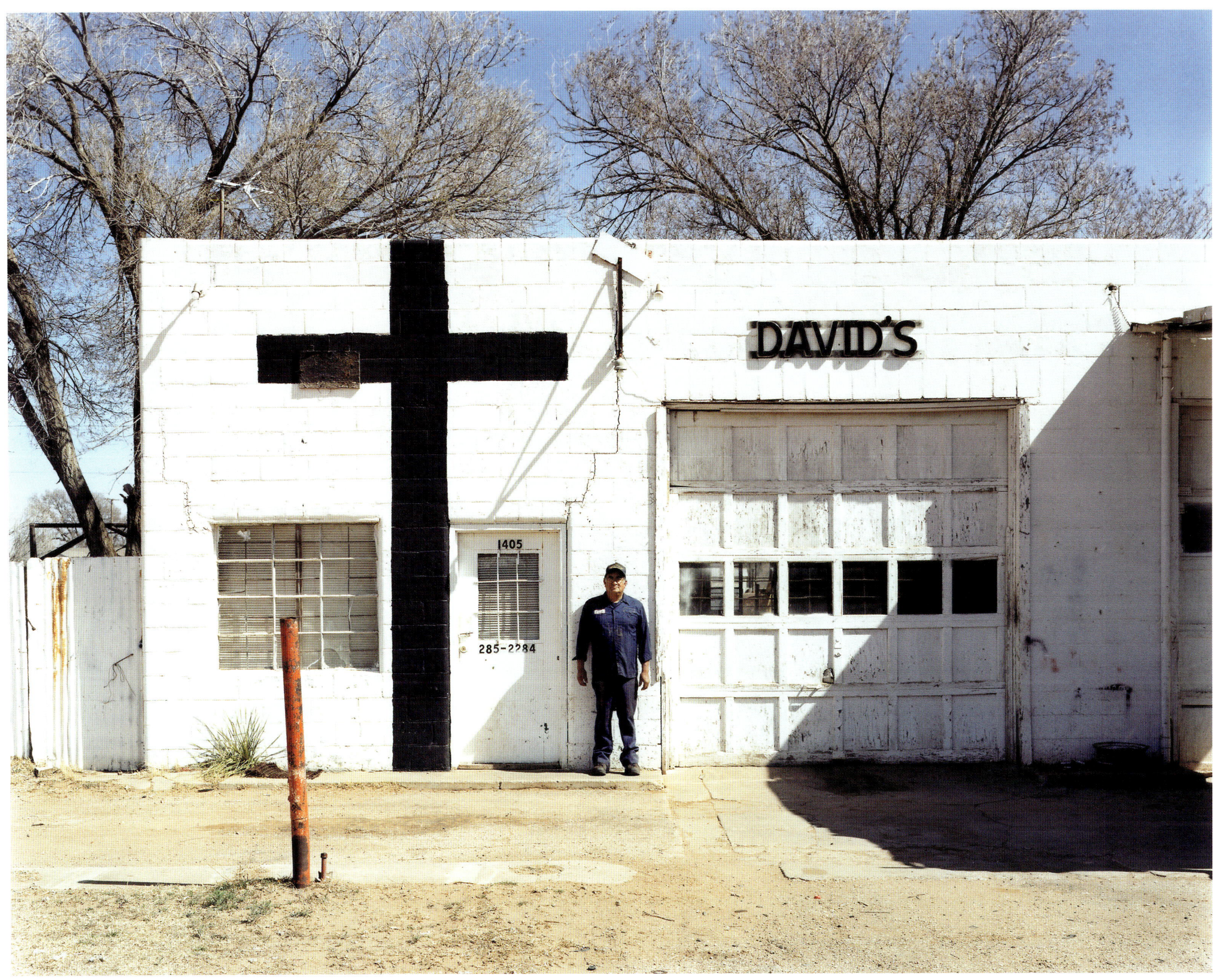
DAVID'S
1405
285-2284

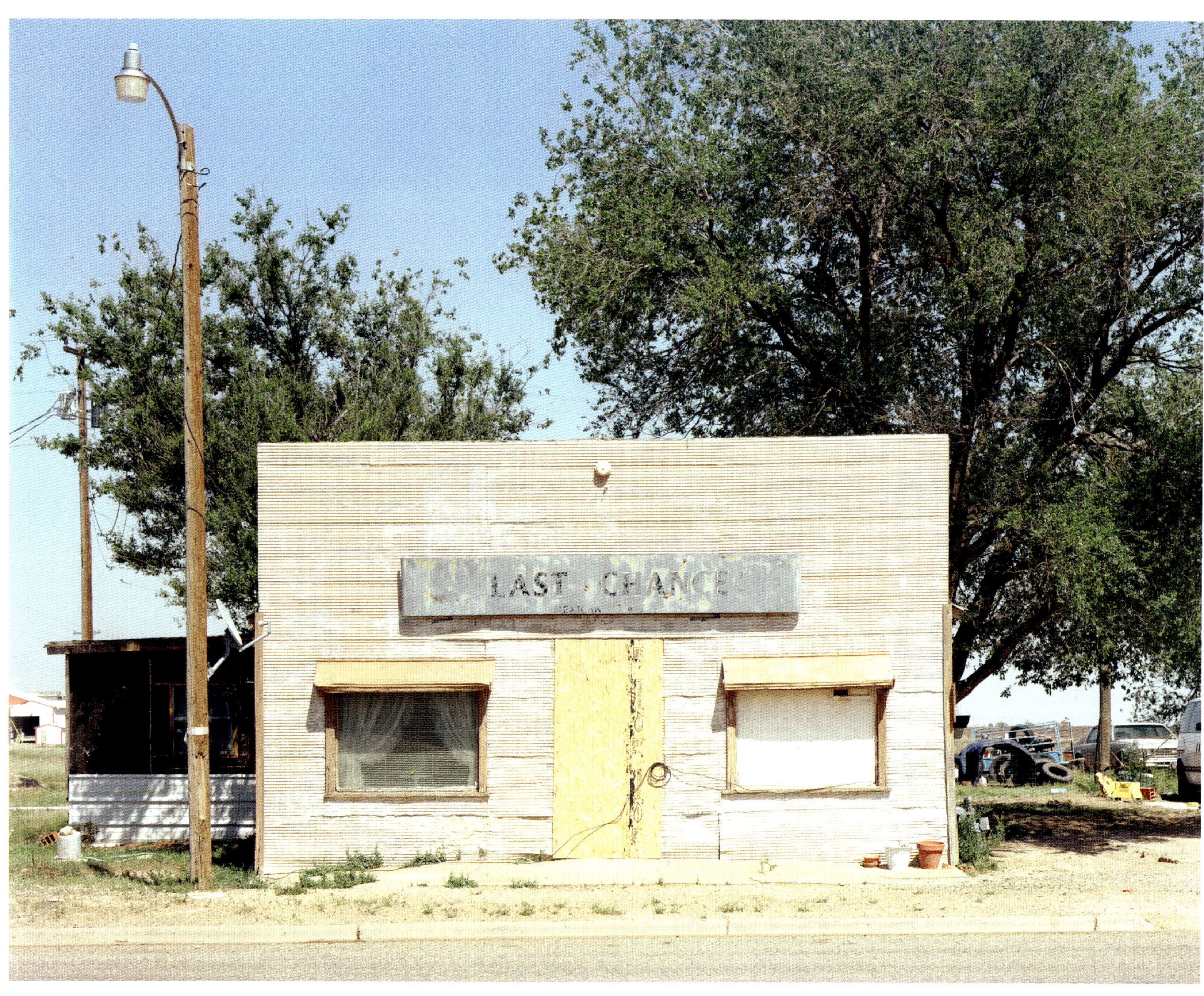

Last Chance Restaurant, Cotton Center, Texas, 2003

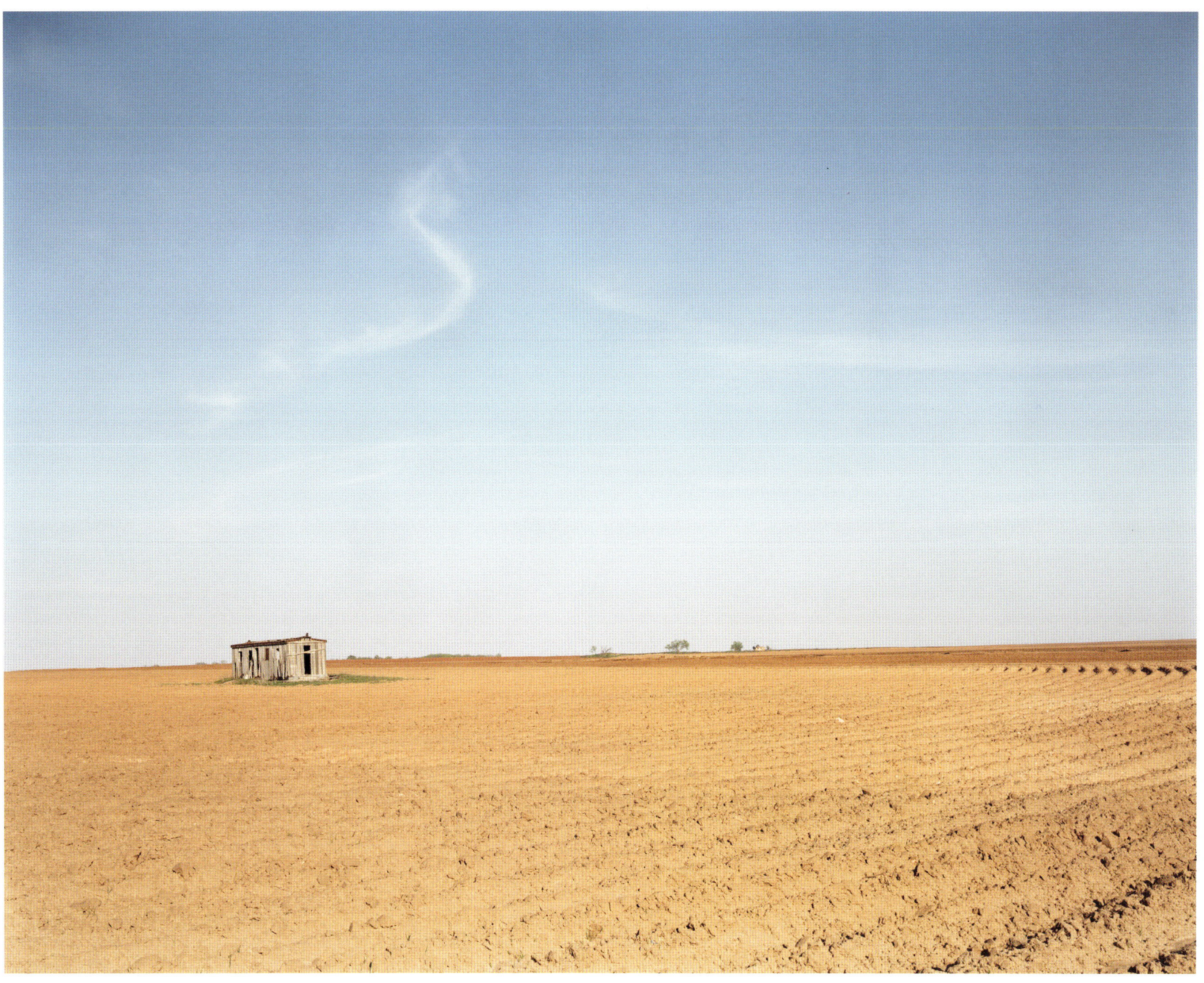

Railroad shack home, Fairview, Texas, 1999

Open space, Grady, New Mexico, 2003

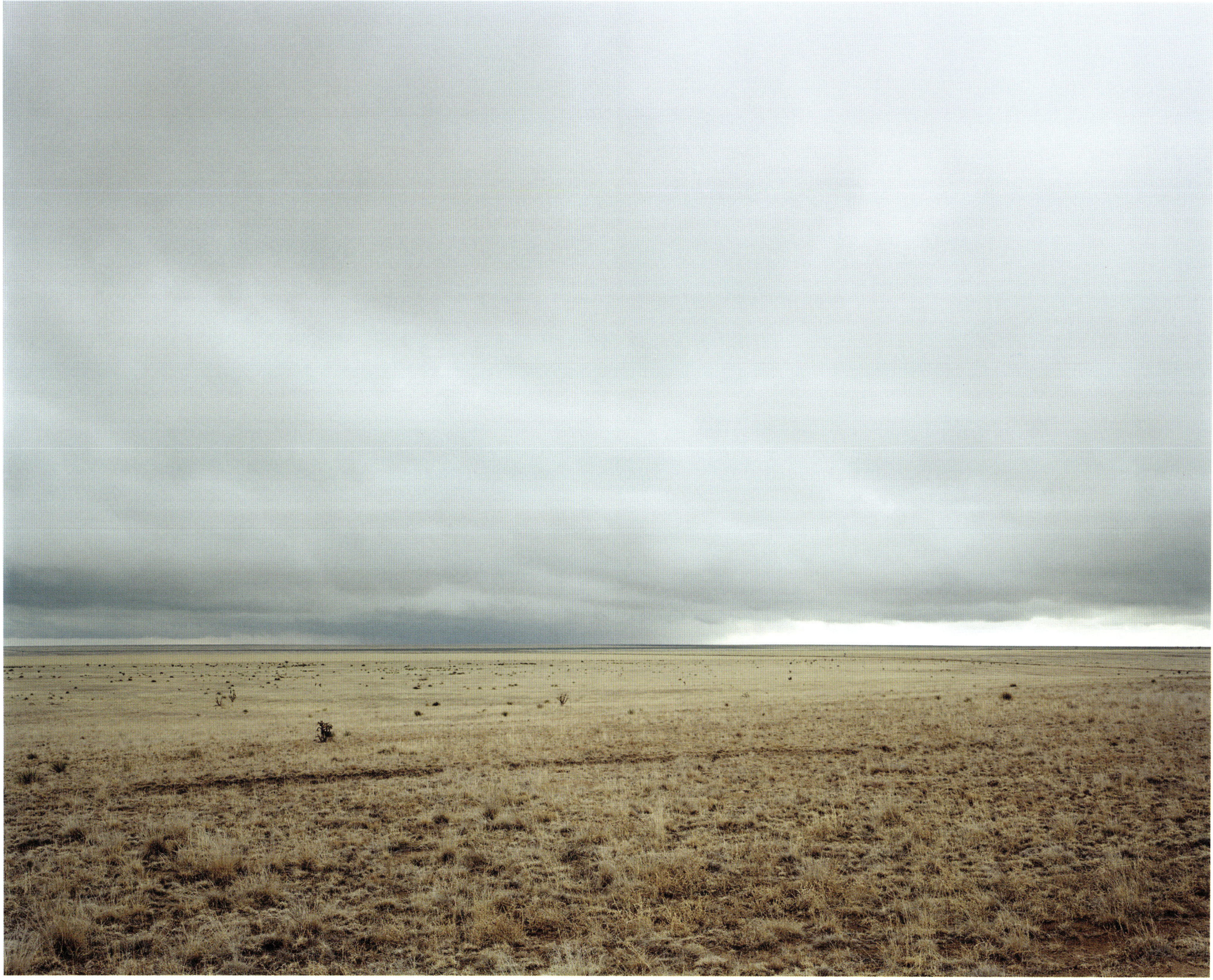

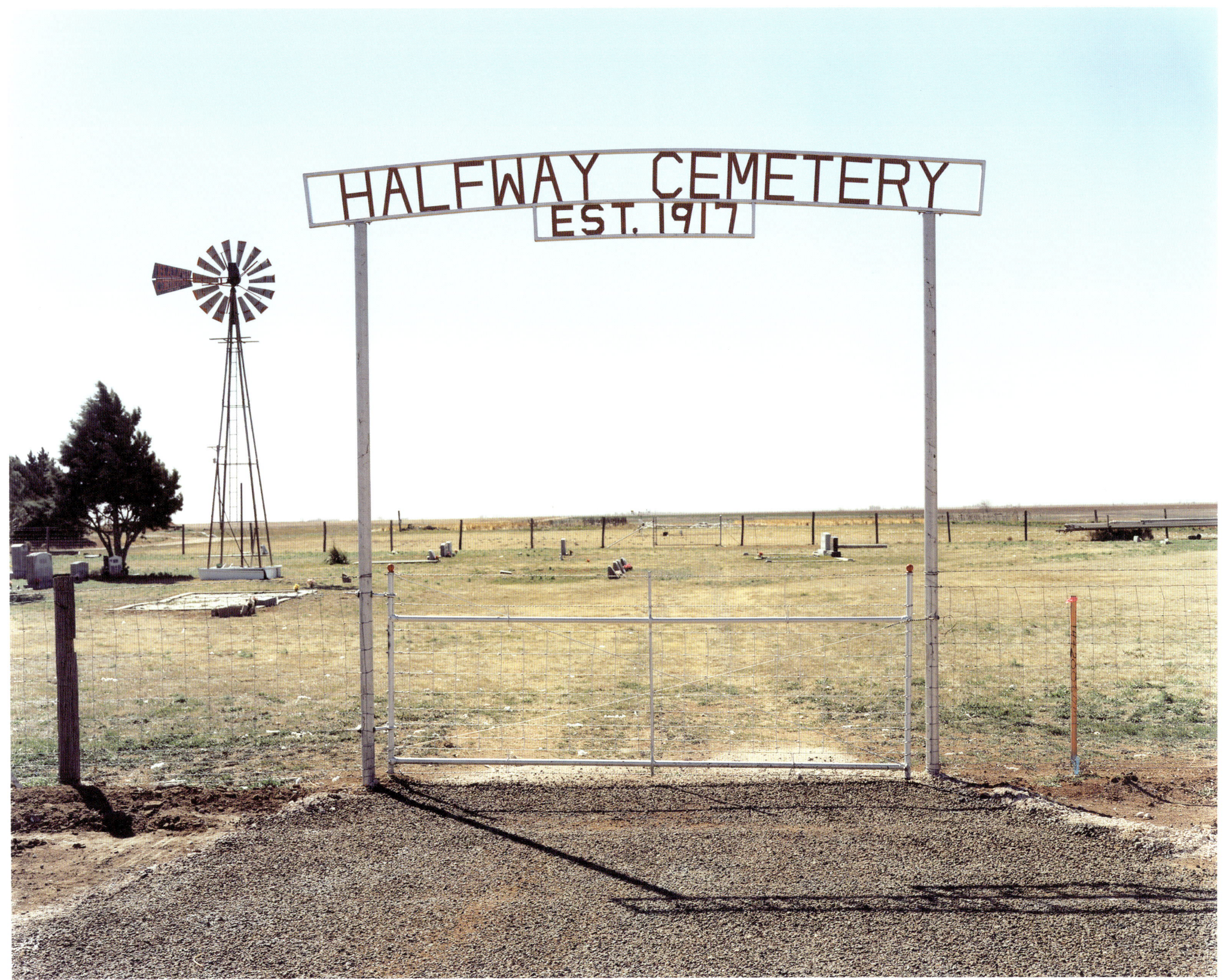
HALFWAY CEMETERY
EST. 1917

Halfway Cemetery, Halfway, Texas, 2003

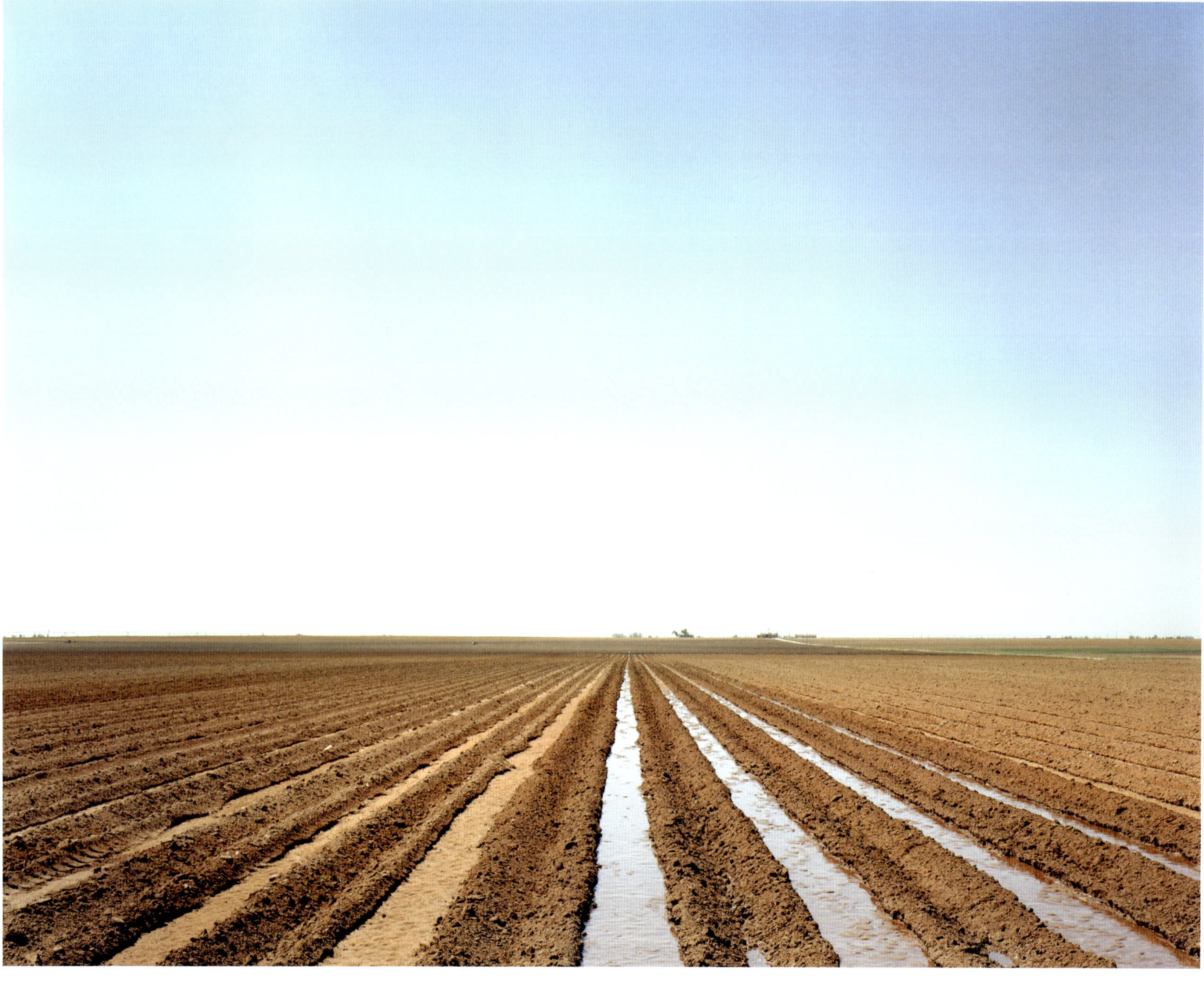

Irrigated field, Levelland, Texas, 2002

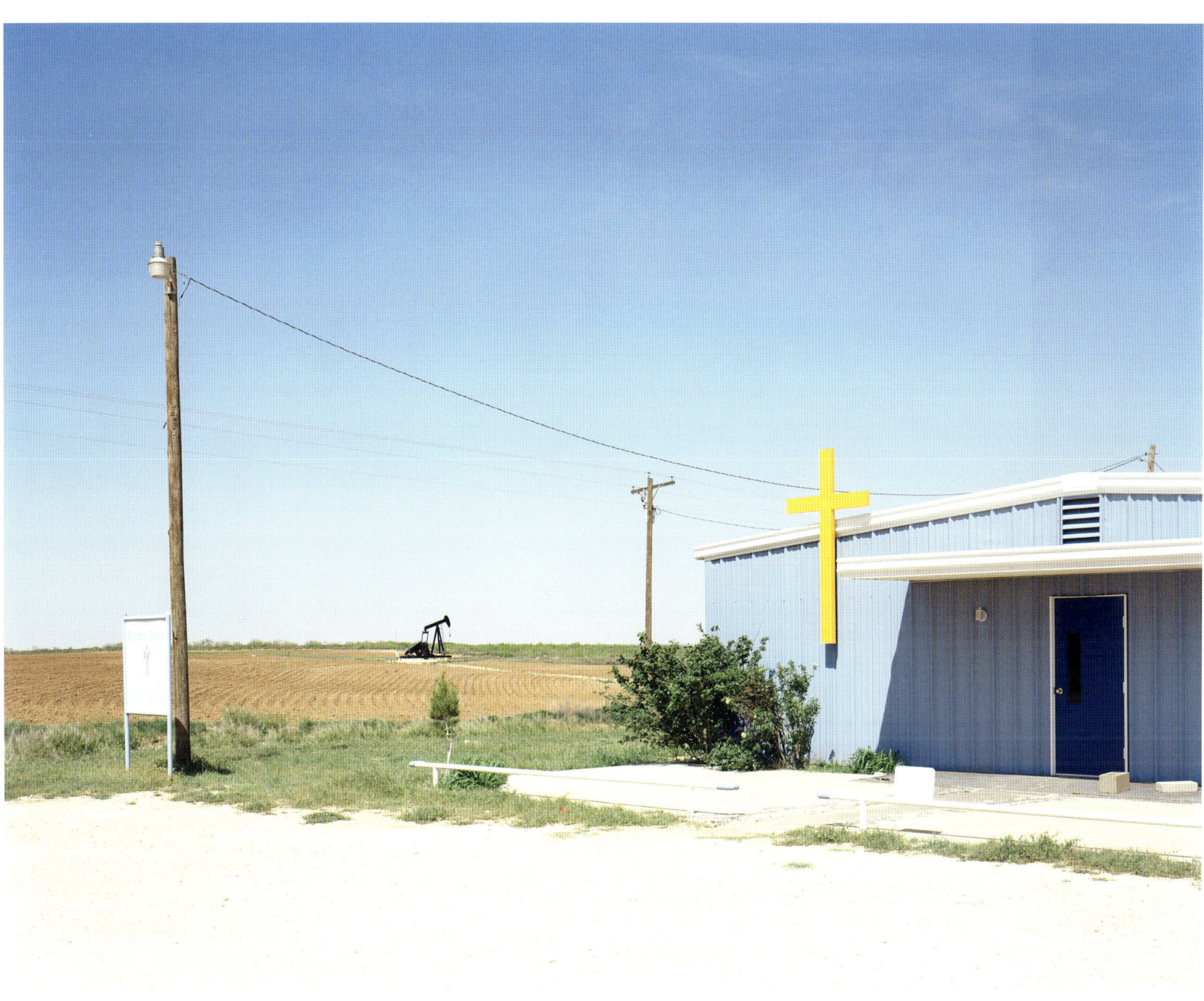

St. Isadore Church, Lenorah, Texas, 2002

Storm, Slaton, Texas, 2002

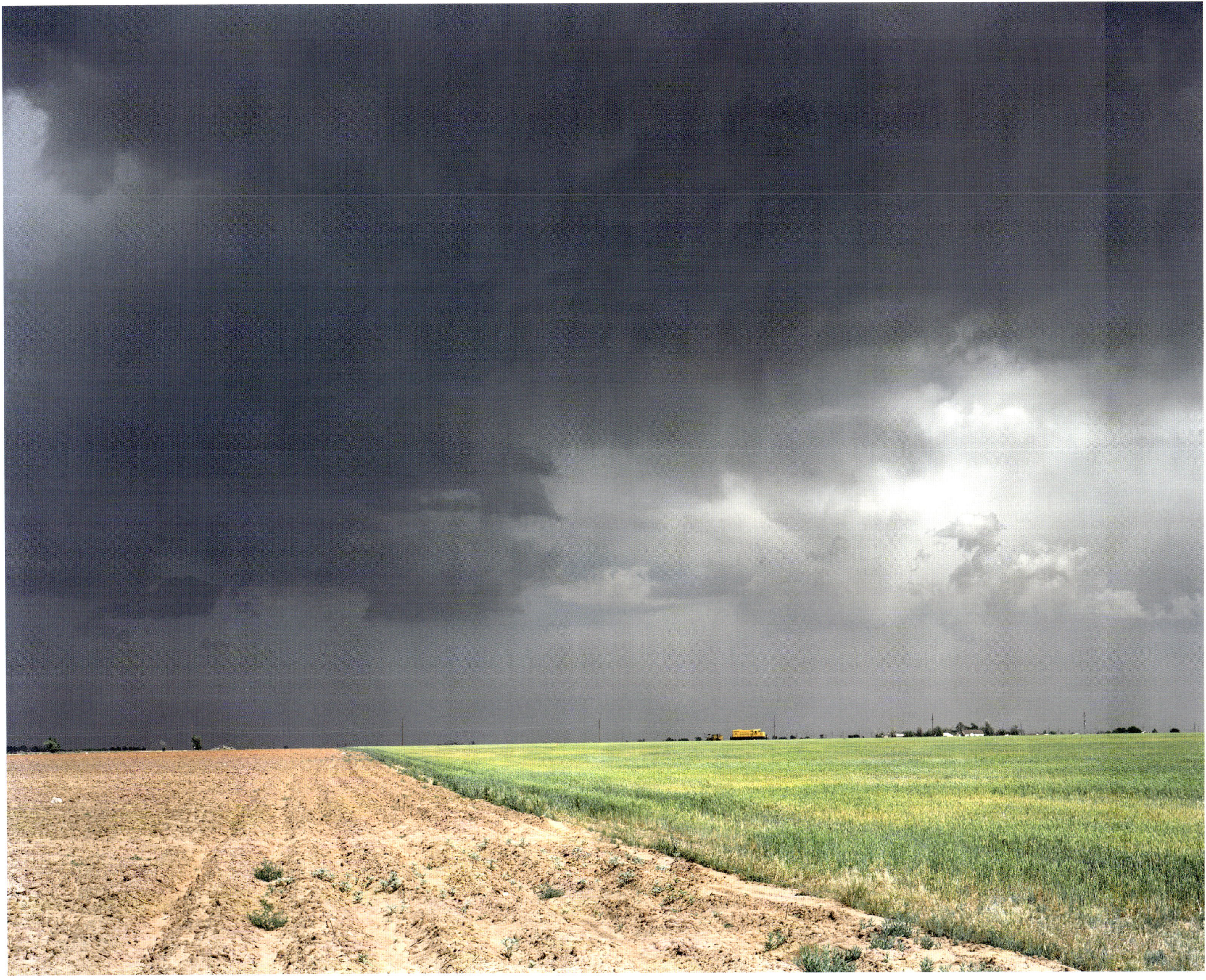

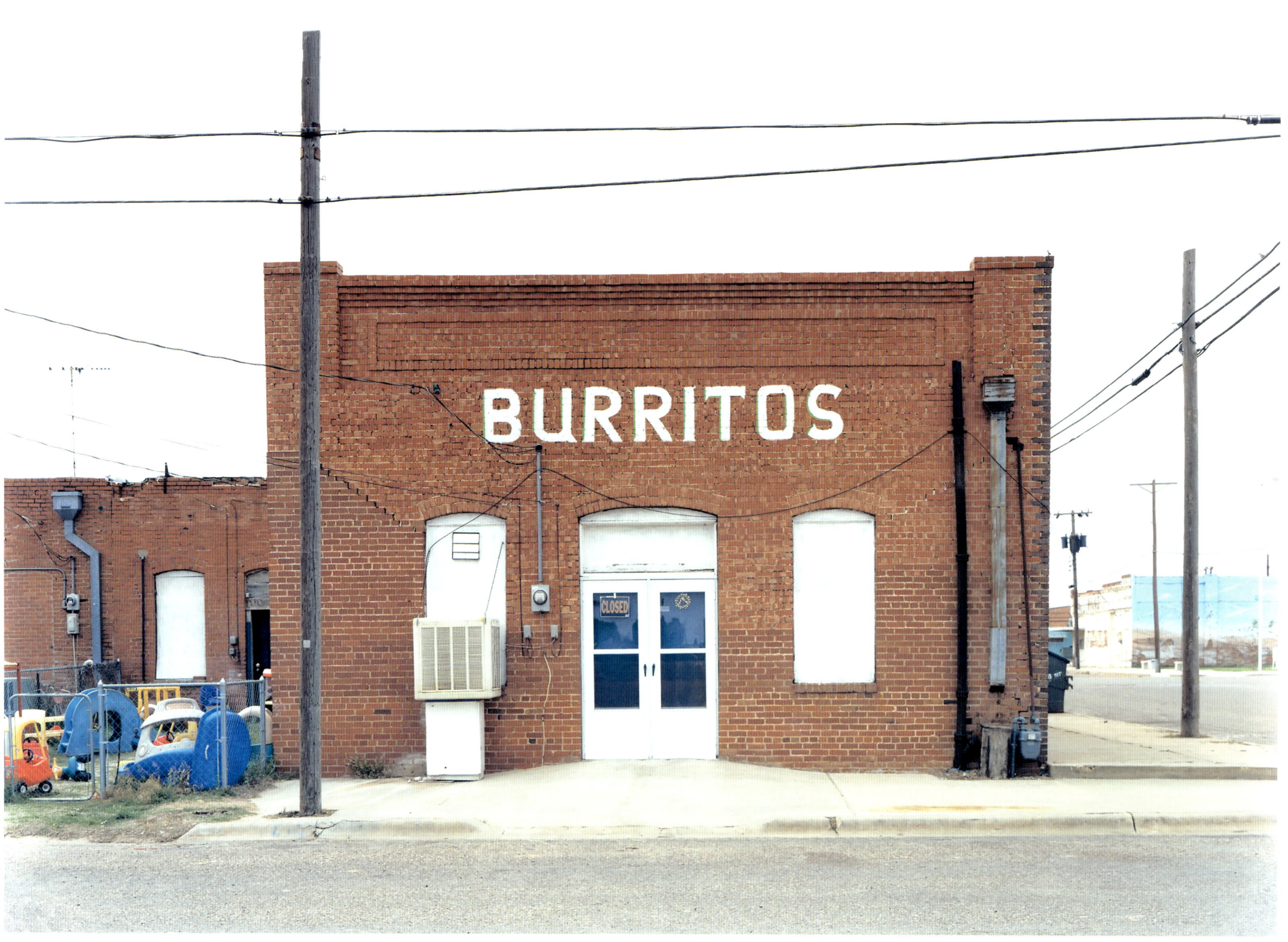
BURRITOS
CLOSED

Burritos, Tahoka, Texas, 2004

Readings

SANDRA SCOFIELD WITH JESSICA SCOFIELD

A PHOTOGRAPH SAYS: *Look at this.*

It evokes in me an immediate response (*I know this place; I like this photograph*) and then something ephemeral and idiosyncratic. Call it meaning.

I tell stories, and I look for them everywhere.

My family moved from Wichita Falls to Odessa, Texas, in 1954, when I was in seventh grade.

My aunt and uncle had lived in various West Texas towns since their marriage in the late forties, and my little sister and I had spent many summer months with them and my cousins. My uncle was a second-generation Halliburton man, moved from town to town until he was based in Monahans in 1959, where they bought a nice brick house on the last eastside street. Not far on the other side of the back fence was the million-barrel site, a huge failed crude oil reservoir.

In Wichita Falls, we had lived with my grandmother in an old northside neighborhood that felt like a small town. I rode the bus to parochial school. Most weekends we went to Devol, Oklahoma, to the dry-land wheat farm of my grandmother's parents. My landscape was a trio of dusty yards: school, North Lamar Street, farm.

West Texas scared me. It was vast and windy and dry. Going west out of Odessa, we passed through a cloud of soot from a carbon-black plant. Once I saw a long scarf of tarantulas scurrying across the highway. We lived in a series of rentals on arid lots on streets with no trees. In Hadicol Camp with my aunt's family over a summer, we kids watched for rattlers and we bathed, sequentially by age, in a washtub. We never went outside the circle of trailers, like children in a wagon train. *Out there* was blinding sun and scorching sand, but my aunt liked to drive out in the evenings to look for jackrabbits.

Once my aunt's family settled down in Monahans, she made a passel of friends. She is the kind of person who makes a good time out of any reason for people to get together. She liked me to visit and kept me close. She hauled me around to the fabric store (she was teaching me to sew), the beauty parlor (set up on a woman's screened in-porch), the five-and-dime, the gas station. She knew someone everywhere we went. She had drawn their blood at the hospital, she had shopped in their stores, she knew their mothers, their children, their pastors. We went to tent revivals, and later the preachers came by to eat cold meat and pie. We dropped by houses where we drank iced tea or Dr. Pepper, and I listened to the women talk about recipes and who was sick or well or off in Dallas for spurious reasons. Sometimes there was a Halliburton party and the men danced with me and said I was getting awful pretty. I listened hard, I remembered.

My mother didn't do any of these things. She was never well enough for friendship.

In high school, I had a bicycle and I experienced my first taste of freedom, speeding along County Road with my mouth closed tight against gnats and dust. I went to early morning Mass, I went to the library, I rode through the green grassy neighborhoods across town. My mother was sick, I was on my own. The city was on a grid, like a checkerboard. I could ride right to the edge; I turned around when the buildings stopped and the last lots were littered with broken-down cars, equipment, barrels, and trash. Once I headed out toward Andrews, and a car sped by so close I veered off and fell over in the ditch. A nice stranger—a woman—in a pickup hauled me home. The March day my mother died, a fierce dust storm dirtied the sky, and later that day it rained mud. I left in 1961.

Then my aunt moved to Lubbock, and for nearly forty years I have been flying in to see her, usually in the spring when the skies are wild. We start down into Lubbock and part of me feels as if I'm coming home, though I know I am a visitor. Home is my aunt and cousins and the huge sky and the ache of my losses, but it isn't where I live. Home is what feels familiar even if I am out of place. I've spent three decades and more in Oregon and Montana, and if you ask me I'll still say I'm from West Texas. I used to think I would grow up and move away and belong somewhere else, but instead I learned that I am who I was when I used to be there, even if I didn't have the sense to take a good look when I could.

FIELDS, SHACKS

Peter Brown's "Railroad Shack Home, Fairview, Texas"

A cockeyed shack in a long plowed field sits on a pad of spring green like a placemat. It's easier to plow around it than to tear it down. There is a real house far across the field on the horizon, and a few mature trees. All the homesteads in these photos are far away, appearing miniscule and tangential to the fields, but aren't they the reward for the immense labor of the farms? Just above the field, a wisp of cloud seems to have carried the last of something away, whatever was left when the people who lived here couldn't take it anymore.

There's a similar tiny oasis, *sans* house, in Rick Dingus's "Old Home Place in a Plowed Field, Posey, Texas." Straggly trees stick up incongruously in a huge dry field. The patch of green is like a docking station; the manipulated curvature of the horizon suggests a drop into space. It feels as if you're viewing the landscape through a bubble window.

In Andrew John Liccardo's "Rangeland, Near Friona, Texas" an old shack leans precipitously, echoing the foreground remnants of fence. There's a sign on a post, but we can't read it and you get the feeling it is probably old news. This field is desolate, because we can't see an end to it, only the ghosts of tire tracks and a ribbon of green on the distant horizon.

GETTING BY

Peter Brown's "David's Garage, Olton, Texas."

The sun is glaring, but the man in the photograph—is it David?—stands away from the swath of shade, near the door, and a huge black painted cross that dominates the picture. Metal blinds on the windows are shut tight. The trees in the background are bare, so it must be winter, but the man doesn't look cold. Blue is the only color—his uniform darker than the sky.

I notice the glare and the contrast between the whitewashed concrete garage, the black cross, and the darkly-clothed figure. Two cracks run like rivulets down the walls behind the man; the old driveway is cracked and broken. This looks like a hard place to feel at ease. The man agreed to pose for the photograph, but there's no sign of vanity. The building has his name on it, but he knows his stature is nothing next to the Lord. The cross is a promise: A good man works here, you'll get an honest deal; and it's a prayer, too, because some times are hard. Our view of the building, flat face front, might suggest there's nothing behind it, but the cross is a pledge of faith.

A stranger comes: *Can I take your picture?* Maybe a man feels some pride, pulls his shoulders back, or maybe he is wary. *What's the picture for?*

He wasn't busy anyway.

"Burritos, Tahoka, Texas" is a photograph of an old square red brick building with tall windows boarded up. The right corner edge of the building has been re-pointed. You can see the bricks crumbling at the top of the building on the left side of the photograph. It must be dim and cool inside. An air conditioner is propped up against one of the windows. There is no sign of life today, no people, no cars, as if everyone in town has been evacuated.

How many transformations has the building gone through? First it might have been a bank or a law or insurance office, before everyone drove to the city for business. Maybe later it was a fabric store, a thrift shop, or just an empty hull, until someone thought, *Burritos.*

The town won't see a Starbucks or a McDonald's. It won't be gentrified. The view is stark. Maybe it's Sunday and everyone is at church. Maybe the building is closed again and nobody had a reason to do something about the sign painted on the red bricks. The power lines stand like sentinels. Extension cords looped across the building's face are for something occupants would need, like a television connection.

Is there a daycare next to the burrito building, or was there once upon a time? And if so, what do the children's mothers do; where is there work? I wonder what it's like to be a child in this parched, treeless place. You could sure ride a bike.

The play yard is full of bright plastic toys. A kiddie pool leans against the chain-link fence. There would hardly be room for children in the space. Maybe the toys will sit in the rain and hail and sun until their color is bleached away, like so many other objects in this landscape.

There is evidence of pride here, though. On the side of the building in the right background is a mural with a bright turquoise sky. Someone painted the plowed fields and barns that stretch away from this small place with its wide streets and blocky buildings.

In the Brown picture, "Last Chance Restaurant, Cotton Center, Texas" (a long-faded sign), there is yet another building that looks like a false front, with a slab of plywood where once there was a door. But there are curtains at the window and something else, maybe a television or a fan. More makeshift connections: cords from a closed window past the front, to a trailer snug against the side of the building. And look at those trees! The patches of green. Three little empty flower pots. Cars. A nearby neighbor's place with the garage open.

Someone lives here. Someone is getting by.

A friend pointed out to me that all my stories have people looking for places to live. It's not something I've ever taken for granted.

MURALS, SKY

In Steve Fitch's "Windmill painting, Panhandle, Texas," a close-up photograph of another building mural, a black windmill stands in stark contrast to the sky and flat horizon. This regional idiom represents the impact of agricultural industry on the landscape, and the wide open sky with its constantly changing moods. Without windmills there would have been no water, no farms, no upturned earth. The mural is a public sign of people's hearts. *See what we have accomplished.* Similarly, seventeenth-century Dutch painters represented national pride when they painted rolling farmland, windmills and dramatic skies. In Texas murals, there is a humility in the way things are singled out for remembrance: Jesus ("Painting of Jesus, Hobbs, New Mexico"), windmills, skies, Indians ("Plains Indian painting along the highway, Muleshoe, Texas"; Rick Dingus's "Buffalo Mural, Hale Center, Texas").

In "Radio tower west of Levelland, Texas," Fitch echoes the simple composition of his mural photograph to dramatic effect. Most of the photograph is taken up by a gray sky, a band of pink light and magnificent gray clouds pierced by a tower. The building at the base of the tower is dwarfed by the structure and the huge sky. Derricks and power lines appear as insignificant details on the horizon. The force of nature is on display in that steely sky, but the photographer seems to be saying: Look what people here can do. Look how powerful technology looms over the horizon. *Look how we are changing.*

Peter Brown turned his focus to the vast horizon, too, in "Open space, Grady, New Mexico." What appears to be a subject reduced to just sky and land reveals more in the context of his other photographs. Here you can read the sky for clues. A storm is looming on the distant horizon. This land is notable for what is not there: no plowed, irrigated furrows; no oil pumps; no satellite towers; no roads or buildings. It goes on forever, this open space. It calls to mind a time when it would have been a sea of yellow grass.

You have to look elsewhere (Rick Dingus's "Oilfield trash, Penwell, Texas") to remember how progress and economic growth have too often degraded the land.

An abandoned house provides further clues to the people who have settled this land. In Steve Fitch's photograph "Hallway in an abandoned house, Claude, Texas" we see what former residents of a house chose for decoration. The wallpaper has peeled off, the framing around the door is gone, but artifacts tell us that these people wanted to live with beauty. They pasted up a print of a landscape painting and an American flag. The painting is of a lush landscape, utterly foreign to this region. Every time the house's residents went up the stairs they saw it, so blue, so green. Maybe it was a reminder of what they had left, maybe a dream of something they never had. Maybe it was just pretty. The image of the American flag over the doorway is on newsprint, not even a poster, but there is a poignancy to the patriotism suggested here on fragile yellow paper that, preserved by aridity, has outlasted the house's occupancy.

And there is melancholy in oddly preserved artifacts: a doll on a cabinet near filled fruit jars ("Inside a house beneath the Caprock between Caprock and Maljimar, New Mexico"), a room scattered with mementos of athletic successes ("Trophies in an abandoned school, Bula, Texas"). These photographs of interiors evoke memory and loss. People left and never returned. It feels as if they hurried. Did they depart in a surge of despair? Did they move on and try again? One wonders how a house suddenly loses all utility, all value. One wonders if a child cried for her dolly.

Miguel Gandert and Tony Gleaton, with their emphasis on portraits (kids at play, cowboys, people in their Sunday best), and on occasions (fireworks, parades, car washes) remind us that West Texas is alive, vibrant, and evolving. There is a gentle irony in the fact that their black and white photographs are filled with light and life. There's no melancholy for a lost past in the faces of a family settled on the curb (Gandert's "Parade Crowd, Western Heritage Day, Portales, New Mexico") to await the princesses and sweethearts ("Parade, Western Heritage Day, Portales, New Mexico") heading their way. The line-up of cowboys on lunch break in Gleaton's "Lisa Regan's Young Son" (family round-up, Caprock Canyons, Texas) includes a boy who looks as if he's dressed for serious business. His expression seems to say:

Whatcha lookin at, anyway?

Miguel Gandert

As I drive across the staked plain of the Llano Estacado, I feel small; my car is a red boat in the middle of a vast ocean. The calm horizon stretches before me, the grasses ripple like waves, which environmental historian Dan Flores refers to as "horizontal yellow." The freight trains, over a hundred a day, travel between Clovis and Belen, tracing ancient trails from other centuries. Comanche riding from their winter home in Palo Duro Canyon crossed this vast sea to raid the communities of the Rio Grande Valley; ghosts of the Spanish-Mexican *ciboleros* still hunt the buffalo here. The landscape resonates with the spirit of history. It is an expanse of land that has been contested many times.

But it is that horizon, the ever-changing light, and the imprints of people, that combine to create the depths that dominate the photographs I have made here, reminding me once again that the Llano Estacado is a place of mystery and beauty.

Freight cars west of Clovis, New Mexico, 2004

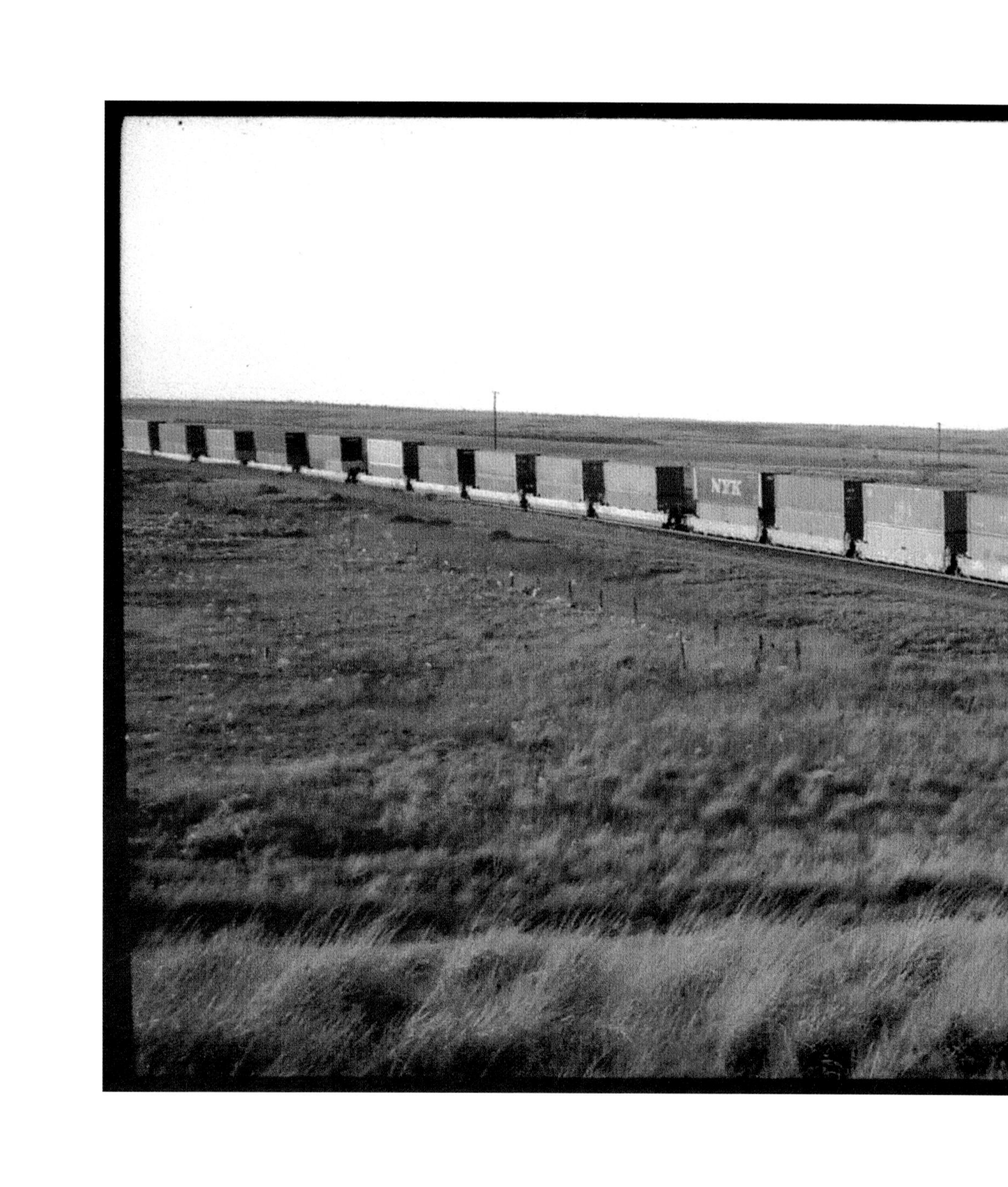

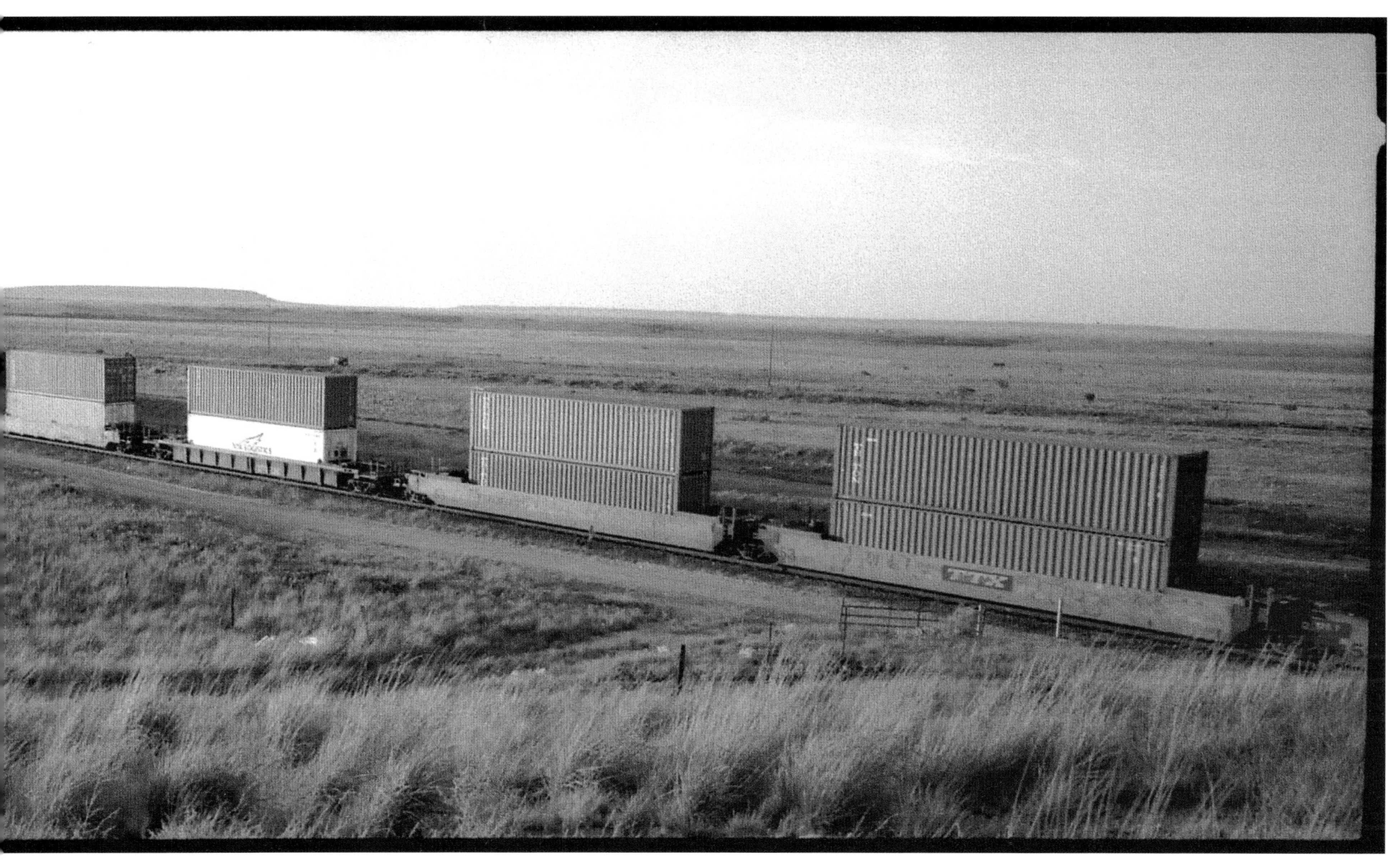

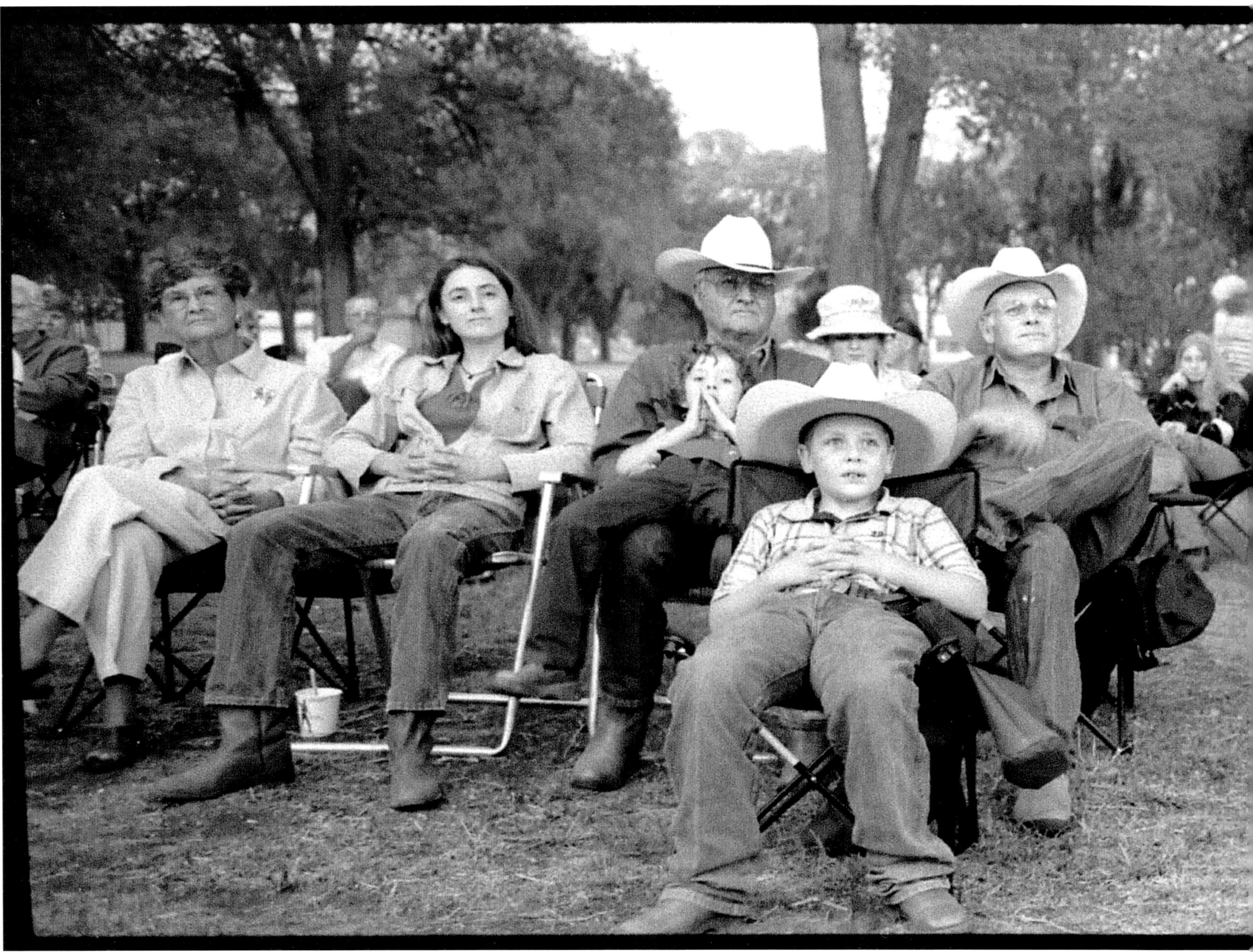

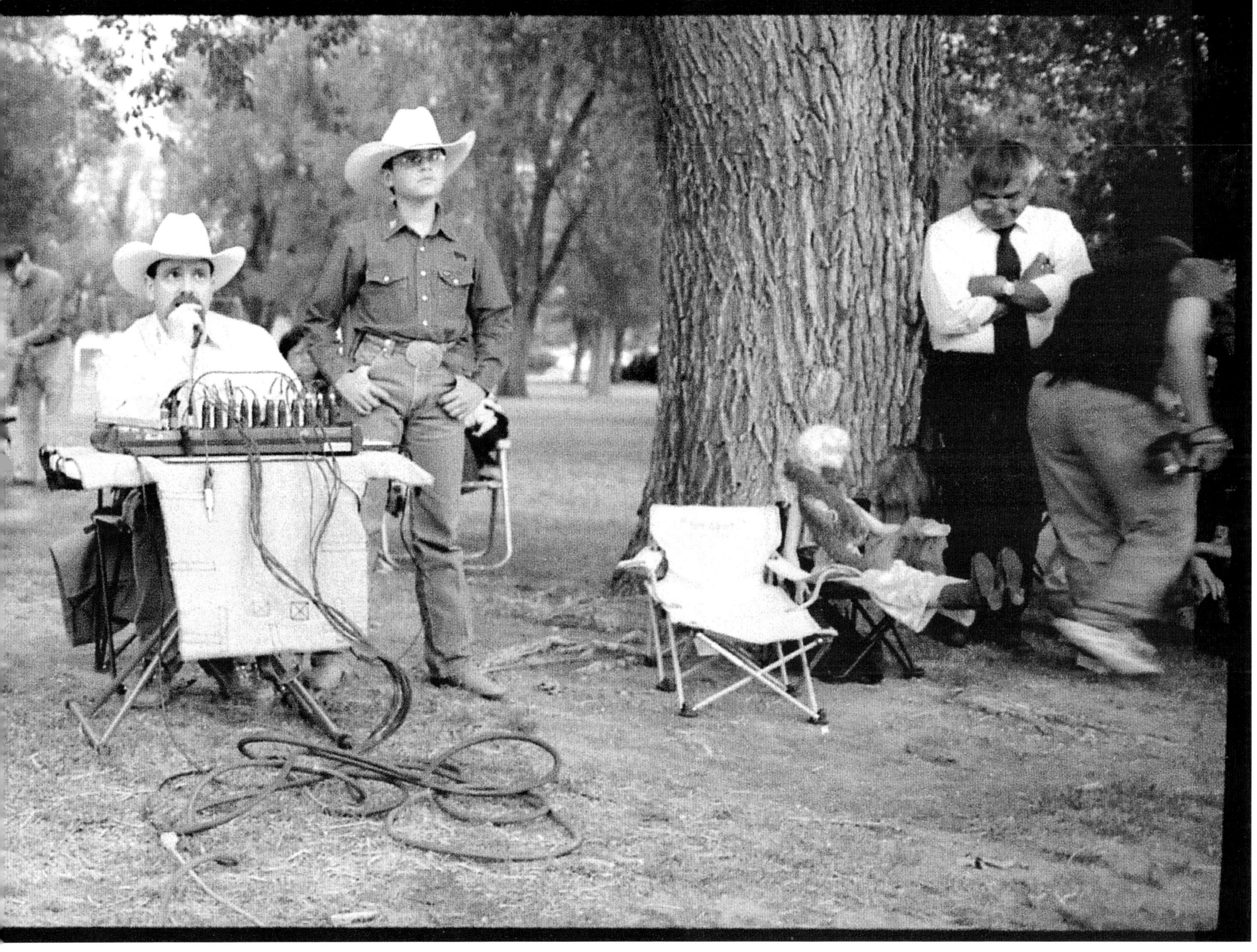

Cowboy hats, Portales, New Mexico, 2004

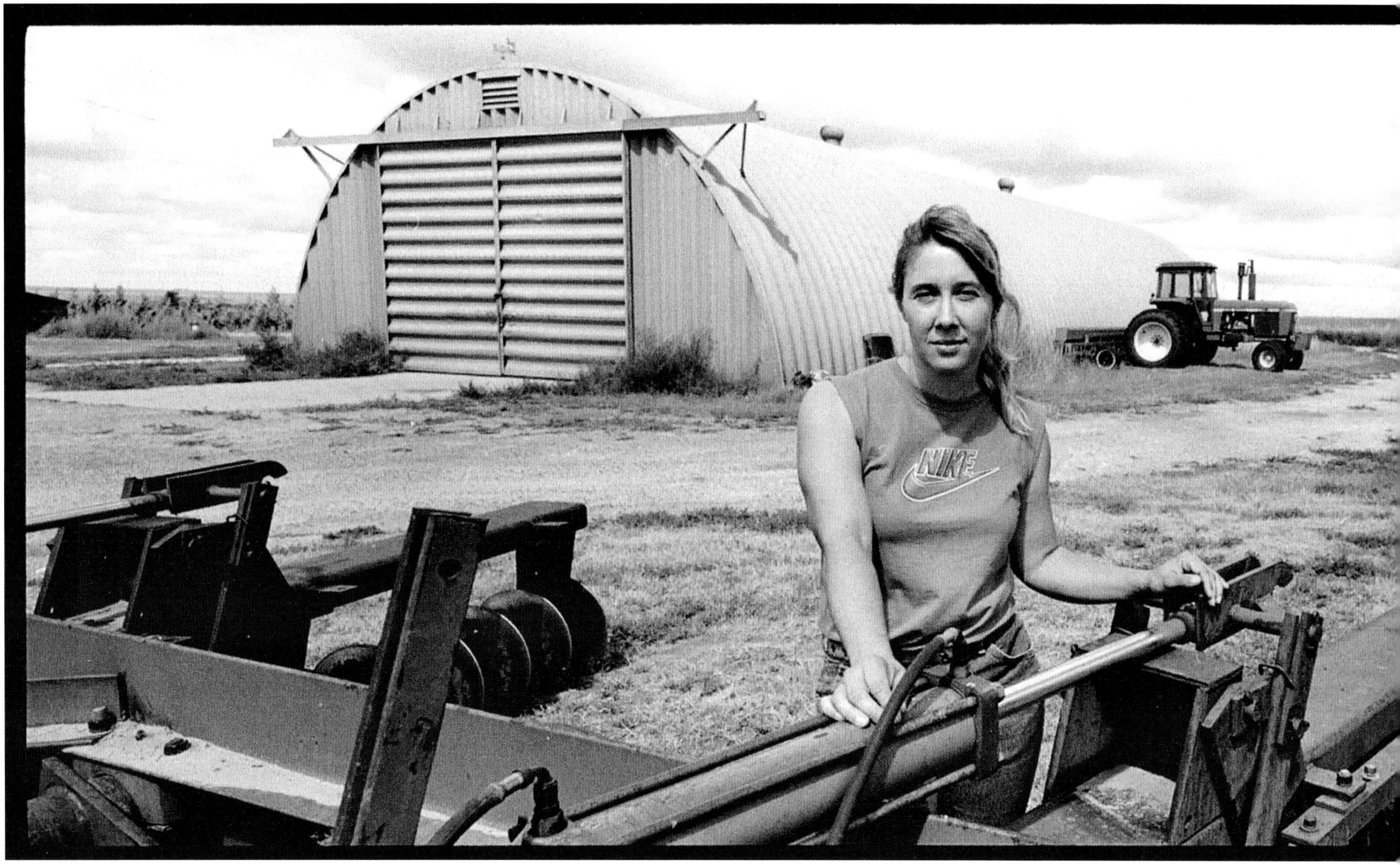

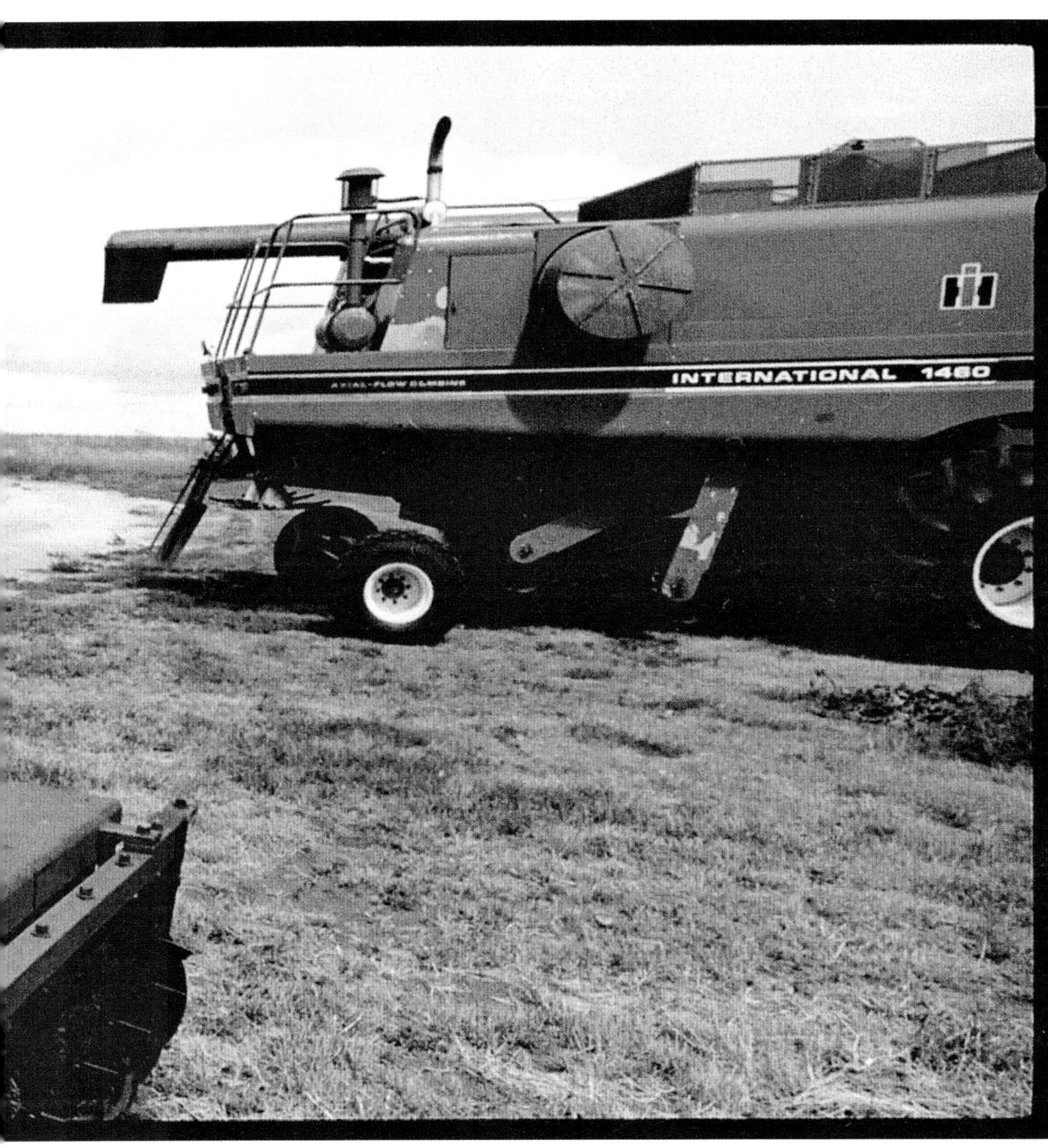

Tammy Vineyard, Clovis, New Mexico, 2005

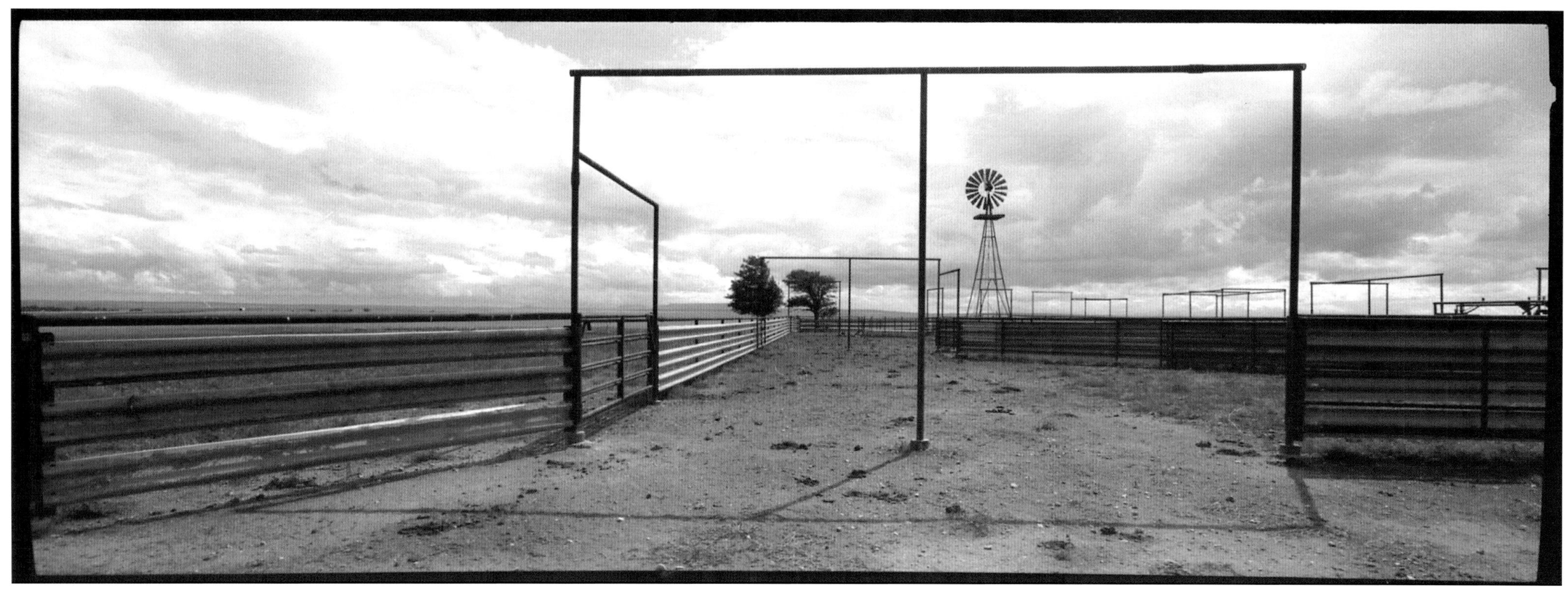

Corral west of Fort Sumner, New Mexico, 2004

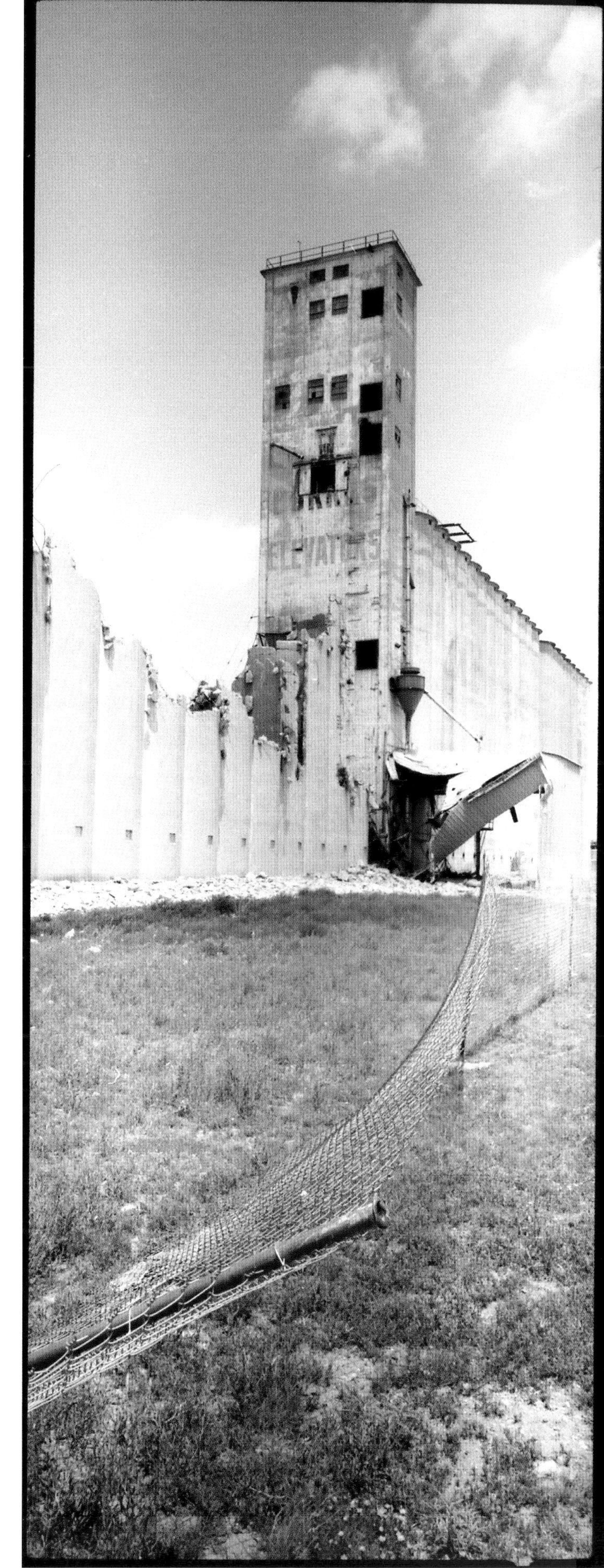

Grain elevator, Lubbock, Texas, 2004

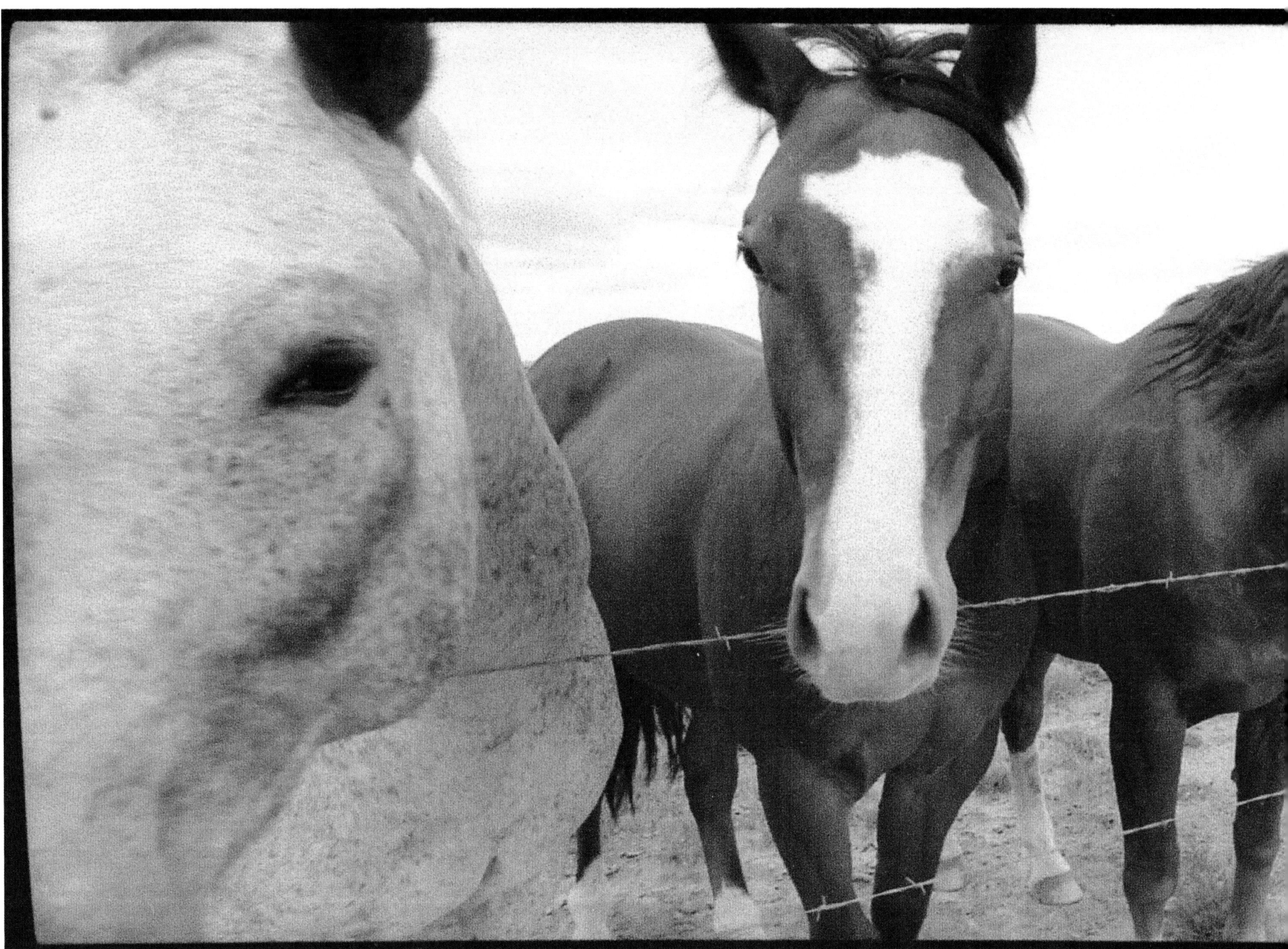

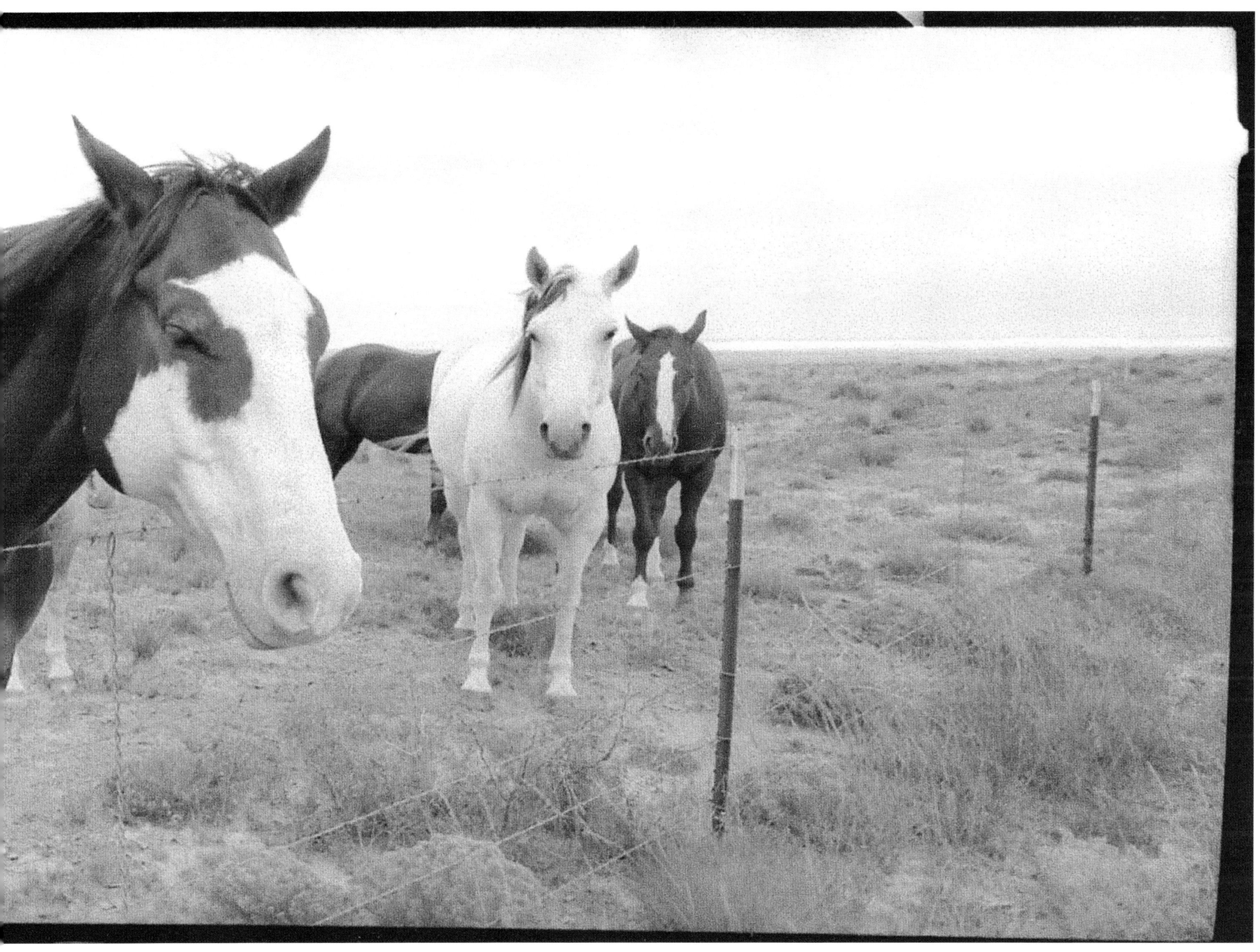

Horses, New Mexico, 2004

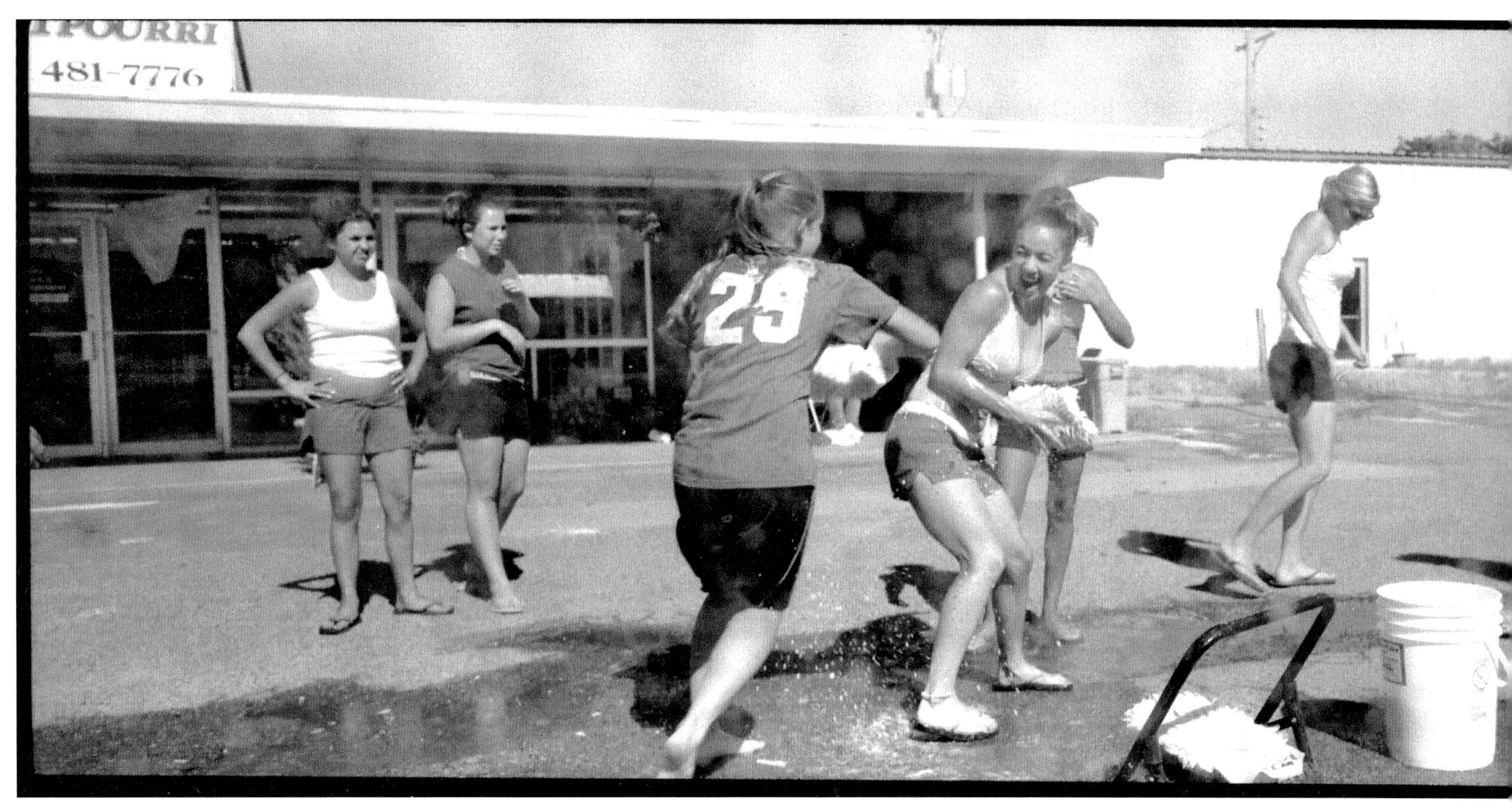
TPOURRI
481-7776
29

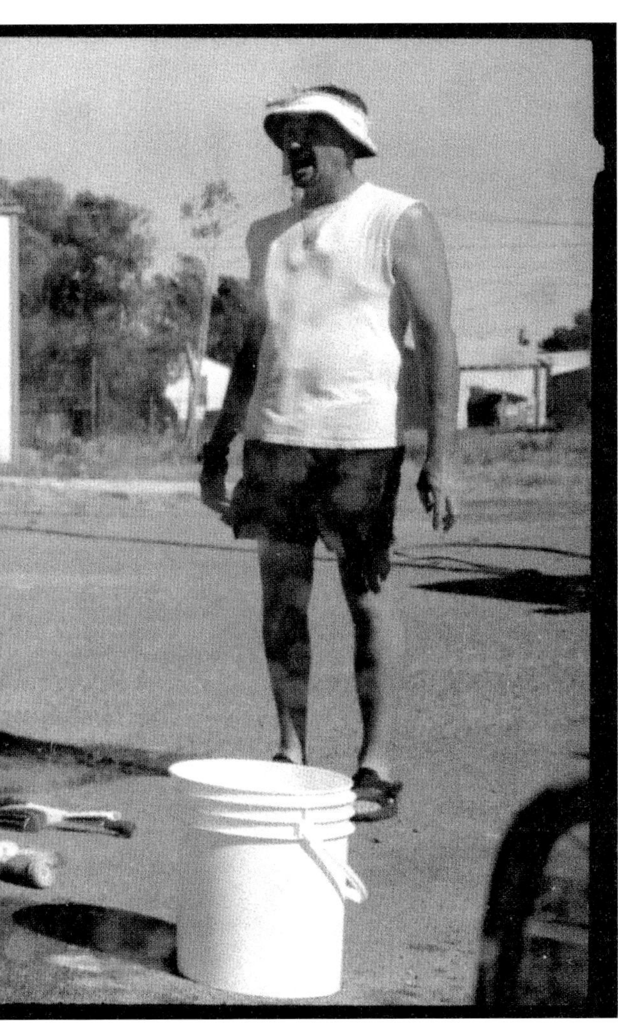

Farwell High School girls' basketball team carwash, Farwell, Texas, 2004

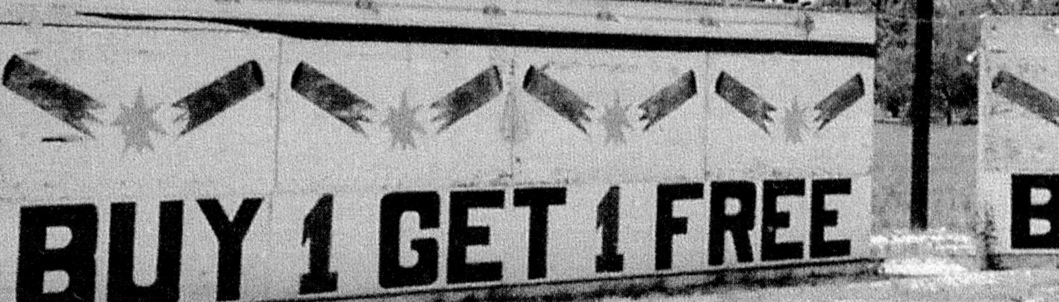
BUY 1 GET 1 FREE
BUY

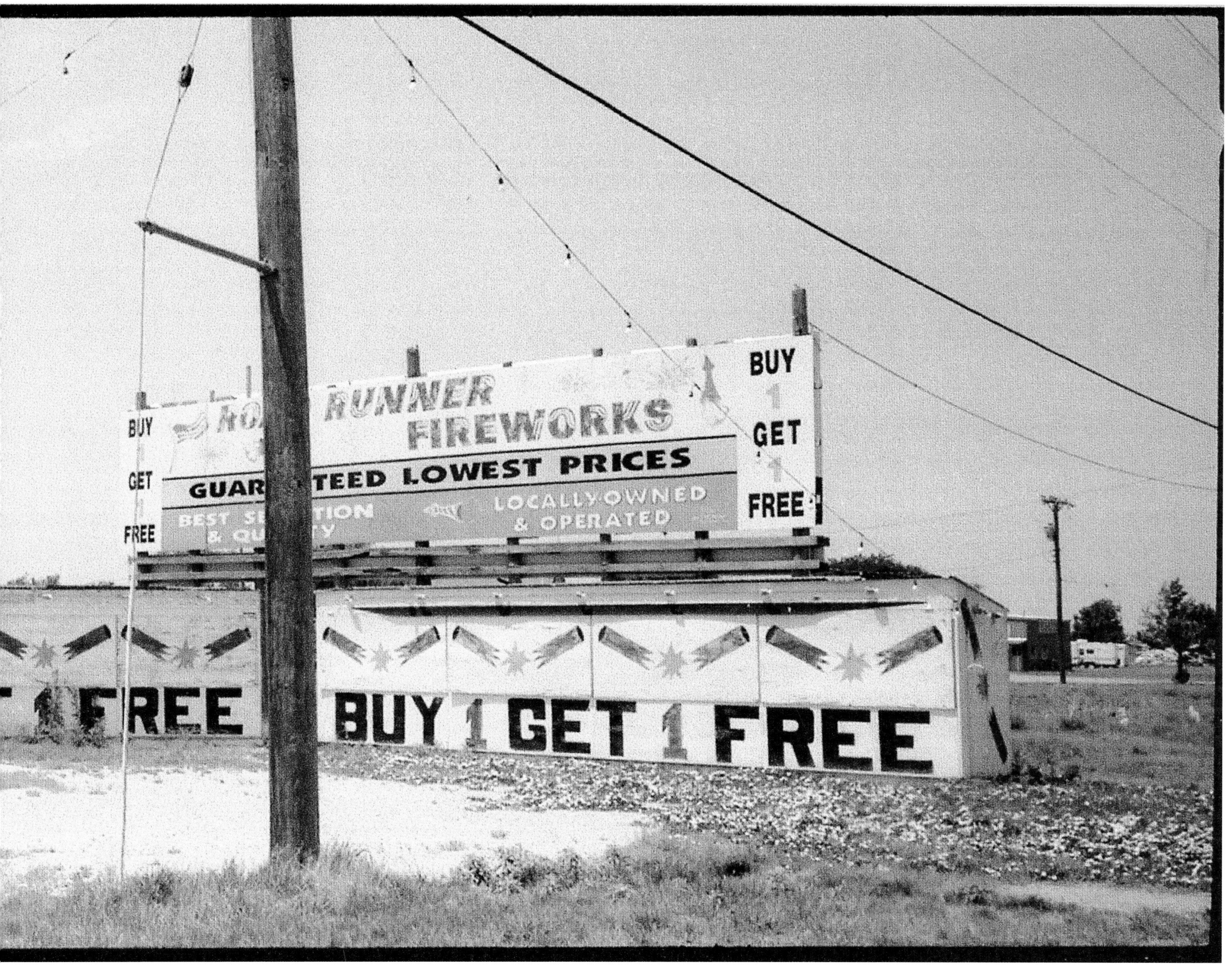

Fireworks vendor near Lubbock, Texas, 2004

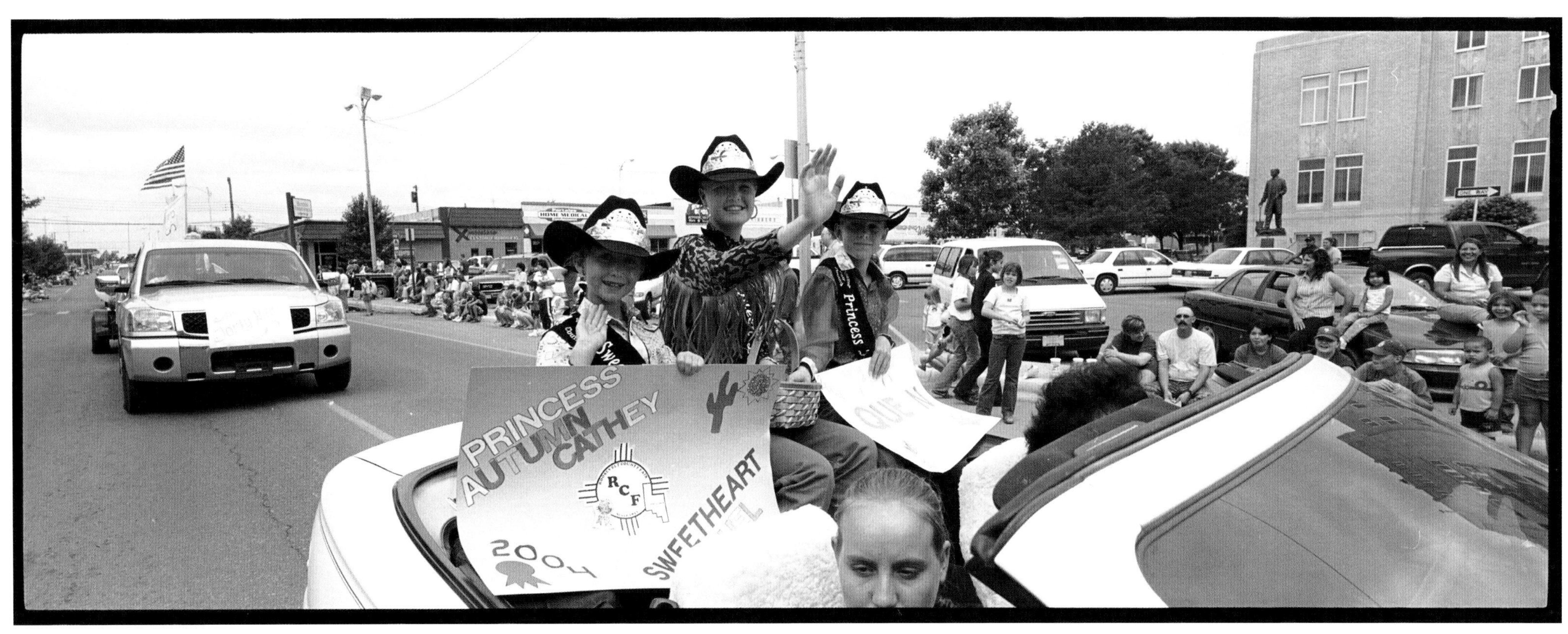

Parade, Western Heritage Day, Portales, New Mexico, 2004

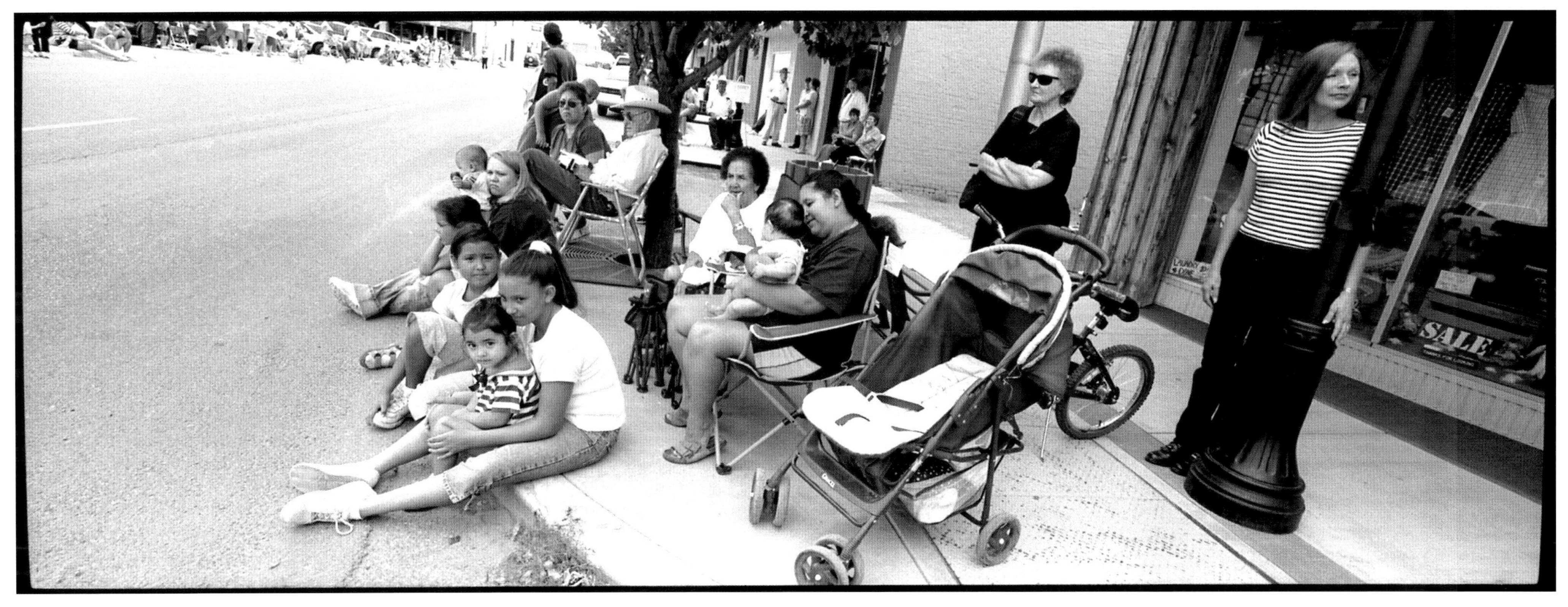

Parade crowd, Western Heritage Day, Portales, New Mexico, 2004

What You Can Remember

STEPHEN GRAHAM JONES

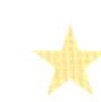

THESE FIELDS. These roads. These pastures.

These people.

These pictures.

Ask me if I ever slept in the furrow of a freshly broke field, no headlights for miles. Ask me if I've pulled a sandfighter back and forth across young cotton, lightning already hitting the utility poles all along the pump road. Ask if I've found big cat tracks in the soft dirt around a hand line at six in the morning, and then looked for a long time in the direction those tracks were going.

Or, no.

Tell me.

Tell me about this kid home sick from school but his mom has to work anyway, so his uncle comes for him, takes him on the tractor all day, showing him how to do wheelies with a 4440, telling the kid to watch out the back glass, see if any shark fins are cutting through the plowed dirt, coming for them. Tell me this kid doesn't still believe in those sharks. Tell me that kid doesn't still close his eyes and pray for those sharks.

Tell me about finding, way out in a field that's been in CRP (Conservation Reserve Program) for years, a rusted shut old monkey wrench, and carrying it around until one of the old guys rolls it in his hand and says this is one of the tools the Model T came with.

Tell me about, when it's blowing too hard to even sandfight anymore, putting goggles on instead and leaning out into the wind, for the arrowheads you can only find on days like that.

Tell me about digging holes in the ground deep enough for the four giant feet of a windmill and then standing under that windmill when the winch truck has it up in the sky, getting down in those holes to guide the feet in like they need to be.

Tell me about farm sale hauls, stringing them together into a carnival of trailers and hitching them home a quarter mile at a time, then never even unloading those trailers.

Tell me, please.

Or let me go there again.

Just that.

To walk with my granddad through the mesquite, looking for a heifer with her first calf and knowing if we find her that she's coming for us, but still we wade through the scrub, my granddad always guiding me behind him, like he's ever been taller than five and a half feet. Let me sling corn out to the turkeys again, let me still believe that shinnery, it's not just a greasy bush but the top of ancient trees long buried. Let me spend the day piling pie melons into the bed of a pick-up until the leaf springs are flat and then back the truck up to a caliche pit and launch those melons one by one into space. Let my great-grandfather, Pop, let him take my hand in his again and then, with his other, latch onto the electric fence. Let me work the fields with him, up one row, back down another, until the light's gone.

Let me walk out to the old broke-down houses some more, and dig through the trash, cut my fingers on the rusted barrels. Find a smoky perfume bottle with the lid still on, so that if I open it, I know I'll be able to smell the old days.

Let the snakes pull at my pantslegs again, let the dogs chase me through the fields when my truck's run out of gas, let me stand up with twenty feet of hand line balanced to either side and listen to the school band two miles away, at Friday night's football game.

Give me those stars so close overhead, I mean.

What I want is to lie on top of an oil tank in the deepest field I can find, no rails around me, and wait for the meteor shower to rip silver lines in the sky. What I want is to get down off another pumpjack and still have both legs. What I want is to fix another busted heater hose with a beer can and duct tape, to find more spring-handled slag hammers in the ditch, to move more trailer houses and then spend the rest of the afternoon chasing down grass fires we've started, using a torch to cut those anchors that were supposed to have held that trailer there forever.

What I want is to drop down into the coolness of the draw one more time, the trees down there like another world. What I want is to be twelve again, chasing a porcupine into a fallen-down house. What I want is to show off for another girl by jumping from the bed of a truck with a .22, crawling into the mesquite after a rattlesnake, ending up face-to-face enough with it that I have to pass the gun back over my shoulder.

No.

What I want is to stand from that mesquite again, my face not swelling up, both my eyes working, and then run into the lake for the rest of the day, fall asleep on a tube, not wake up until I'm on the wrong shore, so that walking back takes until almost midnight, with no shoes.

What I need, though.

What I need is to ride in the parade in Stanton one more time, one last time. To wear my uncle's boots with the silver dollars up their sides and to walk into the drugstore for a double cheeseburger, and know that my dad came here too, and his dad before him.

What I need is to feed the goldfish in my grandmother's stock tank some more, until I'm breaking off pieces of my hand for them, so they can live forever. What I need is to spend a few days digging up the black plastic of an oil pad and stuffing it behind the seat of the truck, because anywhere else and it'll blow away again. What I need is to pull another disc rig across a field that's just had winter wheat growing on it, so it's full of rabbits and mice and snakes that will pull in fifteen hawks by lunch. What I need is to throw bottles and rocks at the hawks, because it's slaughter back there. What I need is to smuggle a rabbit into our halfway paneled bathroom in the middle of another bubonic plague, and then let that rabbit bite me deep in the web of my hand, and have that rabbit die two hours later, for no reason I can see.

What I need is to lie in my bed again, my hand swollen and hidden, and listen to the butane pumps popping out there, as far as I can imagine.

What I don't need, don't want anyway, is to go out to the square of concrete I played all my basketball on, go out there the morning we get the bad news about somebody, go out there and shoot shot after shot, until my cousin she comes out and just sits there by the concrete pad watching me, not saying anything.

What I don't need is another third grade recess, to lose the ball over the fence, have to go into the cemetery for it, and on each of those headstones, part of my name's there.

You can only hold your breath so long, too.

But it's not all like that.

There's racing your trucks down the back roads, having to use other trucks to pull them from fences and ditches, and from each other. There's shooting bottles from fence posts all day and into the night. There's the drive-in you'll take your kids to someday, the bugs swimming in that dusty finger of light like they want to live there too. And there's the dances.

Give me those dances again, please.

Put me anywhere—up against a carpeted wall in sixth grade, all the other guys in my grade standing there too, none of us sure what to do, or years later, leave me walking into a dance in Big Spring, my best hat on, clean enough boots, shiny buckle, no gas in the truck whatsoever, so we're going to have to find a girl with her dad's keys, her dad the manager out at the gin, and then leave me at that gin too. Let me wait for morning, so I can listen to the old men lie, so they can grub peanuts up from the tilted table and tell me what a strange world it was when the cars first came to town, how all the men had their arms in slings for a while, from the cranks. Let my Pop tell me again about the men who were old when he was young, the men driving tractors for the first time, standing up at the turnrows to lean back on the traces, falling instead off the tractor. It's where he learned a lot of his more choice words, he used to tell me, rapping his knuckles on the table in something a lot like laughter. And I can see them, those old men falling back. I can see all of them, can still feel the electricity passing through my Pop, directly to me.

It's still there.

So, yeah, ask me if I came out of that fell-down house with a quill or not, ask me if I ever dug skunks and squirrels from the plugs of hand lines and then drank from those hand lines. Ask me if a cow will eat mesquite beans if it's a dry enough summer, ask me if you can watch the horses to know if a tornado's coming. Ask me what you do when you've fallen down into a storm cellar so old the house it used to go with is gone. Ask me what you do when you have no light, when a bullsnake's pushed up against the wall opposite you in that cellar. Ask me what that sounds like when a bullsnake does its hissing little roar in the dark, so that you can feel it on your face, and don't yet know it's just a bullsnake. Ask me what it's like to ease along a circle system at night, checking the sprinkler heads, your yellow beams full of mist, owls watching you from the bowed spine of the circle.

Or, find one of those owls yourself, scuttling through the cotton just after it's been sprayed in November. Find one of those owls, find two, three, six, none of them even a foot tall but their eyes so big, swimming with the poison. Find them and fill your truck with them, drive around for the rest of the day like you can save them. Let them watch you from the floorboard, their heads turning with one mind.

Maybe start climbing things, too. The radio towers if they're insulated. Or truck stop signs. Truck stop signs go nearly as high, and will have flat places up there you can sit, dangle your legs down into all that open air.

Spend algebra and lunch and English on top of the school some days. Just watching. Knowing the sharks are out there. They have to be.

Or go see your Pop at the home, all of you, cousins and uncles and everybody, and push his wheelchair up and down the hall, answer his questions about where his wife is, and isn't, and then suddenly be the last one with your hands on that wheelchair, everybody else already in the parking lot, so that it's just you and him, and then realize that you don't know how to let go of these two handles. That you can't.

What you can do, I think, the only thing to do, your cousin watching from her place by the concrete, is shoot shot after shot, the horses in their corral watching you, and let her throw the ball back to you when you miss, and know that it all counts for something. That it has to.

What you can remember instead, if you want—and you do, you have to—is standing in a field of young cotton at daybreak. What you can remember from a thousand miles away, from twenty years down the line, is how, when the sun first breaks over that flat edge of the world, how every leaf for three hundred acres around, it turns for that heat, that light. And you can too. Just close your eyes and let it wash over you.

These fields. These roads. These pastures.

This place.

I'm still there.

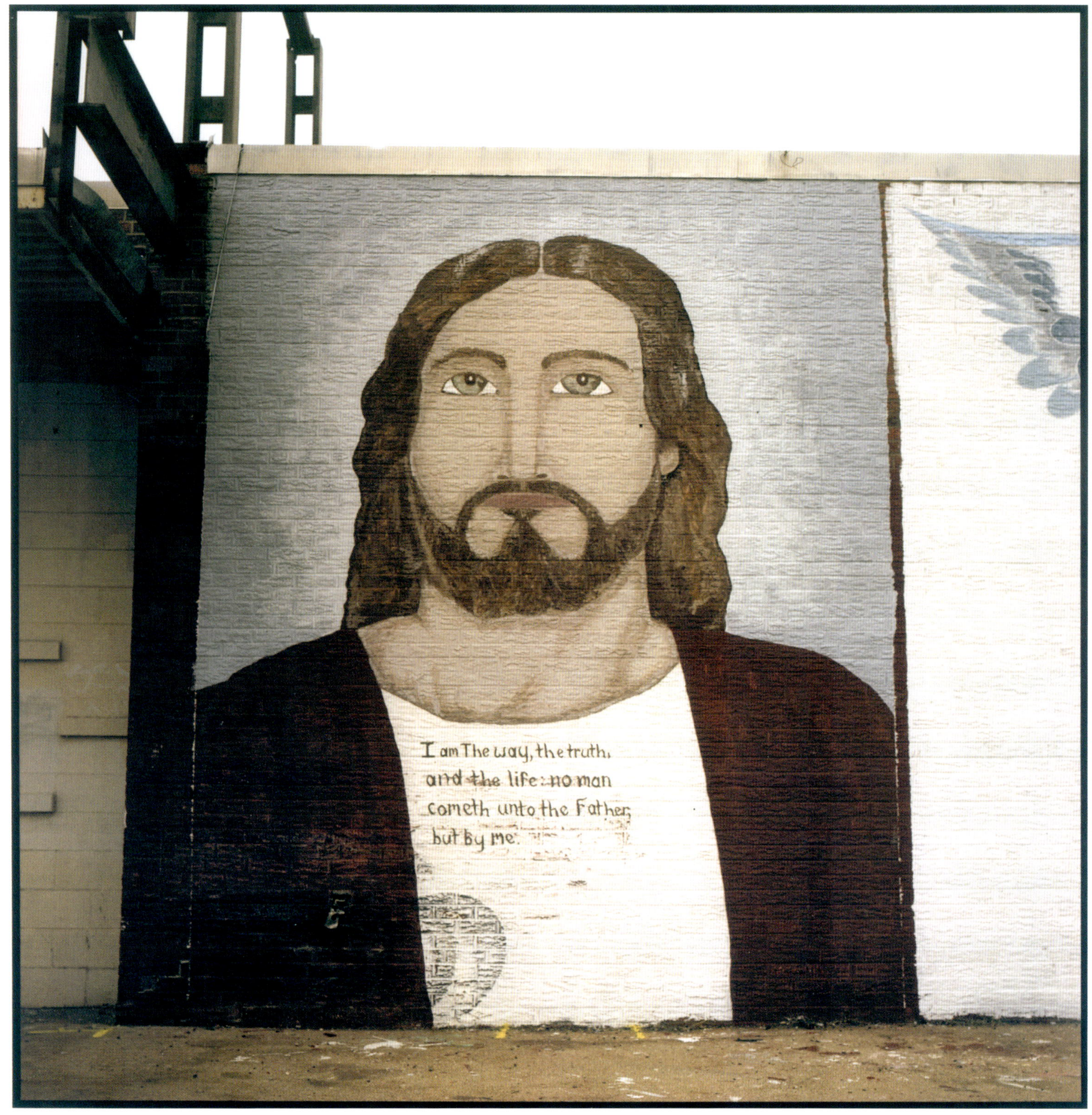

Painting of Jesus, Hobbs, New Mexico, 2004

Steve Fitch

Beginning in 1971, nearly all of my photographs have been made on various trips of exploration, which evolve from a starting idea followed by a period of travel and discovery, and conclude with the struggle of editing and selection. The three groups of my Llano Estacado images included in this book were made in a similar manner.

For my first book, published in 1976, *Diesels and Dinosaurs: Photographs from the American Highway*, I took photographs of vernacular subjects such as billboards, neon signs at night, drive-in movie theater murals, snakepit and dinosaur park sculptures, and other phenomena that gave me an insight into the American roadside psyche. I believe my recent photographs of mural paintings and signs do a similar thing for the Llano Estacado: each is a window through which we can peer into the particular, often funny and eccentric, history and world view that has evolved on the Llano Estacado.

A more recent photographic project of mine—published in 2003 in the book *Gone: Photographs of Abandonment on the High Plains*—involved traveling the length and breadth of the American High Plains photographing the interiors of the many abandoned buildings that are found there. Over a ten-year period, I made numerous exploring trips in my pickup, crisscrossing the High Plains portions of North and South Dakota; Montana and Wyoming; Nebraska, Colorado, Kansas, and Oklahoma; West Texas and eastern New Mexico. A good portion of the Llano Estacado, like the rest of the High Plains, has lost much of its rural population over the past hundred years or so, and the signs of this loss are evident in the many abandoned structures that dot the region. The interior photographs included here are an outgrowth of the earlier project that resulted in the book *Gone*.

The third group of my photographs included in this book, the radio tower images, are, perhaps, the ones that come most specifically from my explorations on the Llano. Some parts of this region are so surprisingly flat that anything that sticks up vertically from the landscape takes on an overwhelming presence. In these images, one can see the technological intricacies of the towers themselves and feel the mystical beauty of the big, atmospheric sky that floods over the wide terrain of the Llano Estacado. The tower photographs catalyze an awareness and appreciation of this powerful, often intimidating landscape.

Radio tower near Field, New Mexico, 2004

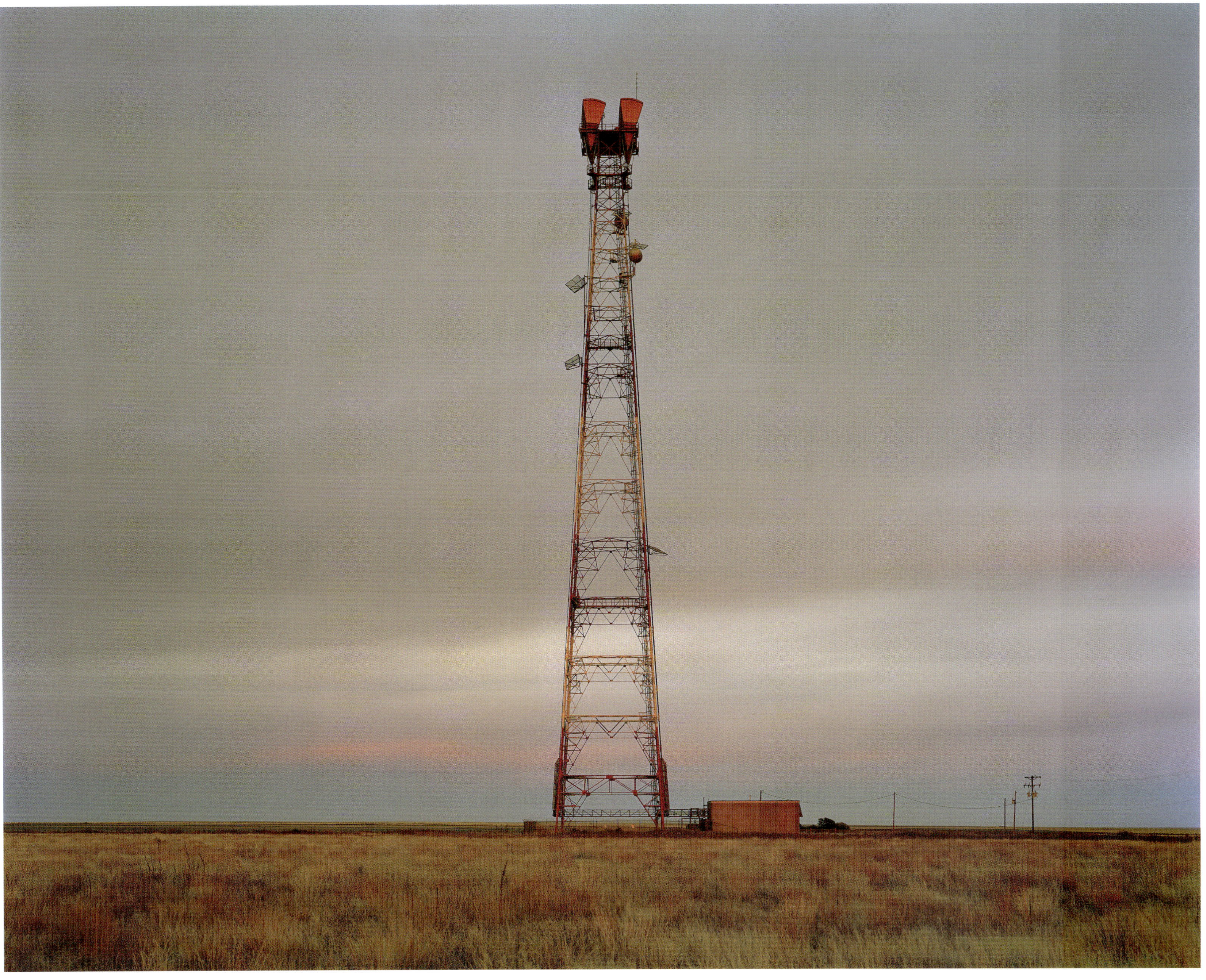

Hallway in an abandoned house, Claude, Texas, 2004

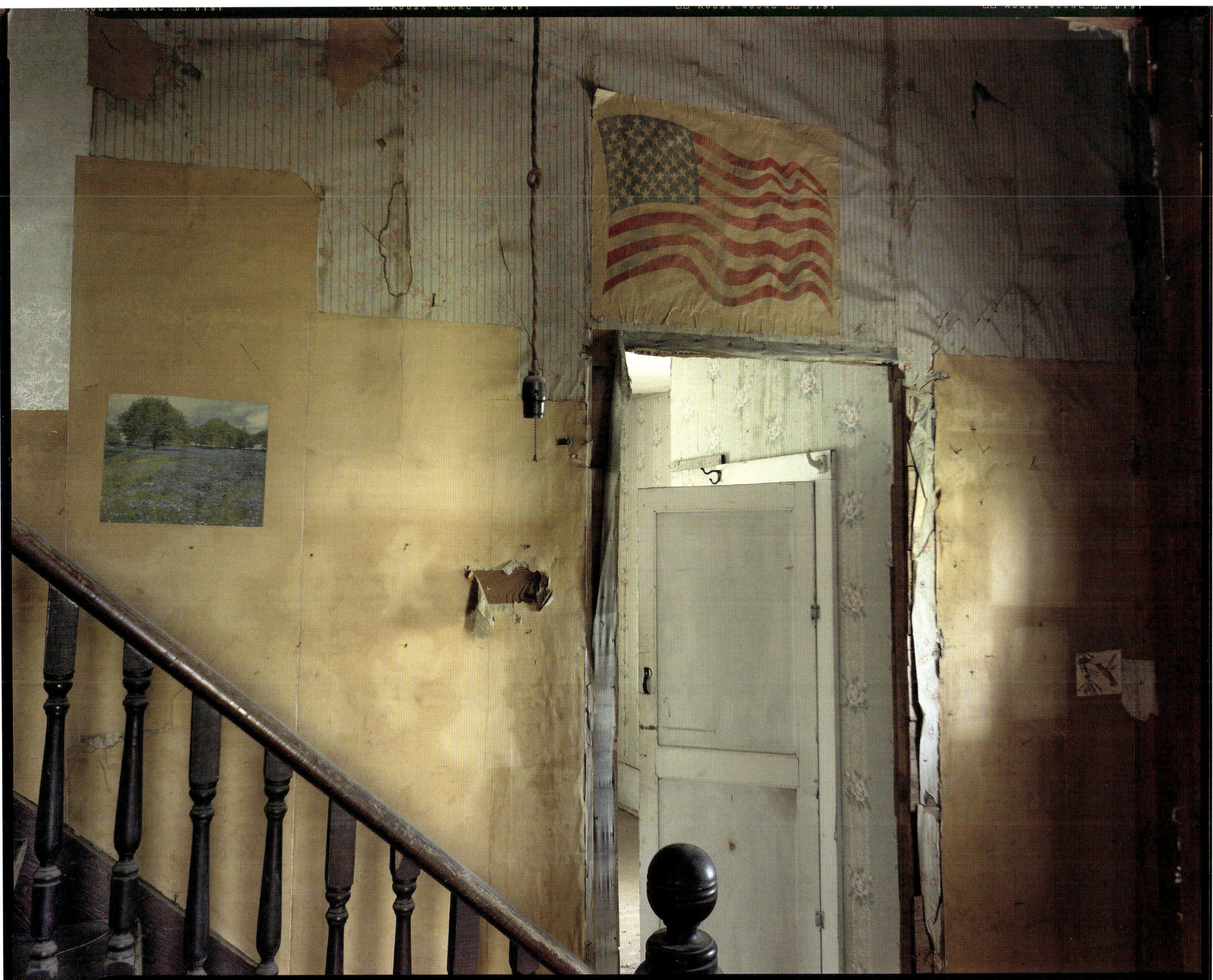

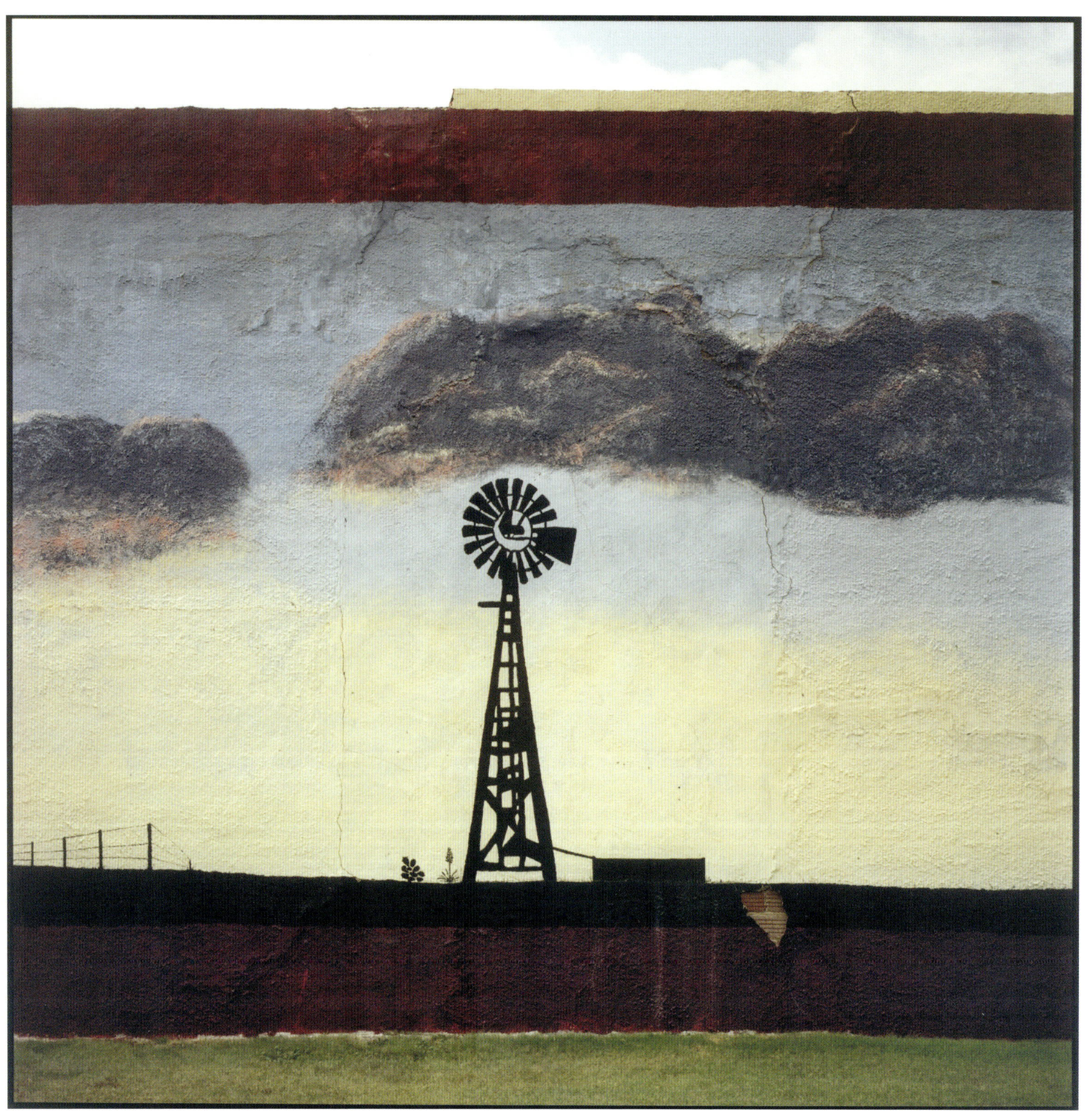

Windmill painting, Panhandle, Texas, 2005

Radio tower west of Levelland, Texas, 2004

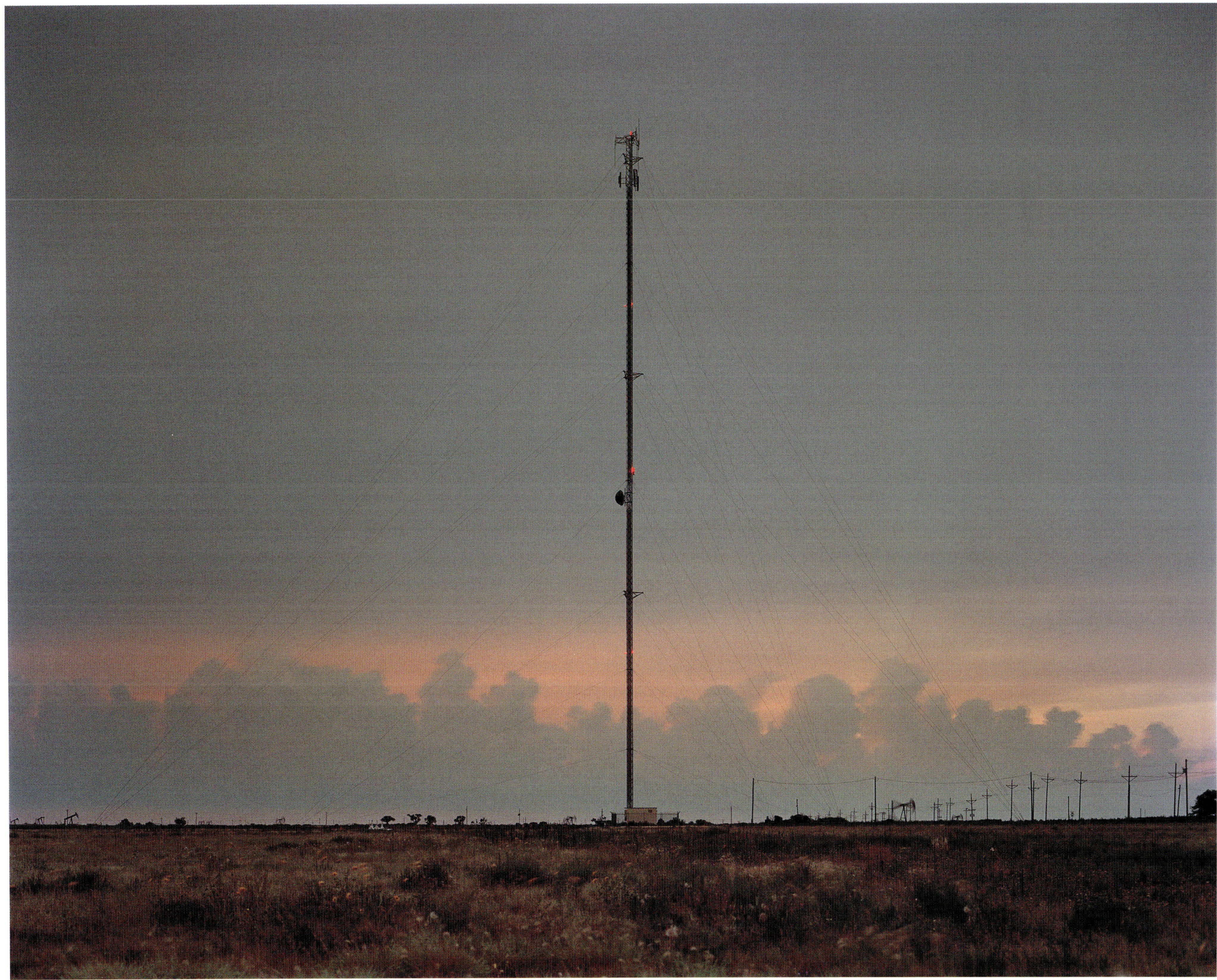

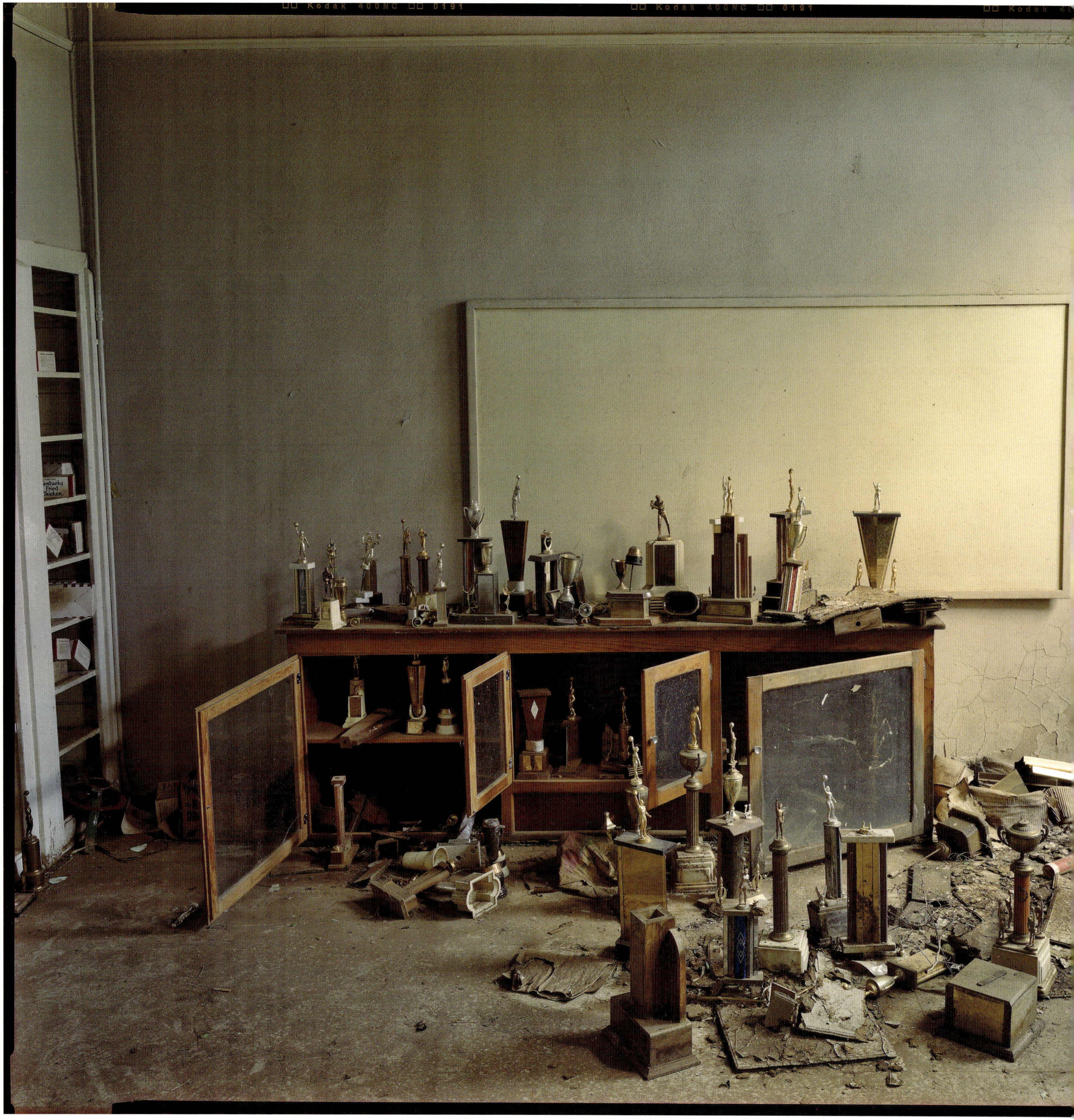

Trophies in an abandoned school, Bula, Texas, 2004

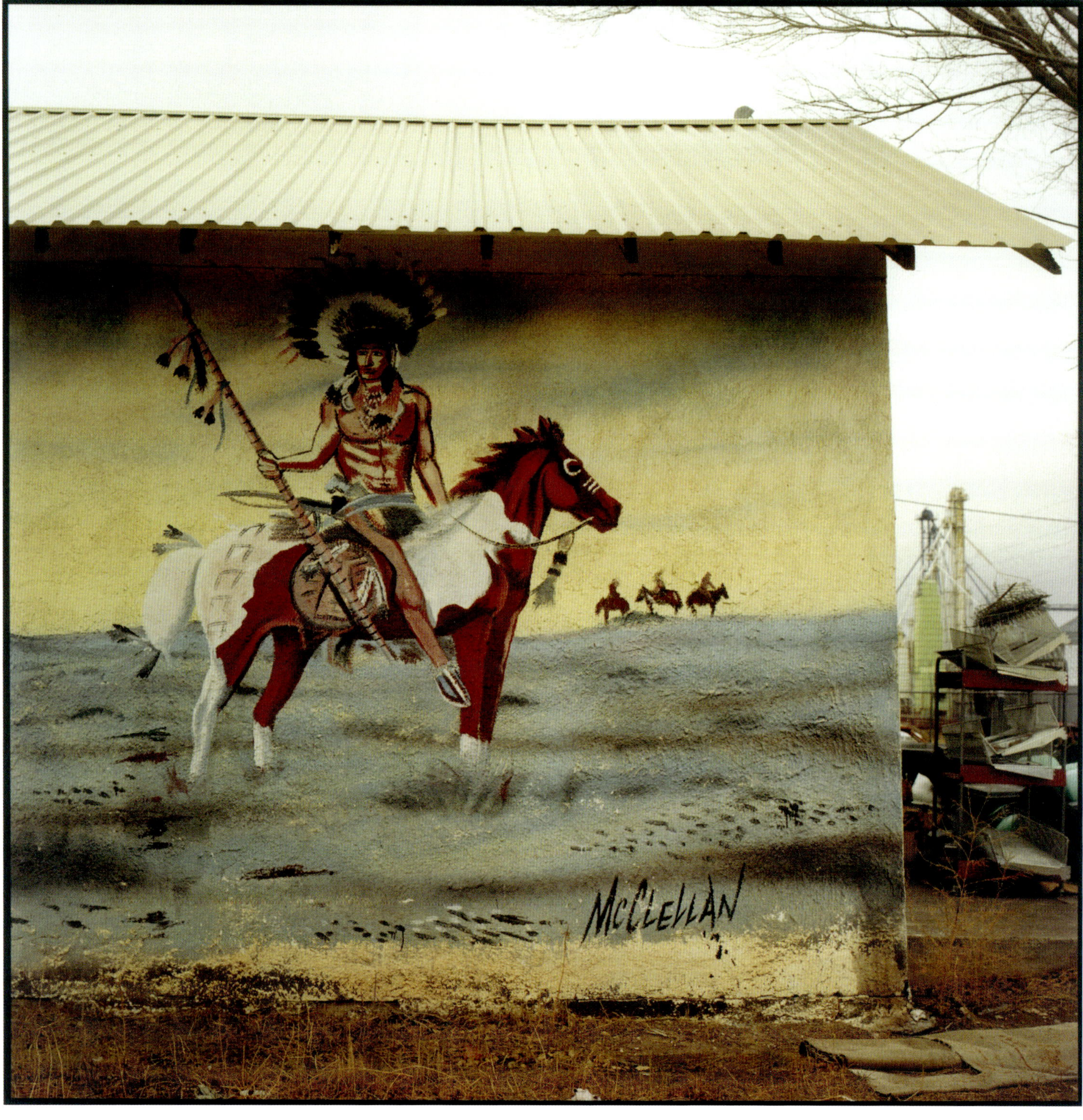

Plains Indian painting along the highway, Muleshoe, Texas, 2004

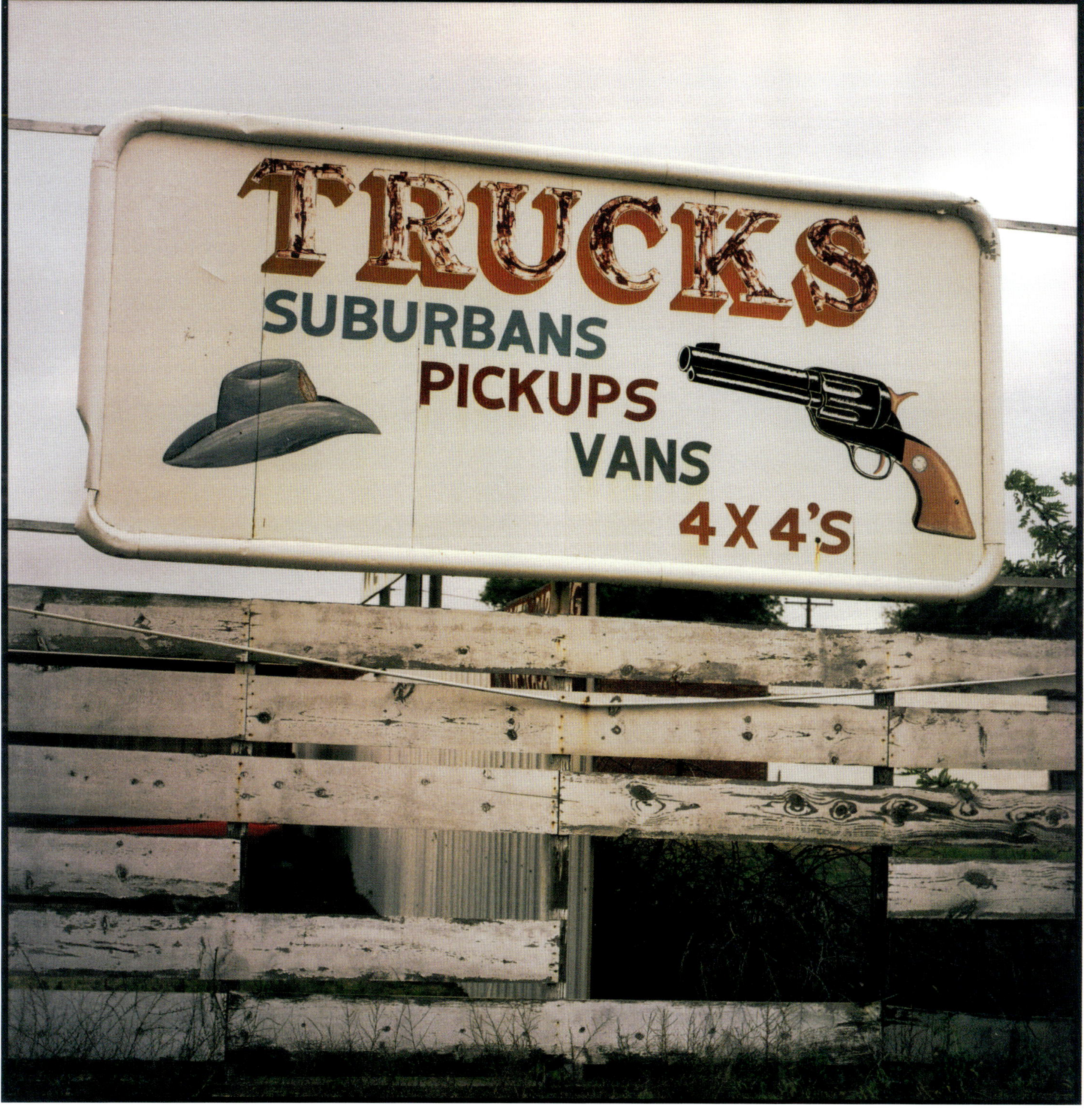

Sign, downtown Pampa, Texas, 2004

Inside a house beneath the Caprock between Caprock and Maljimar, New Mexico, 2006

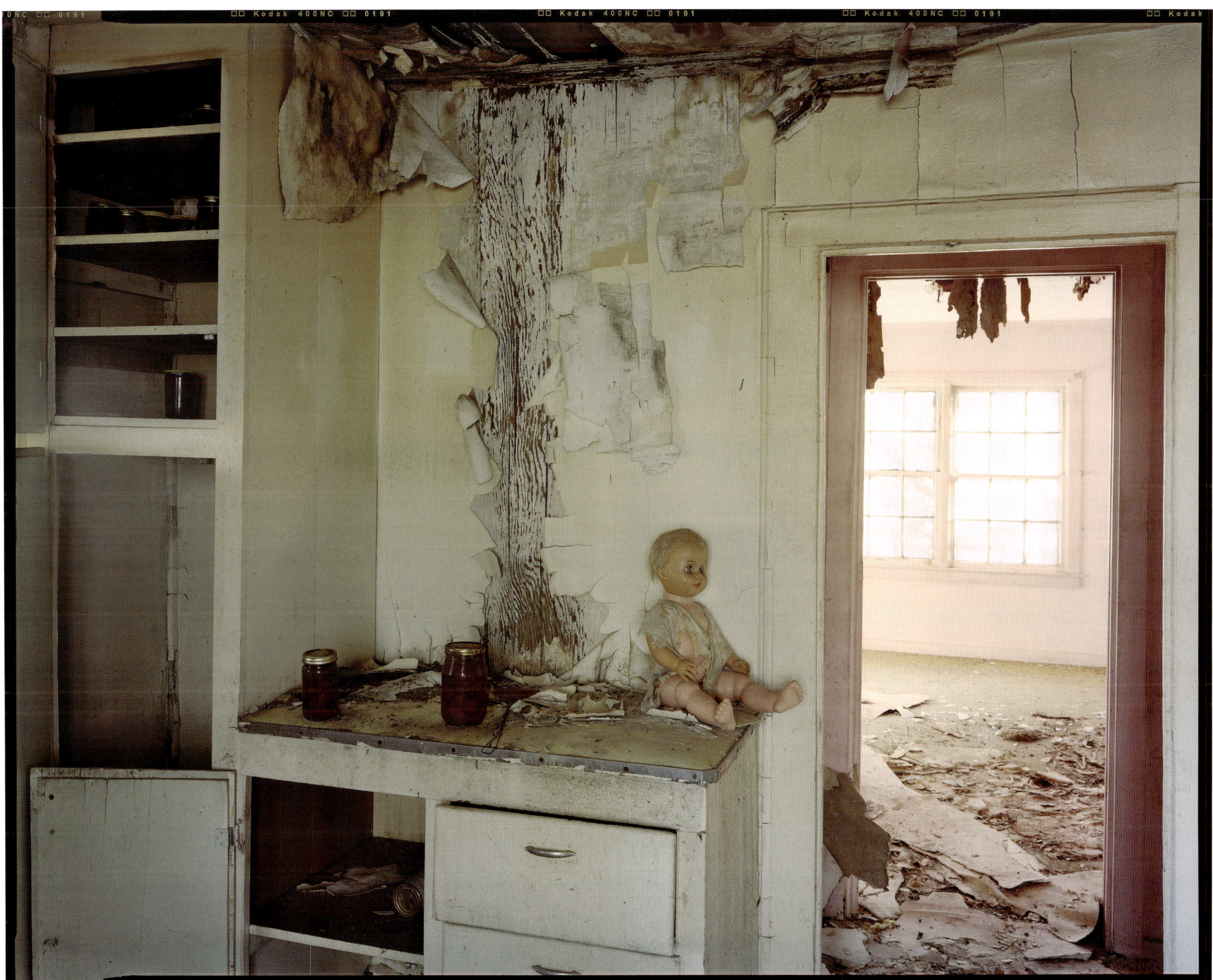

Kodak 400NC 0191
Kodak 400NC 0191
Kodak 400NC 0191
Kodak

Radio tower near Umbarger, Texas, 2005

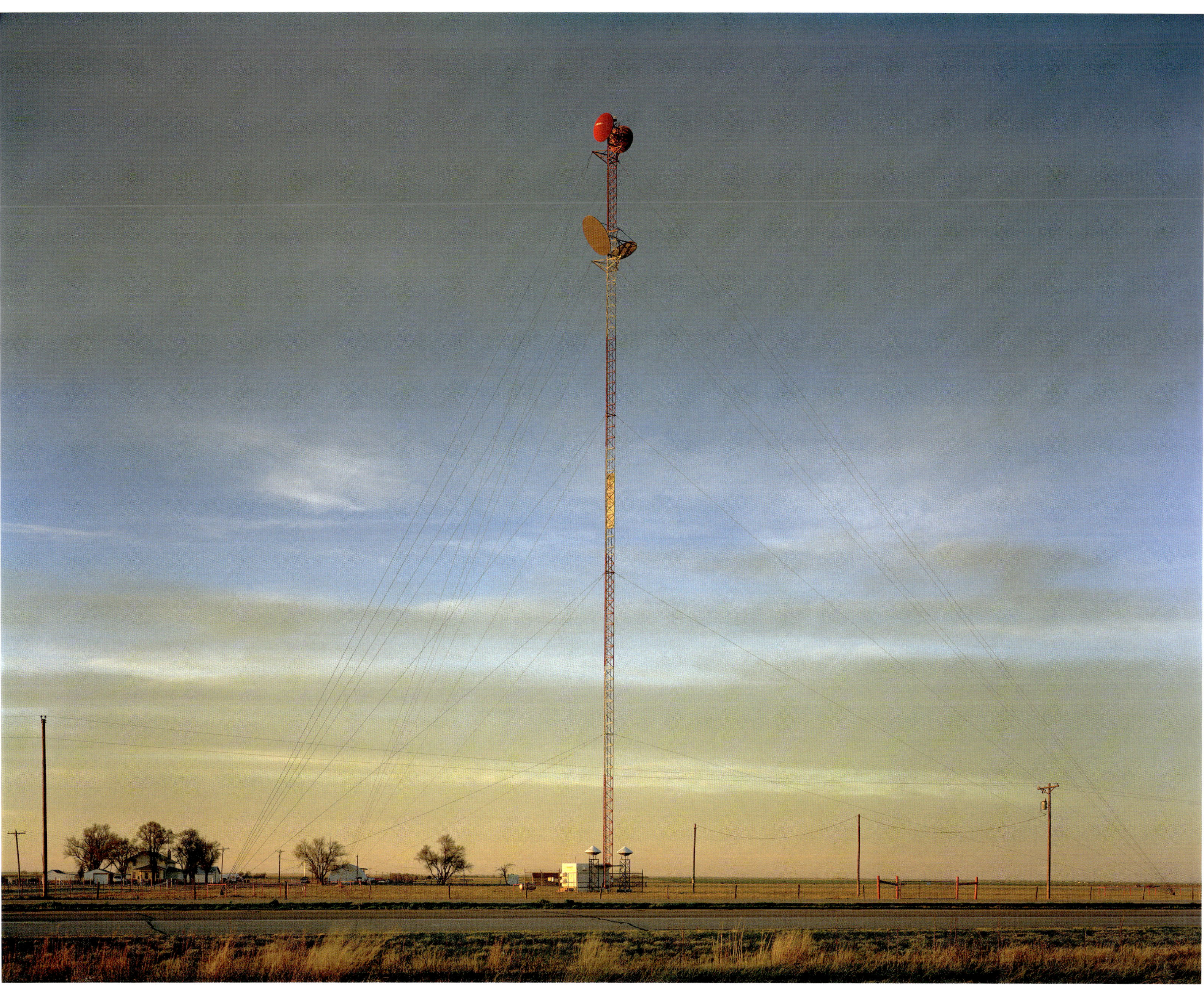

Waiting

RICK BASS

WHAT CURIOUS CREATURES WE ARE, capable of holding two complex emotions at once, often in a tortured amalgam. It's true that we tend to see what we want to see, but it's also true enough that there are times when the camera doesn't lie. As a Texan, I came to the viewing of these photographs anticipating one thing—a celebration, perhaps slightly tinged by the weathering of myth, of austerity, endurance, and a self-sufficiency forged in part by geographic isolation—but I have witnessed here, for the most part, quite another thing, a thing to which I cannot yet quite place a name. And I have to wonder if perhaps it was this kind of expectation, this same cheap or unearned hope, with which so many others have first come to the Llano, and, in trying to bend the landscape and their lives around that internal and already-made or dreamed map, have ultimately foundered instead and run hard aground.

I was already familiar with the rural photographs of Peter Brown, of whom I am a huge fan. Call me sentimental and subjective, but it seems to me his photographs usually possess a unique mix of humor, reverence, beauty, and even—to push further into the realm of the kind of abstraction that makes talking about art, or, for that matter, landscape, so difficult—courage.

Looking at his Llano Estacado photographs, however, I experienced a different kind of resonance. His celebrated photos of courage and integrity seem almost to be, in this instance, a kind of burial of this landscape, and of this time and culture of man. Being Peter Brown, however, he does so with dignity, respect, love, and even—you can see it there if you want to see it, in the edges between the living and the dead, the dying and the not-yet-dead—with hope.

Maybe.

Somehow it seems to me that there is rarely anything that is clean and simple about any of us any more, and the way in which we behold the world. Unless I am just imagining this—and I do not think I am—it seems to me that always, our world now consists of two things, rather than one, and that it does so in unsustainable conflict or paradox: hope yielding to despair, presence yielding to absence.

In Brown's "St. Isadore Church, Lenorah, Texas" we see a dazzling caliche of brilliant aridity, the shores of which lap right up to the vertical coolwater blue of the church, and the skull-and-crossbones pumpjack in the background, grinning at the wind-whittled wooden spar of power line, which is echoed then, like a cast shadow, by the sunny little yellow cross that strives brightly to remain in the foreground.

In Brown's "Railroad shack home, Fairview, Texas," we gaze with some nameless mix of horror, bemusement, regret, and familiarity at the curious and isolated shack perched on the gnawed-down worn-out landscape (the dry soil appearing incapable of yielding anything, though still it is furrowed, prepared, made ready for our ceaseless hopes or expectations), the shack seeming to await almost patiently, —as if yearning for the Rapture— the impending wisp-away tornado-suck of the slender cloud that hangs just overhead, canted down and coming, it seems, for the shack. And what bitter story or truth it is, that such an insubstantial cloud is all that is required to hoist up such an insubstantial and storyless assemblage of lumber.

The Tony Gleaton and Miguel Gandert photos—the portraits—rattle me further. On some days I have looked at them and admired the artistry of them, have found hope in the whimsy of composition and the elements—the round windmill-fan and two solo windmill-dependent trees amidst all-else horizontal grids in Gandert's "Corral west of Fort Sumner, New Mexico," and the giant billboard pistol aiming at the giant hat beneath the even-larger lettering of the word "Trucks" (an advertisement for road rage!) in Steve Fitch's "Sign, downtown Pampa, Texas." In other viewings, a kind of doubt begins to creep into me; or rather, a doubt that was surely already within me connects with certain of these photos, and begins to uncoil, finds outlet back into the world. Is it my imagination, or do many of the subjects in these portraits appear to be waiting, and not with patience, or the nobility of tested endurance, and not with resolve or hard-gotten pride, but instead, with a mix of visible fatigue and some degree of confusion?

Is it me reading this into some of the portraits (and landscapes), or is it the subjects themselves, and the land itself?

And if it is the latter, what comes next?

In some ways, the landscape photos, such as those of Andrew John Liccardo and Rick Dingus (whose title "Horse, Wheatland" I misread initially as "Horror, Wheatland") are easier for me to interpret; for whatever reason, I feel less uncertain about interpreting the nature of landscapes—even damaged or severely altered landscapes—than the nature of men and women, who are fairly practiced at keeping their internal registries obscured, masked, withheld for as long as possible.

Again and again (maybe we don't always see what we want to see; maybe we can be instructed, or re-instructed, yet, to see things differently), I witness in these photos not the scrappy pride of yore nor the calm content of relative (or perceived) self-sufficiency in the subjects, but instead the outer edges of despair. I do not want to see despair or confusion, nor passivity or waiting, but there it is, again and again.

I see it particularly in the Gleaton portraits. A pallor and stillness in a woman standing with hands clasped, a what-next assessment by a man seated in a dark garage. The young woman reclining in the passenger seat, soda cans in the console.

This same waiting is in some of the children (and young adults) in Gandert's "Parade crowd, Western Heritage Day, Portales, New Mexico" and "Parade crowd, Western Heritage Day, Portales, New Mexico," where the participants as well as the spectators somehow—despite their youth—seem aware already that they are trapped in a parody. *Oh, here we are watching a parade, this is what you are supposed to do, this is how you are supposed to feel.* They suggest to me actors and actresses on a stage in a play that has not ended, but one where the pages and script have gone blank; there don't seem to be any parts left, just empty pages without scene or dialogue, without direction.

There seems to me likewise to be an unsettling quality of deep and perhaps unquestioned spectatorship in Gandert's intergenerational "Cowboy hats, Portales, New Mexico." I'm not judging anyone for how they wear a hat, or for wearing one—how many of us anywhere really consider the things we do, the small and familiar gestures that accumulate in our lives?—but instead that beneath and within these photos—the slump of shoulders, a flatness of gaze—there lurks, I fear, once again, that waiting, which is quite a different thing from anticipating.

There is one photo in which I do not see despair or confusion. It is the image by Tony Gleaton of the middle-aged black man lighting his cigarette—taking what appears to me to be the first drag. Here, finally, is an image of a man in the middle, who seems neither confused nor fearful nor overly fatigued—who seems confident, retained within himself, aware somehow of capabilities as well as limitations, and unplagued by his recognition of either of these borders—and yet it occurs to me only now that, hell, maybe that expression of relative serenity on his face comes not so much from within, but from the quick rush of the morning's first contact with the nicotine he might rely upon, to which he might be addicted.

And yet still I think I see, or want to see, a dignity in, or balance with, that relationship.

Waiting

RICK BASS

Doubt is a bitter, weakening thing, as debilitating, I think, as regret. I want to believe I am not seeing what I think I am seeing.

About those landscape photos: they strip away my childhood memories of a more spacious and vibrant and resilient relationship—the towns and communities of the Llano, at the healthy edge of further, farther, less-managed landscapes—and reveal, like a surprising glance in the mirror for the first time at a lined face and graybeard stubble—*how can this be?*—a land stretched very, very thin. And upon that living canvas, that fabric, our species has made mistakes; unremarkable, uncomplicated mistakes, generally involving overreaching, often but not always tinged with greed, or at the very least a lack of respect for anything beyond ourselves, and then, fairly quickly, as things sagged or went away, a lack of respect even for ourselves. Simple mistakes and assumptions made on a large canvas repeatedly across time, out in the wide open, in a land not of bounty but, more often than not, relative paucity. Mistakes made not in the remote backcountry of the West, nor paved and chromed over by the glitter of urban dreams and desires, nor masked by the vegetative uproar and foliated disguise and clamor of either the Northeast or the deep South, but instead, mistakes made out in the clear wide-open, illuminated by a brilliant aridity that is, in the end, less forgiving than other landscapes, and, I fear, less resilient.

Maybe the main mistake wasn't of overreaching, but instead of failing to imagine a future. Maybe we set up shop on the Llano too hurriedly, without taking time to attach properly and firmly to the substrate. But aren't we all guilty of that, almost every day? Doesn't such attachment elude us still, more than ever?

I am not judging. Maybe there wasn't time. I am not suggesting any of us would have done any differently. I am just looking at the evidence, or what seems like evidence, in these photos.

Maybe that's the hope to be gotten here, from these images of confusion and weariness. Maybe that recognition of the places that so lucidly reveal to us where we have made mistakes will be one of the first steps in our turning away from those mistakes. And we will hope that there is still a place left toward which we can turn.

I am not by nature a pessimist, but the further and farther we go on this journey, the more irritated I become with false or reflexive hope, as opposed to the more difficult brand of earned hope. I hope that someone, somewhere, somehow, will rescue us from this jackpot we seem to have suddenly gotten into. But it seems disrespectful, as well as foolish, to bank on it, and to simply wait. If my heart knows anything, it is that the road does not necessarily go on forever, and that some parties do finally end.

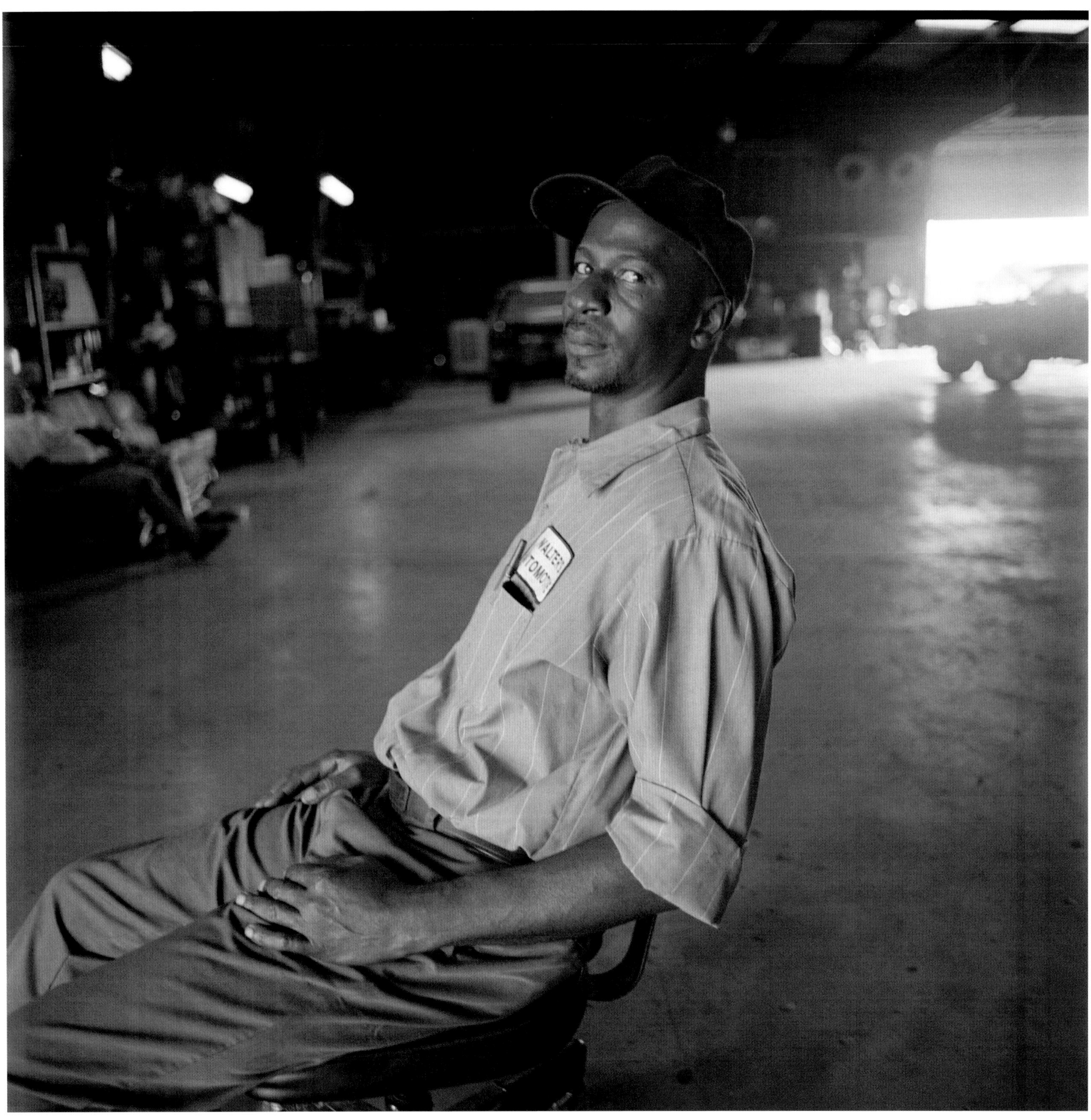

James White, Proprietor, Walter's Garage, East Lubbock, Texas, 2006

Tony Gleaton

My work comes out of my need to comment on the social condition of the "other." The images that I produce, more often than not, depict elements of society that are in a way invisible to the majority culture. In crafting visual images of these nonpersonages, I am attempting to manifest a parallel iconography equal to yet inclusive of the modes of representation that are predominant in "mainstream" representational tropes.

I love the "other," those people who are separated from any dominant social group. My work examines our common elements and the disparities which, in making us different, also bind us together in the human condition. My photographs are a metaphor for the state of grace which lies within us all.

These photographs that I create are as much an effort to define my own life, with its heritage encompassing Africa and Europe, as an endeavor to throw open the discourse on the broader aspects of *mestizaje*, the "assimilation" of Asians, Africans, and Europeans with indigenous Americans.

Darren and Donna Robertson's Home, the old south headquarters of the Spade Ranch, East Highway 114, Levelland, Texas, 2008

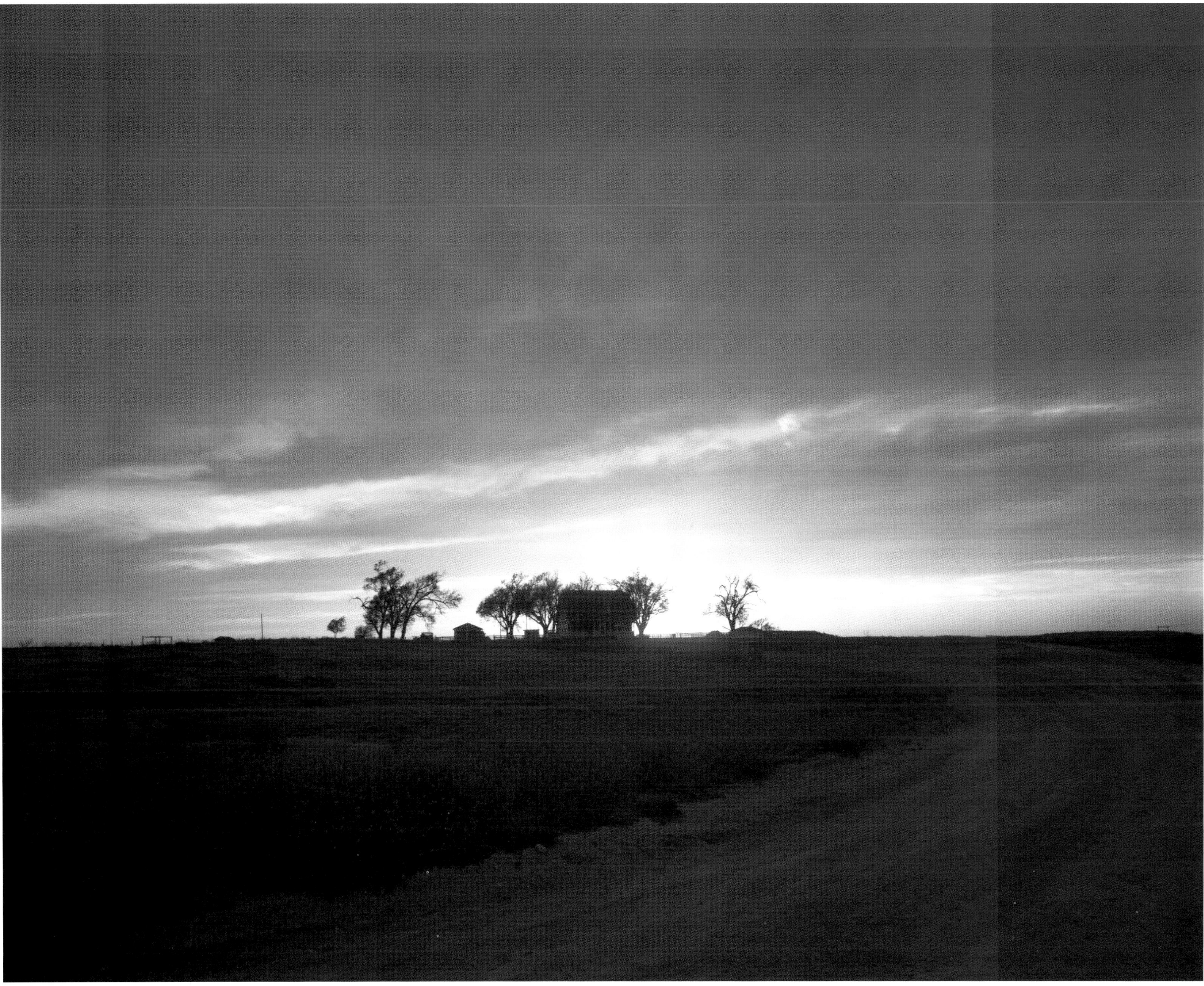

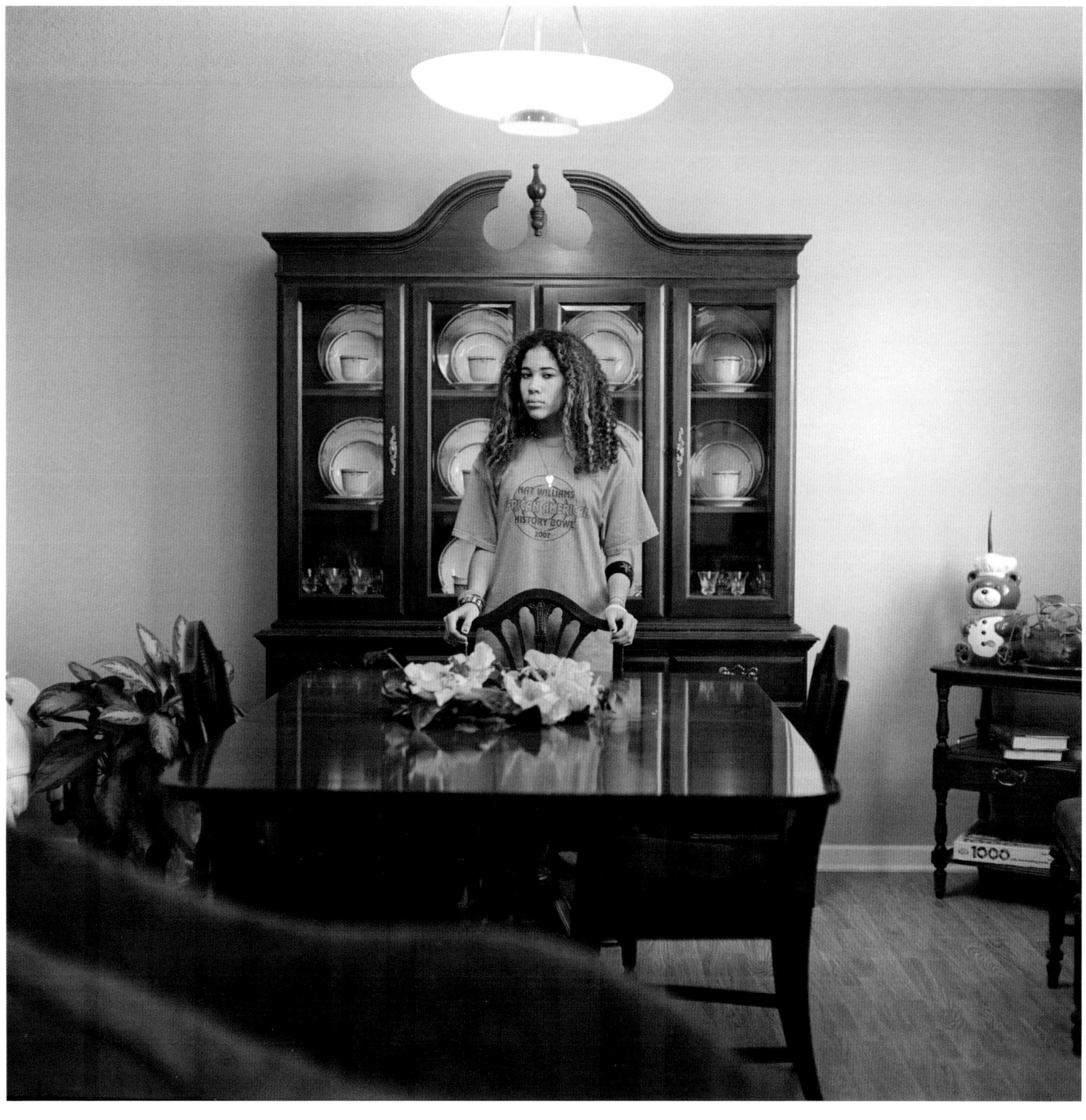

Portrait of Ron McLaurin's Daughter, Lubbock, Texas, 2006

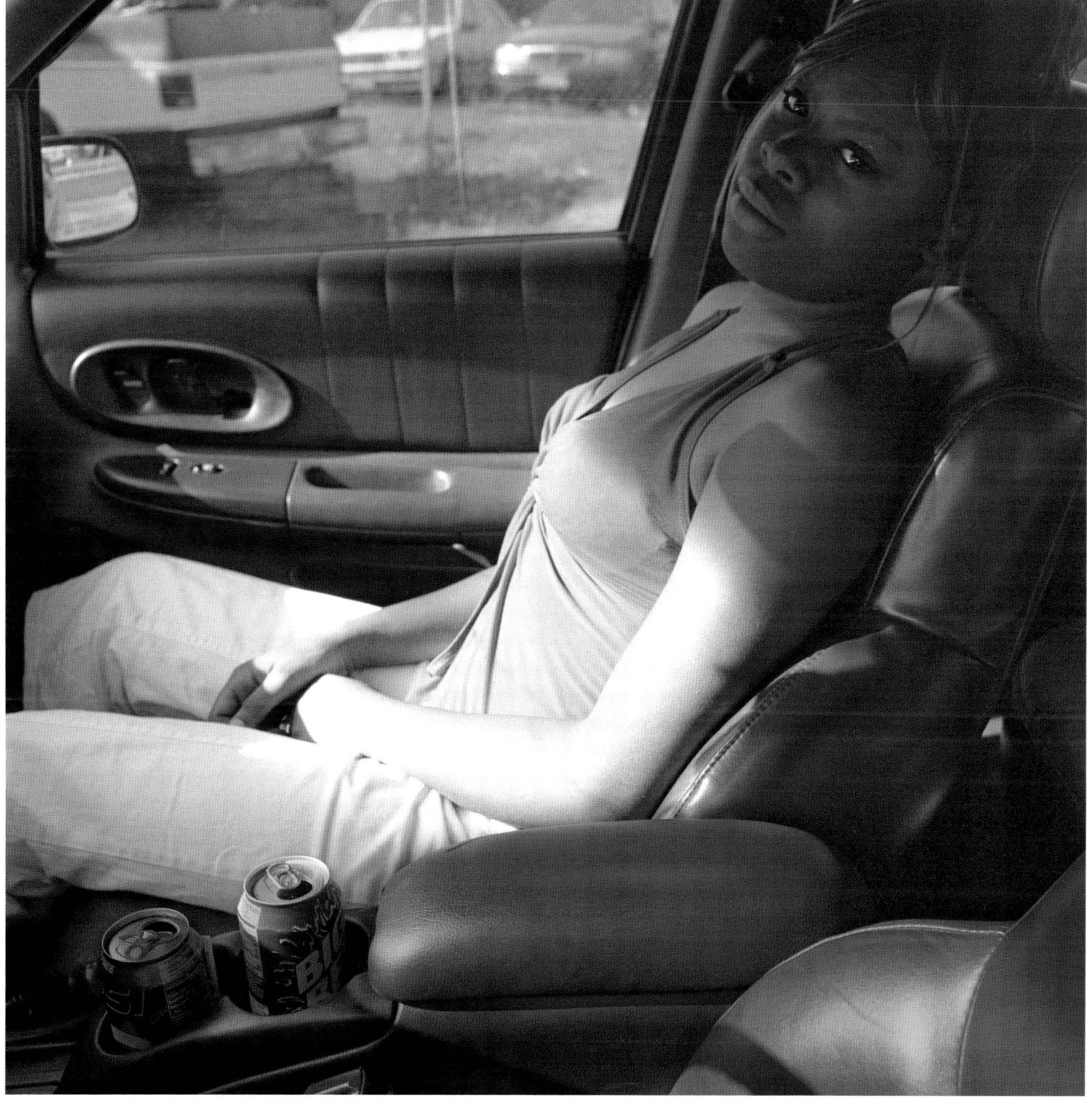

Girl with Pearl Earring, Walter's Garage, East Lubbock, Texas, 2006

Parishioner, Macedonia Baptist Church, Anton, Texas, 2006

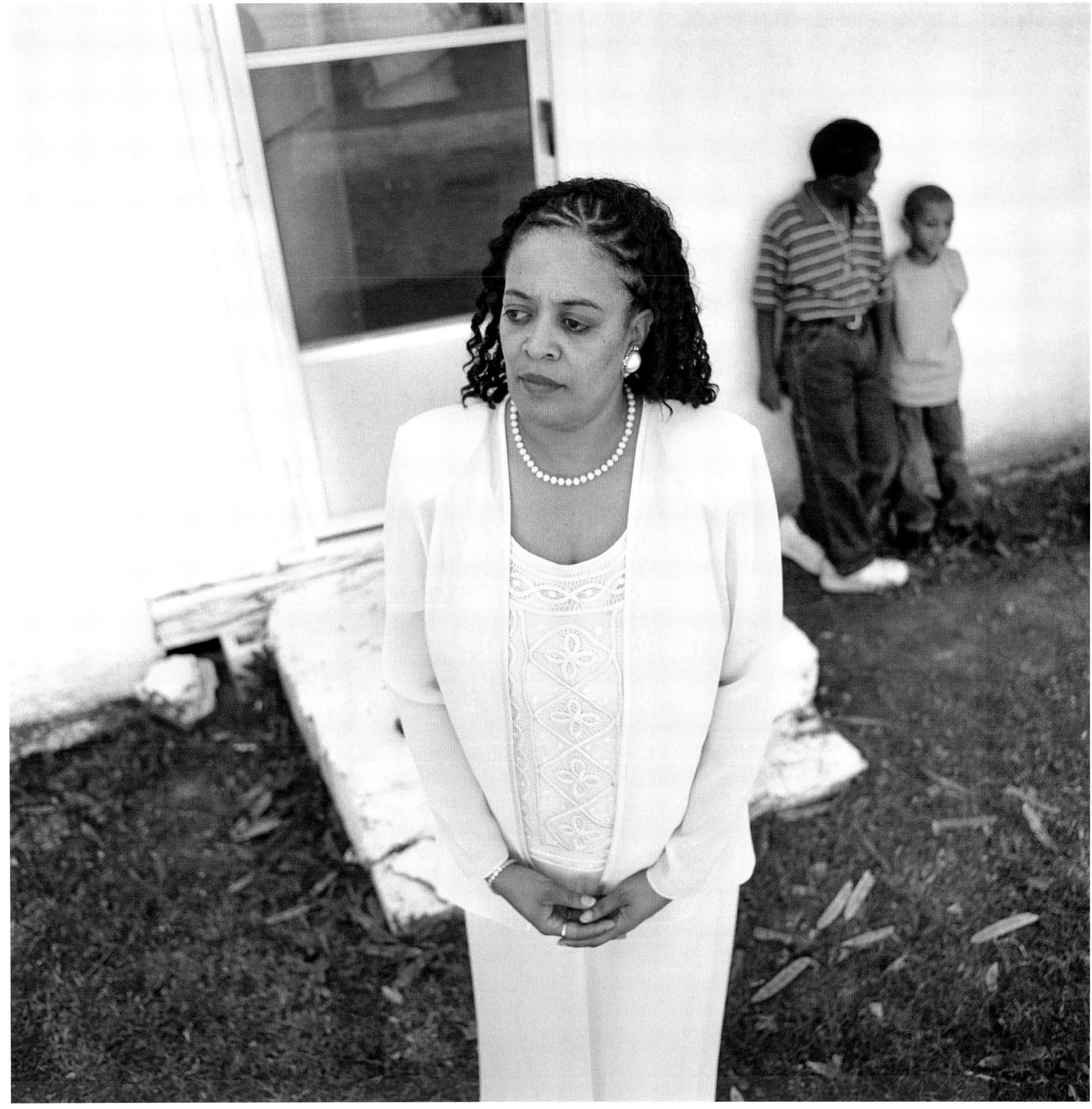

Bobby Crosslin, Cowboy, Carl and Dorothy Bomar's place, the old McMurtry Ranch, Silverton, Texas, 2006

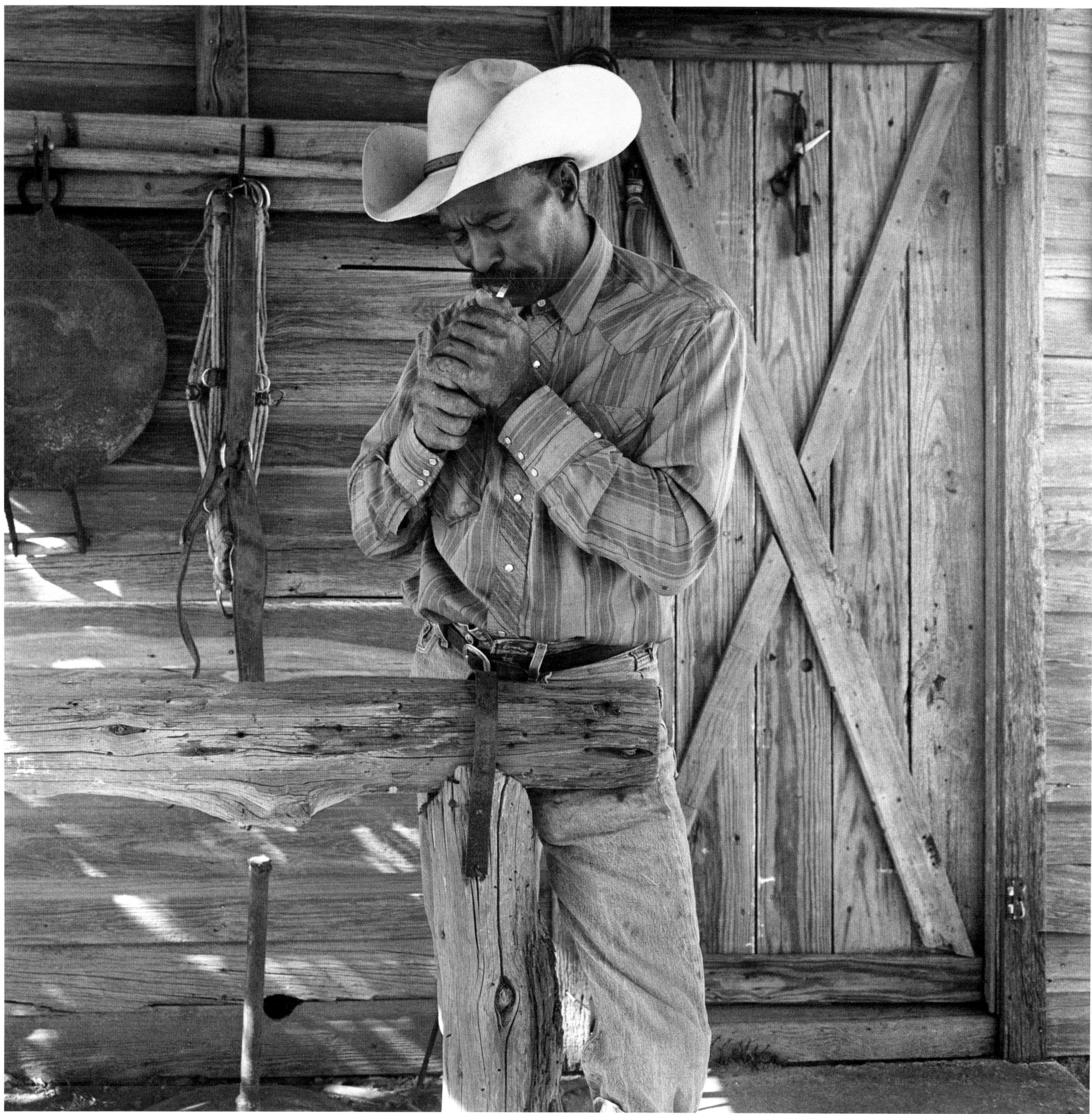

80

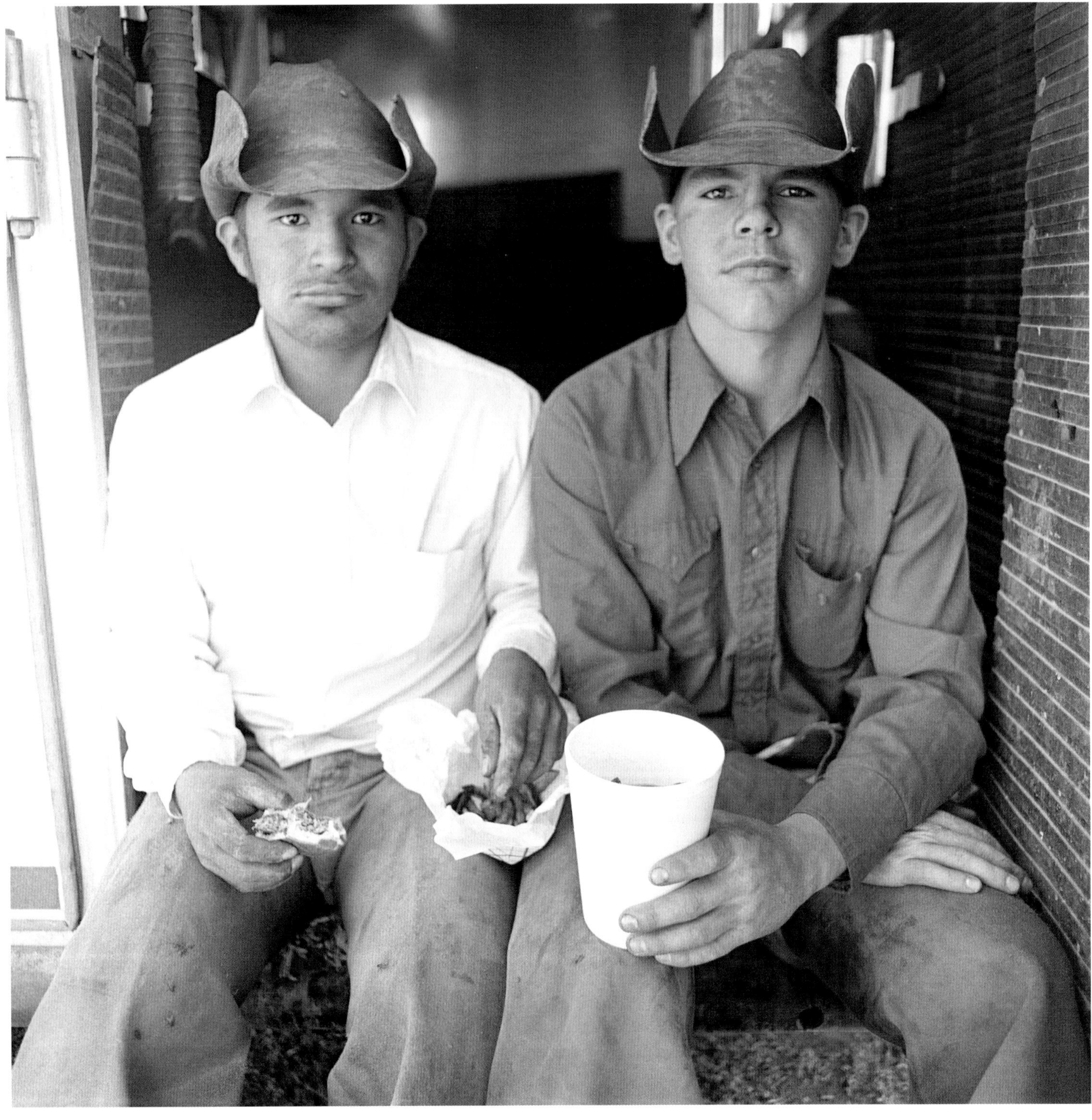

Untitled, family round-up, Caprock Canyons, Texas, 2008

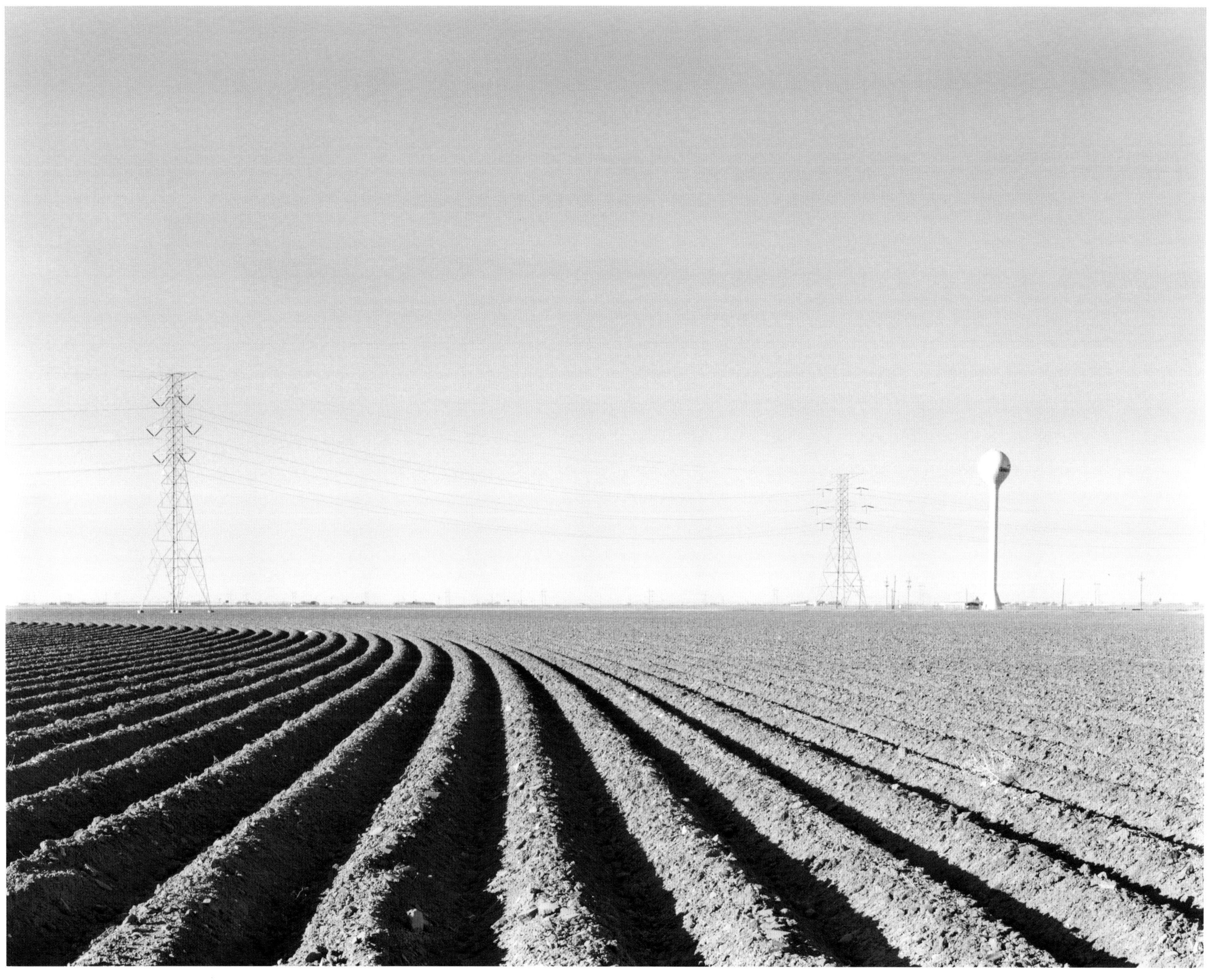

Untitled, Highway 84 southeast of Lubbock, Texas, 2008

Untitled, Slaton Monument Inc., Slaton, Texas, 2007

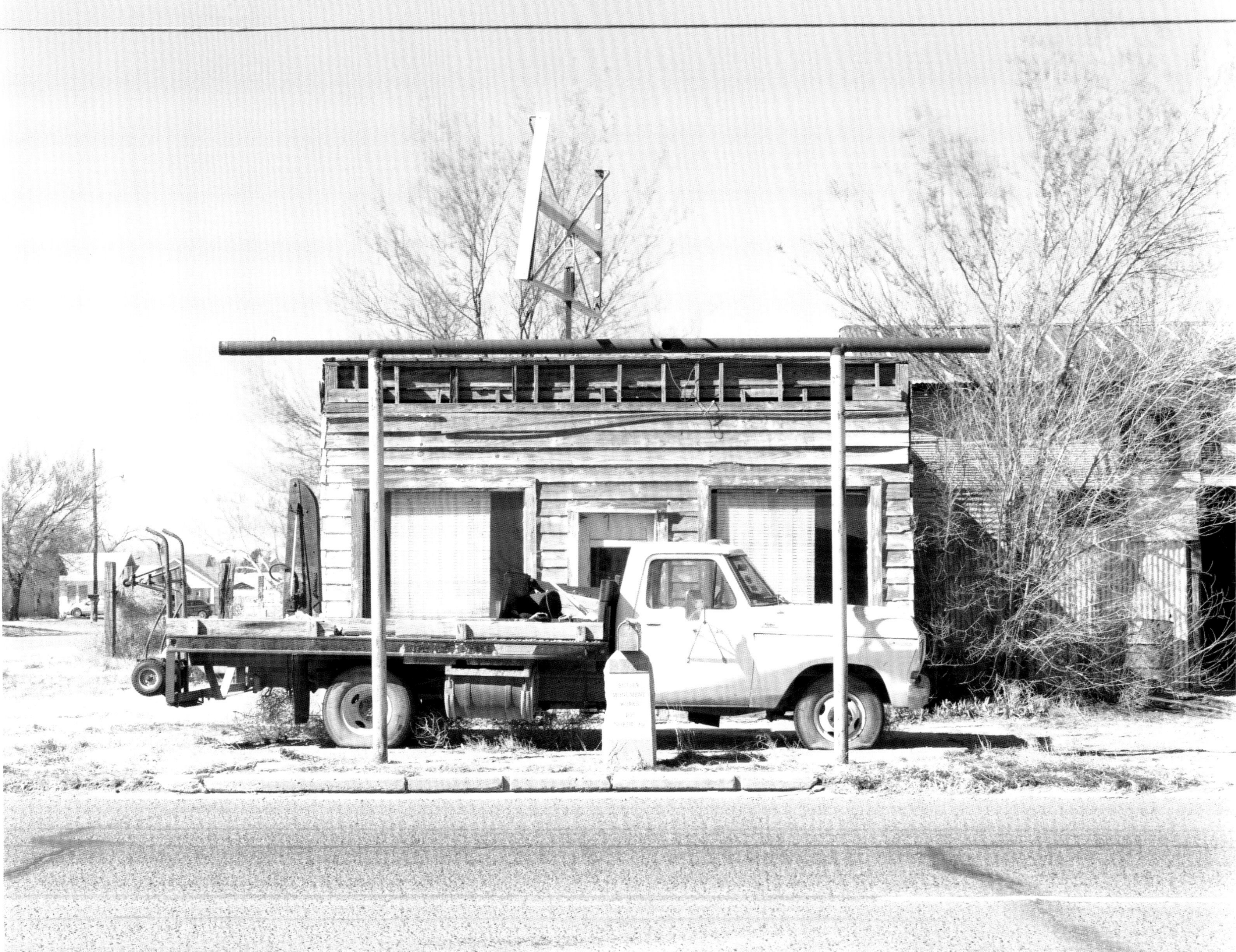
MONUMENT
WORKS

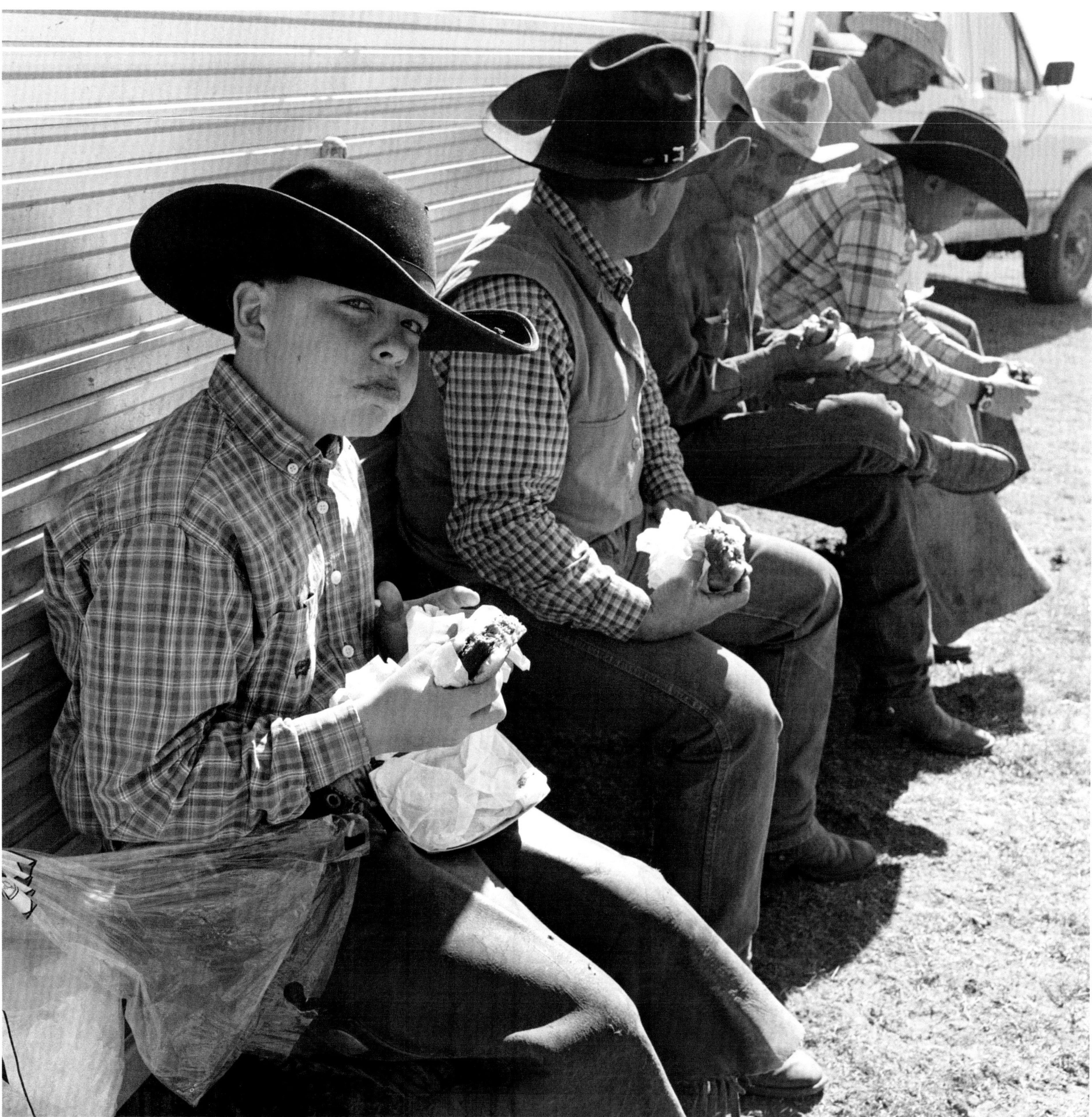

Lisa Regan's Young Son, family round-up, Caprock Canyons, Texas, 2008

Max Crawford and the Palisade Plains

WILLIAM KITTREDGE

OUR FUNDAMENTAL EMOTIONAL CONNECTIONS and consequent defining stories are most often derived from families, neighborhoods, even regions, both urban and rural. The Llano Estacado, high plains in West Texas, in recent decades irrigated with deep waters pumped up from the Ogallala Aquifer and bounded by the Caprock in the east and west, constitute such a neighborhood. Max Crawford is the premier storyteller from that territory so far as I can tell.

During the fall of 1973, lonely on a fellowship in Palo Alto, I bought a half case of cheap beer and went to visit a newfound friend in his student house off El Camino Real, the Spanish mission road east of Stanford University. Max showed up to join us. We'd met only a few days before. He was from West Texas and I'd come from the sagebrush deserts of Oregon (think Nevada). Max and I both knew flatland horizons and irrigation agriculture and buying your books off circular racks in drug stores, and so we had hit it off.

Max brought the news that his first novel was to be published by Farrar, Straus and Giroux, and titled *The Yellow Rose of Texas*, after a famous tune recorded by Bob Wills and his Texas Playboys from Turkey, Texas, on the eastern edge of Max's homeland. I was seriously envious. We didn't have live music in the Oregon outback. Nothing beyond Ray Charles and "I Can't Stop Loving You" on the jukebox in the Indian Village, a local eatery. That first afternoon we got into the beer and celebrated, and my friend and I talked Max into usurping Ernest Tubb and changing the title of his novel to *Waltz Across Texas*.

By 1975, when *Waltz* came out, Max was in Missoula, where I live. He'd come to visit and stayed. That was the way with Max, he moved a lot. The reviews of *Waltz* were mixed. While the opening and ending range with acerbic authority, the middle was over-complicated and scrambled. Anyway, damn the reviews. There came along a full-page photograph of Max in the *US News and World Report*. Max scowled at the world from out front of the old Turf Bar in Missoula. He'd been picked as the most promising young novelist in the nation. He was our golden boy. Couldn't miss.

Max escaped the irrigated cotton fields on the Staked Plains, majored in economics at the University of Texas, and hung out with young prairie intellectuals. His roommate, Bill C. Malone, in 1981 compiled a definitive country/western music collection for the Smithsonian. Max found Karl Marx, and became a "card-carrying" communist, if not a purist with no mind to pleasures. Friends in later years took to calling him "the Rhinestone Commie."

There were stories of Max in Houston, and traveling city to city with Larry McMurtry, from one enormous dusty used-book store to another, "looking for one-dollar books I could sell for ten." McMurtry encouraged him to try writing, and Max landed a prestigious Stegner Fellowship at Stanford. But soon he was deep into the radical Bay Area politics of the late 1960s and let his writing slip for a year or so. Max was "a general officer in that army" according to a mutual friend. His political intentions were rude and urgent. Fairness first, and first things first.

After *Waltz*, he got back at the typewriter. *The Backslider*, a satirical West Texas novel about "fundamentalist" religion amid farmers and wives and preachers, came out in 1976. In 1978 Max moved to London, where he made a point of arriving early at the British Museum so no one could beat him to the chair where Karl Marx sat and wrote. In 1979, *The Bad Communist*, a Bay Area political novel, came along while Max was living above North Beach in San Francisco, making the hippie-beat scene in Gino and Carlo's and moving on for happy hours in the Washington Square Bar and Grill. By 1980 he was back in Missoula, getting in some summers of golf, a game he'd loved since boyhood on a nine-hole layout in a shallow canyon outside of Floydada.

More to the point, he was also remembering Texas and the early history of the High Plains, and working on his masterpiece, *Lords of the Plain*, to be published in 1985. The author's note is a muted celebration of his homeland. "Max Crawford was born and raised near Mount Blanco, Texas. This community is gone now, but once it could be found in the country between Floydada, Crosbyton, Matador, and Dickens, Texas, on the southern rim of the *Llano Estacado*, less than a mile from the caprock of Blanco Canyon."

Lords of the Plain came out the same year as Larry McMurtry's *Lonesome Dove* and Cormac McCarthy's *Blood Meridian*. Rotten timing, the three hall-of-fame Texas historical novels in the same year. Max got far less attention than the others. But by that time he'd left again, heading for European seaports.

In April of 1991, Annick Smith and I were in New Orleans, making ready to drive home to Montana. Max had been in London and southern France, but I found that he was temporarily back in Texas, at his childhood home in Floydada. We didn't connect on the phone, but why not detour through Lubbock and hunt him down?

On a Sunday afternoon we pulled off at the little town of Post, where just below the bluffs of the Caprock, C. W. Post, of Postum and Kellogg's Post Toasties fame, once tried to set up a civil utopia. We intruded at the golf course clubhouse, and introduced ourselves to farmers and ranchers playing in big hats and spiked boots, a laughing and congenial Sunday afternoon community. They bought us beer and chatted us up as we all watched the last hour of the Master's golf tournament on a huge TV screen. West Texas looked cordial enough to me.

Annick and I drove away from Post and up over the Caprock in twilight, the palisade Max describes resembling "a bank of stone clouds." We encountered those landforms as they were in *Lords of the Plain*. "Only two miles distant stood the great wall of the *Llano Estacado*. The sloping canyon walls were a fiery brick red dotted with dark green clumps of brush, the Caprock escarpment mottled yellow and white, the sky behind the escarpment a curtain of black blue pierced by a bright solitary star mockingly luring us forward."

From a motel in Lubbock, I finally got Max on the phone. He was in fact in Floydada, thirty miles away, but definitely didn't want to see us. "Don't have time," he said. "Going to Archer City and see McMurtry first thing in the morning. A day's drive." Some line like that which I took to mean, "Leave me alone." So we did. Max had his moods, no use getting upset. The next morning, Annick and I took a look anyway. We drove over to Floydada and stopped by the little apple-tree-and-golf-ball-strewn canyon where he'd played lonely boy golf, and down from the Caprock to the village of Matador where one of the great Texas/Montana cattle empires had headquartered. After traveling the flatlands west into New Mexico, we escaped the plains as Texans are inclined to do, and slept at an Indian gaming resort just outside the pine-forest mountain town of Ruidoso (famous for putting on the richest high-stakes Texan quarter horse races in the world).

Max was a long-time friend, and ducking us. Why? I took it to mean that he, for his own reasons, didn't want to display his origins. I understood. What I'd seen of the level lands of irrigated agriculture, mainly cotton around Lubbock, was inhabited by a culture similar to what I experienced on the eastern Oregon outback where I'd grown up, dusty and culturally denuded, cut off from the "great world" and savagely defensive, brutally acquisitive. If you aren't reasonably selfish in the outback American West, at least in decisions involving dollars and property, you're most often thought of as brain dead or too rich to be responsible.

In *Studies in Classic American Literature*, D. H. Lawrence says, talking of settlement history in America, "Something in the soul perished, the softness, the floweriness, the natural tenderness. How could it survive the sheer brutality of the fight with the American wilderness, which is so big, vast and obdurate? The savage America was conquered and subdued at the expense of the instinctive and intuitive sympathy of the human soul. The fight was too brutal." Sounds true, but is that an excuse for anything?

We evolved as inherently generous to those with whom we share the dinner table, blood relatives and friends. But, even at that level of intimacy, balancing generosity against selfishness is complex and wrenching. That's why we rely on laws, codes of institutionalized fairness. But lawyers and laws can obviously be skewed to favor the wealthy and well connected. Unfairness and selfishness so often win.

At the end of his 2009 Bancroft Prize history *Comanche Empire*, Pekka Hämäläinen says, "Unleashing its overwhelming economic and technological might, the United States pushed the remains of Comanche power aside with a brief, concentrated scorched-earth campaign." The Comanche were one of history's great horse-borne warrior cultures. For more than a hundred years they ruthlessly ran the southern center of the United States, fending off Indian cultures like the Apache, and the Spanish and the French. *Comanche Empire* compares them to the Mongols. But in the autumn of 1874 their dominance came to an end. Vast herds of buffalo had been killed off by white hunters. Great stacks of bison bones decorated the Llano Estacado. And an enormous Comanche herd of horses was slaughtered by the U.S. military. The Comanche were left afoot: proud and often violent, shrewd people left with only the silences of generational reservation life and dole food, they were essentially destroyed. They didn't want to die in houses like white folks.

Lords of the Plain focuses on the 1874 military campaign that brought them down. A fictional Captain Phillip Chapman, of the U.S. 2nd Cavalry, is stationed in West Texas under command of Colonel John James MacSwain, a careerist obviously based on Colonel Ranald Mackenzie, the real life Indian fighter who saw to the end of the Comanche and a decade later went irrevocably insane.

As Max says in *Lords of the Plain*, "To the west of the hundredth meridian was a place alien to civilization." In that setting, the military was at first instructed to keep the peace on the Staked Plains. But those orders soon changed. After a futile Comanche attack on a trading post at Adobe Walls on the Canadian River, President Grant and the United States government said enough was enough. The army went on attack. Captain Chapman and his men marched north across the Llano Estacado. A summer of minor warfare and visits with the buffalo hunters serves as backdrop to Chapman's romantic idyll in a tiny paradise below the Caprock with a privileged woman from the East (involving only the fortunate Captain).

Then Chapman's men hooked up with Colonel MacSwain again, and on September 28, 1874, discovered several hundred Comanche camped in the spectacularly eroded depths of Palo Duro Canyon, just below the Caprock. A surprise attack was orchestrated. As the Comanche fled onto the plains, the army burned their possessions. Our Indian wars were over, but for a final blow.

That blow fell on the next day. More than 1,100 Comanche horses were shot, their bones later hauled away, like the bones of buffalo, to be used as fertilizer. This section of Max's novel is close to what actually transpired. In the novel, the killing of the horses is a bloody, heartless, and heartbreaking nightmare. As it was in life. But a good strategic move: Comanche on foot were close to helpless.

Why do we love our warrior stories? During World War II, the French philosopher Simone Weil, explaining the timeless attractions of the *Iliad*, wrote of "the poetry of power." Some "poetry of power" movie may very well be playing at your local cinema this evening. They make money. There we sit, powerless in the dark, citizens of a conquest culture, dreaming of glory, or what? Imagining that we might get even with the world's transgressions?

We're all familiar with twentieth-century instances of power corrupted by visionary madness: the muddy trenches across Flanders Fields, starved bodies stacked like cordwood in the Nazi camps, Rwanda and Stalin, Pol Pot and the killing fields, and the Disappeared in Chile and Argentina. The list could go on for pages. Fantasies about power and its uses are obviously profoundly addictive, and have led to endless destruction as our nations and cultures and leaders shape the world and its peoples to their purposes.

In *Waltz Across Texas*, a wealthy and influential fellow named Son Cunningham says, "Making money is a funny thing, son. It doesn't come out of thin air, or out of the ground, and it doesn't grow on trees or little plants. You've got to take it away from somebody. You can take it with a gun, or you can take it with your head. Now there ain't much doubt which way to go, is there?"

That voice echoes across America. People who explain themselves in such ways are determined to get theirs and apt to attempt running you down if you get in their way. They populate storytelling, both urban and rural, from around the world, Dostoevsky and Faulkner and Marquez and the crime novels. Like us, folks in those stories have their reasons. But does that excuse anything?

Several years ago, at a conference over east beyond the Rockies Front, I found myself shooting my mouth off about the way the vast Ogallala Aquifer, which underlies the short-grass plains from central Texas to the Sand Hills of Nebraska, was being pumped irrevocably dry. "One day it's going to be gone for good. What then?" A woman stood in the audience. "My people been prospering off that water since the 1950s, when we got the electric pumps. If you think me and my old man are saving a gallon of it for the grandchildren you're out of your mind. That'll be their problem." I was stunned. "Says it all," I said. That was my answer.

Max Crawford's work spins around two themes. First, his reverence for his home territory. Second, the degree to which he deplores what people have done and are doing to it, and to themselves. This, even as he acknowledges how difficult it is to inhabit that freezing, arid, sun-baked distancing landscape; such difficulties harden. The Comanche were terrifying and monstrously brutal. Genitals stuffed in the mouths of the dead, that sort of thing. The white culture was at times also barbaric and brutal. We continue pumping another transmogrified version of the world dry.

Max recently died in Missoula. After *Lords of the Plain*, he moved to southern France, and worked for years on an ultimately unpublished novel about the fallout after the Russian revolution, called *The Red and the White*, along with various other manuscripts. One of them, *Wamba*, a novel about a man struggling against suicide as he drinks and scribbles and tries to resolve his relationship with his legendary mother and the equally legendary Llano Estacado that she represents, was published in 2002. It might be a masterpiece. Time will settle that one. To think about it, I'd have to reread it, and I can't. That might be your task. My memories of it are too close to the bone, as they might have been for Max.

Rick Dingus

Remembering that a map is not the same as the territory that it depicts, I consider photographs as related to mapping. Each is a translation of information, a rendering to be reconsidered for different interpretative purposes in varying contexts. Maps usually contain legends to aid their reading, and photographs often have titles. But while maps most often strive for physically accurate depictions of space, I think of my photographs as urban legends or rural myths that might yield new narratives each time they are seen. Inspired by interdisciplinary roundtable discussions, I record vernacular markers of conflicting tensions and unresolved issues that are current on the Llano and everywhere: technology, disappearing resources, oil, water, constructed realities, and mythical histories.

"*Llano Estacado*: the Staked Plains." As I set out to photograph for this project, I contemplated an aphorism that my father used to recite: "You can't put a row of stakes in a straight line without walking backwards." By that he meant we should learn from the past, use it to orient our understanding of where we are now, and allow it to inform where we choose to go from here. I wonder: How will people in the distant future read the photographs we make today, and how might that reading inform the experience of their time and place? What do our pictures reveal or conceal about the world, about us, and about the choices we have made?

Globe with Lubbock marked, International Cultural Center, Lubbock, Texas, 2004–2006

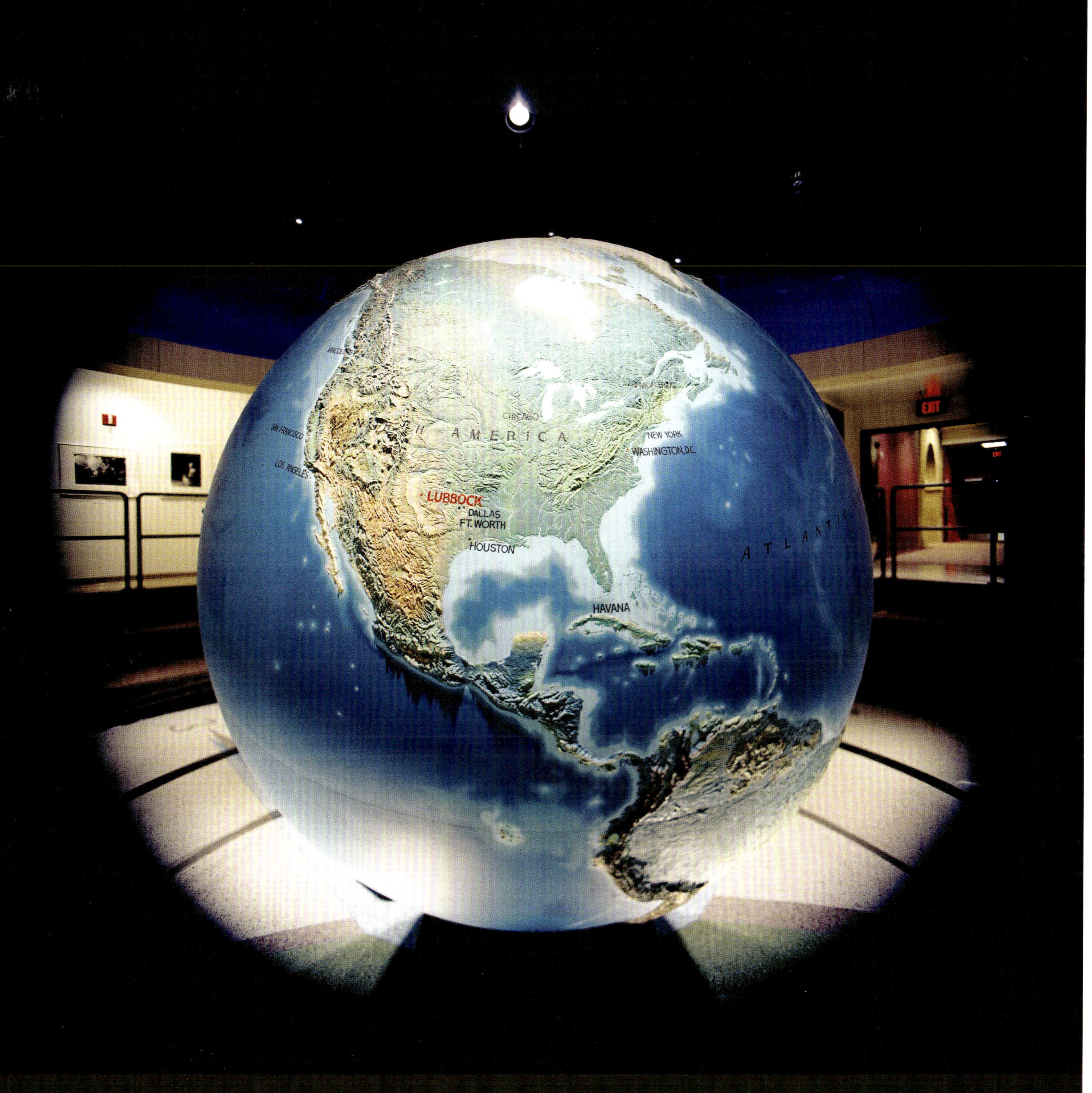

CHICAGO
NEW YORK
WASHINGTON, D.C.
SAN FRANCISCO
LOS ANGELES
LUBBOCK
DALLAS
FT. WORTH
HOUSTON
HAVANA
EXIT

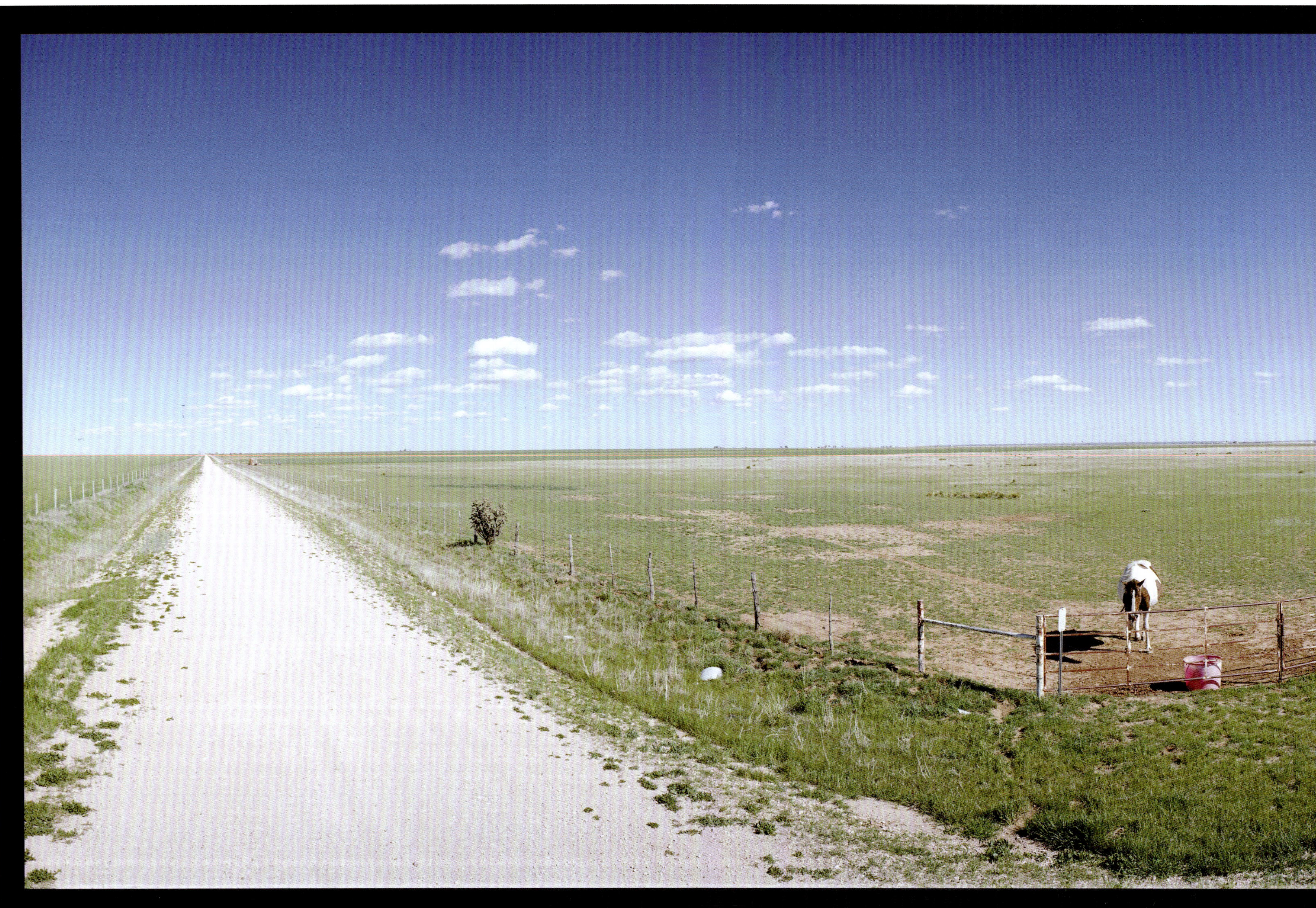

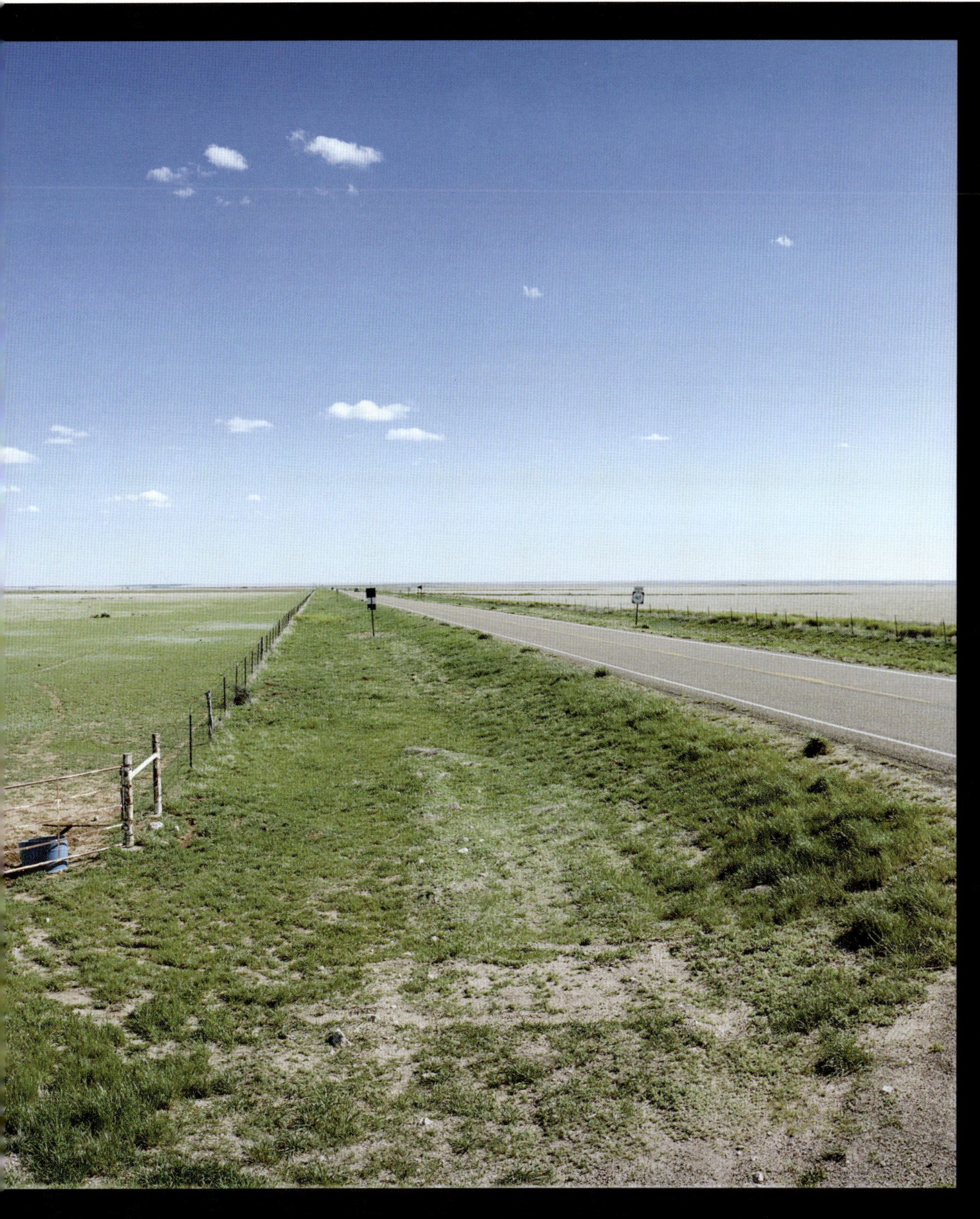

Horse, Wheatland, New Mexico, 2004–2006

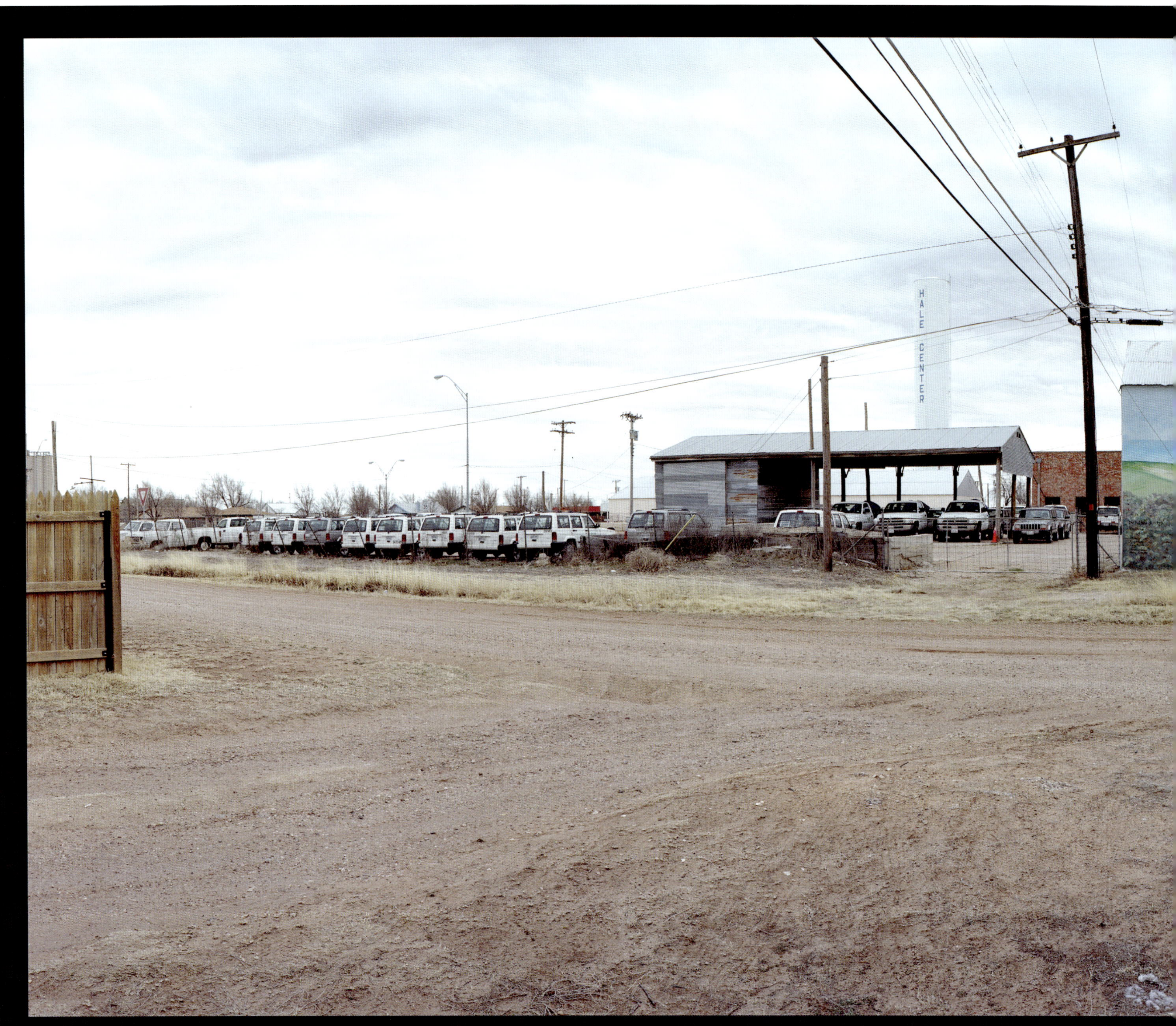
HALE CENTER

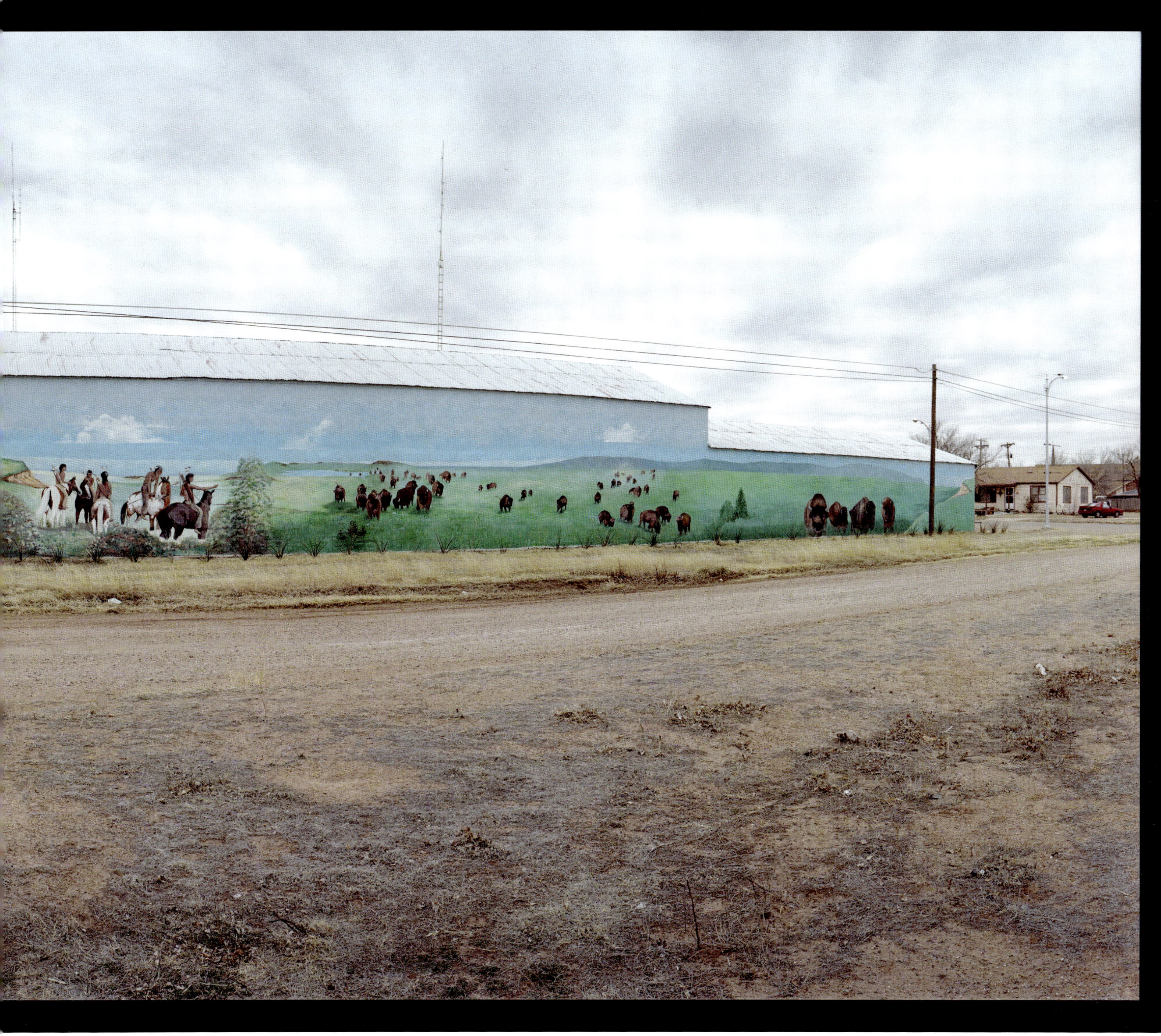

Buffalo mural, Hale Center, Texas, 2004–2006

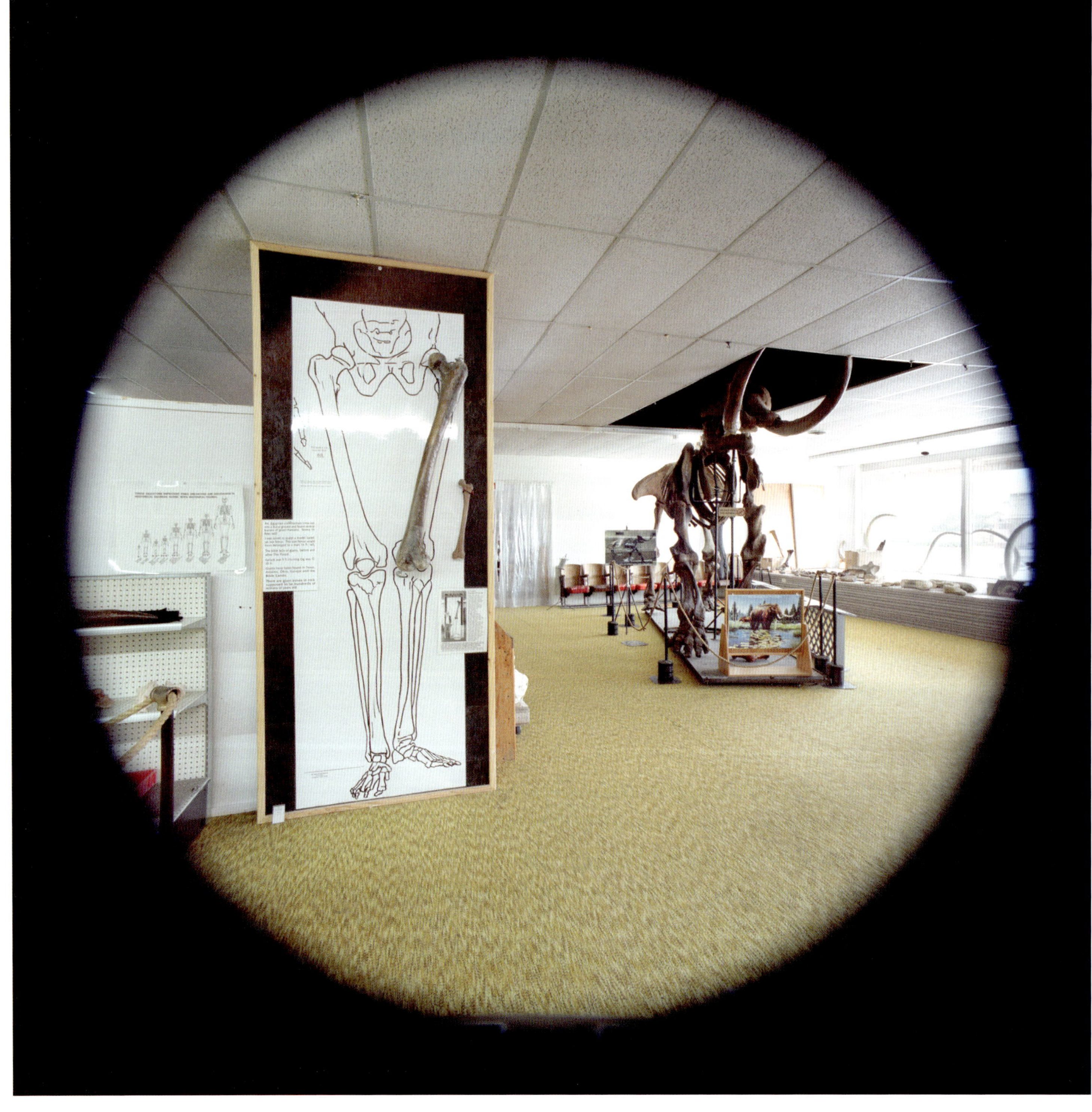

Giant femur, Mt. Blanco Fossil Museum, Crosbyton, Texas, 2005–2006

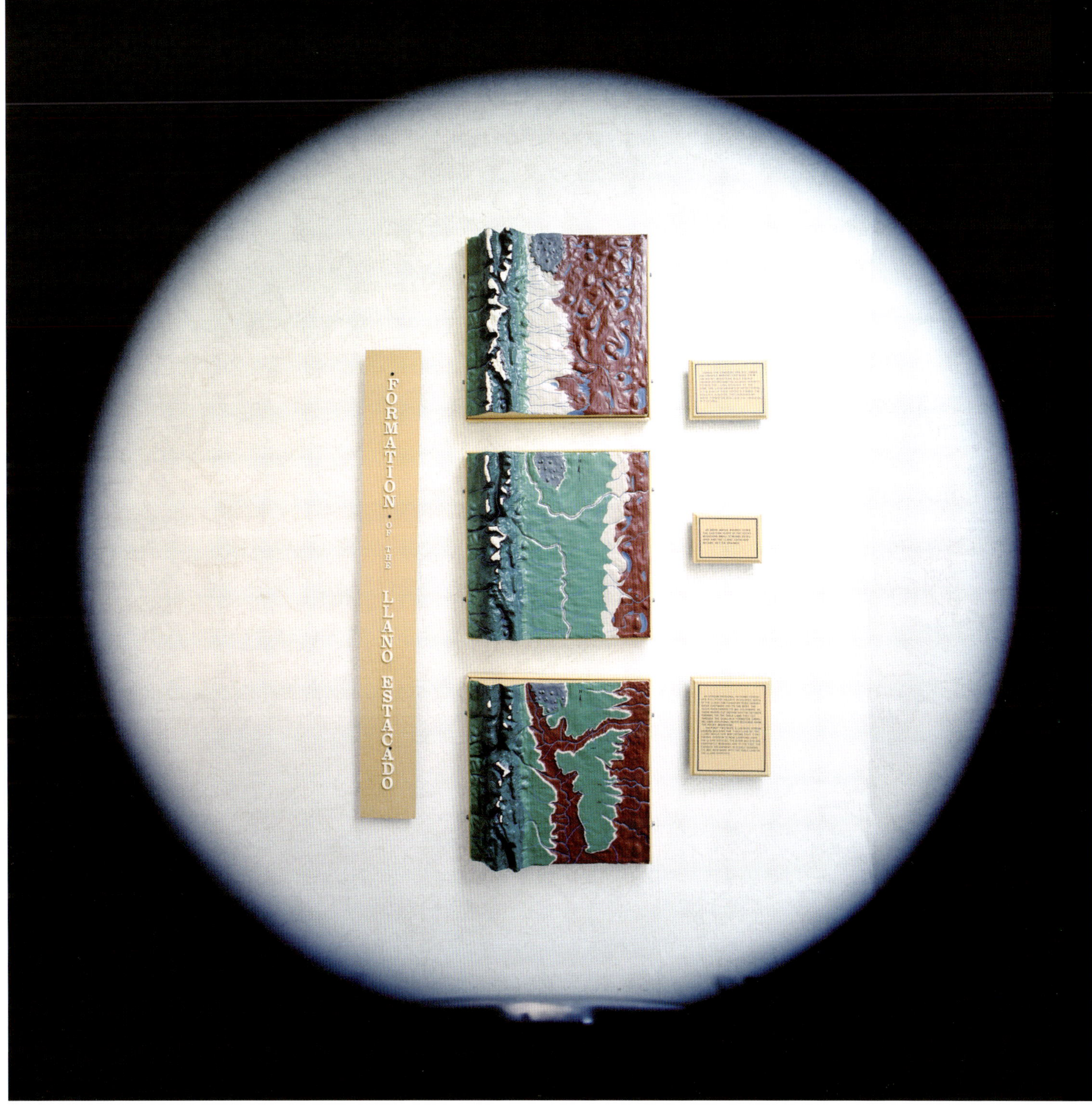

Geologic conception, Museum of the Llano Estacado, Plainview, Texas, 2004–2006

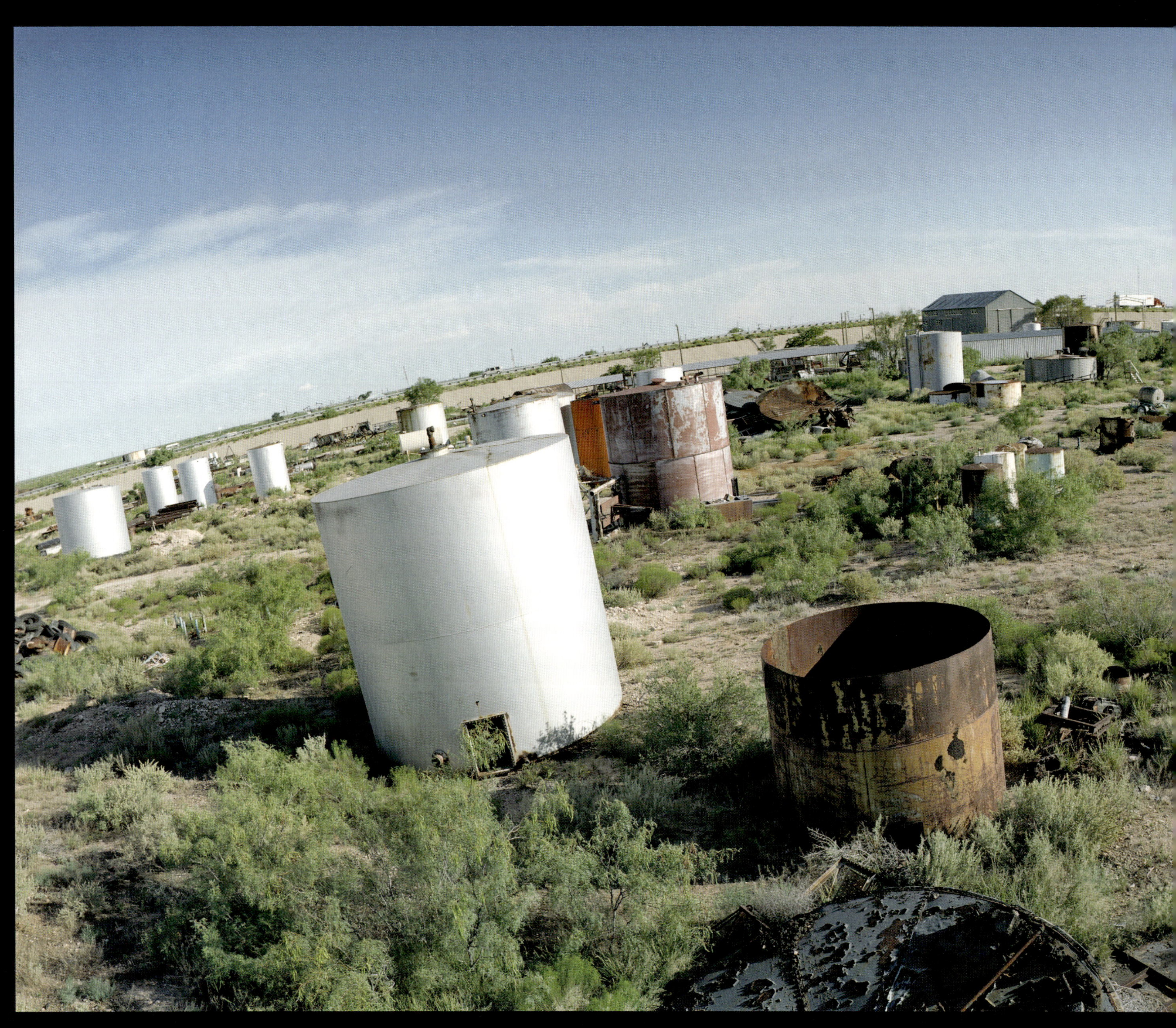

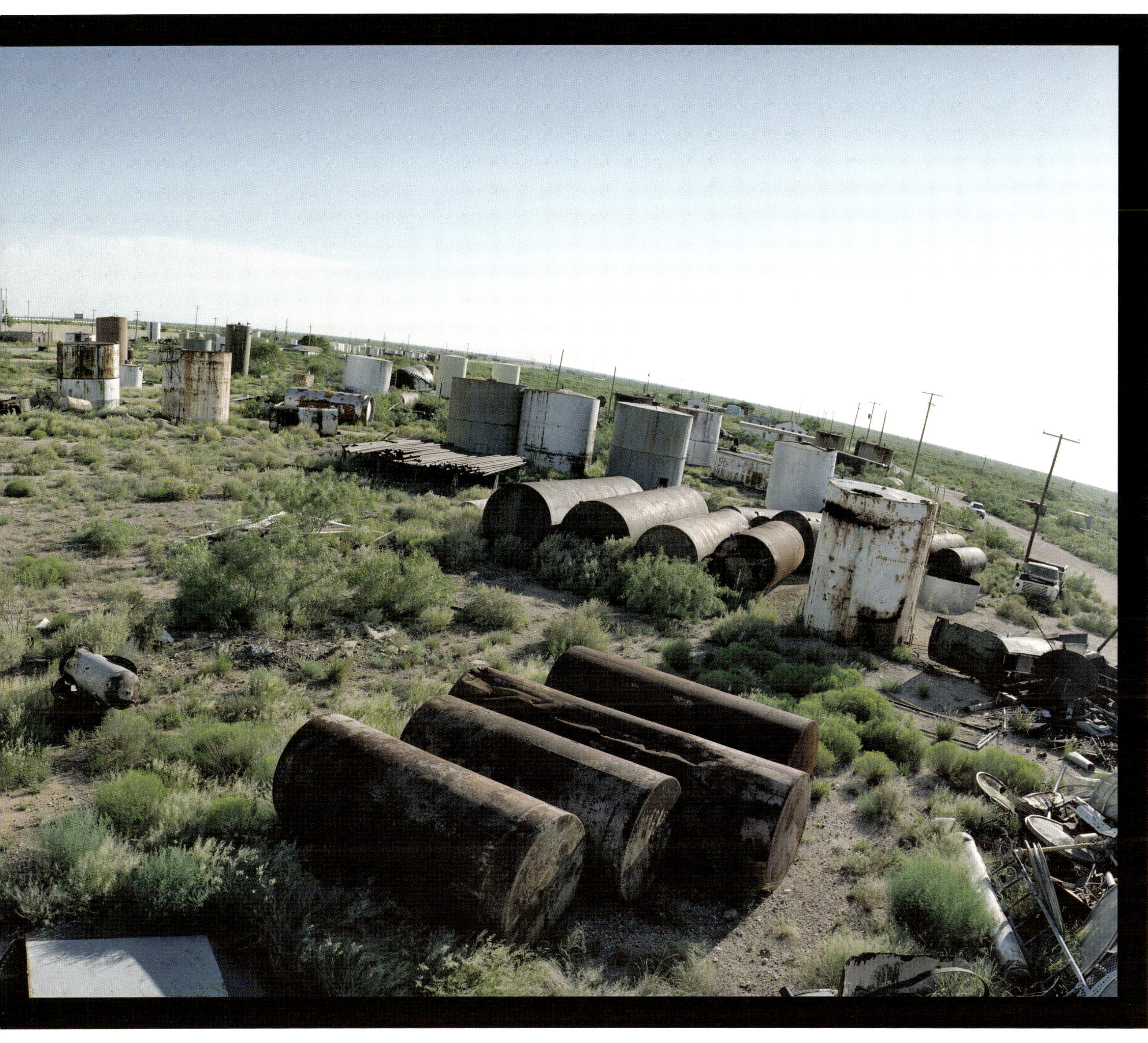

Oilfield trash, Penwell, Texas, 2004–2006

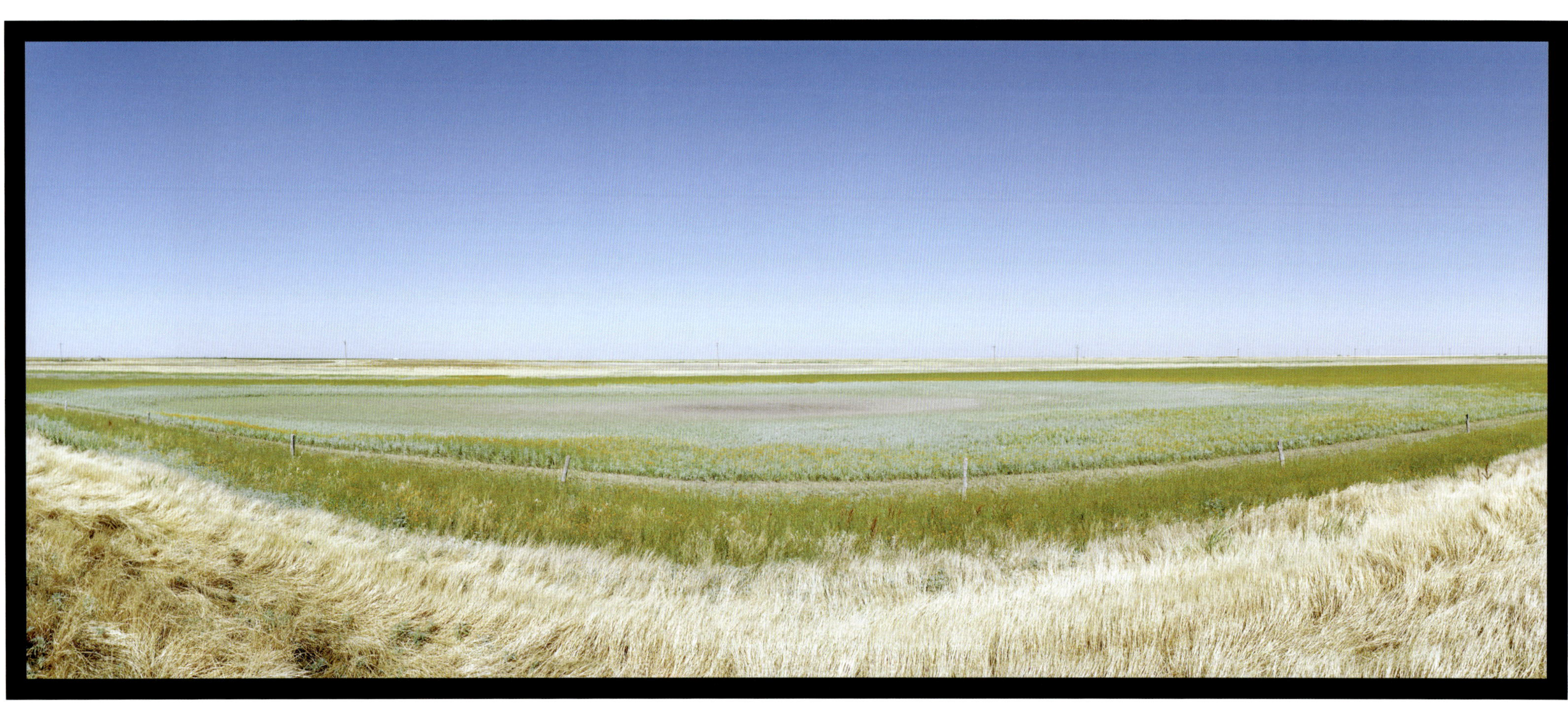

Dry playa lake near Nazareth, Texas, 2004–2006

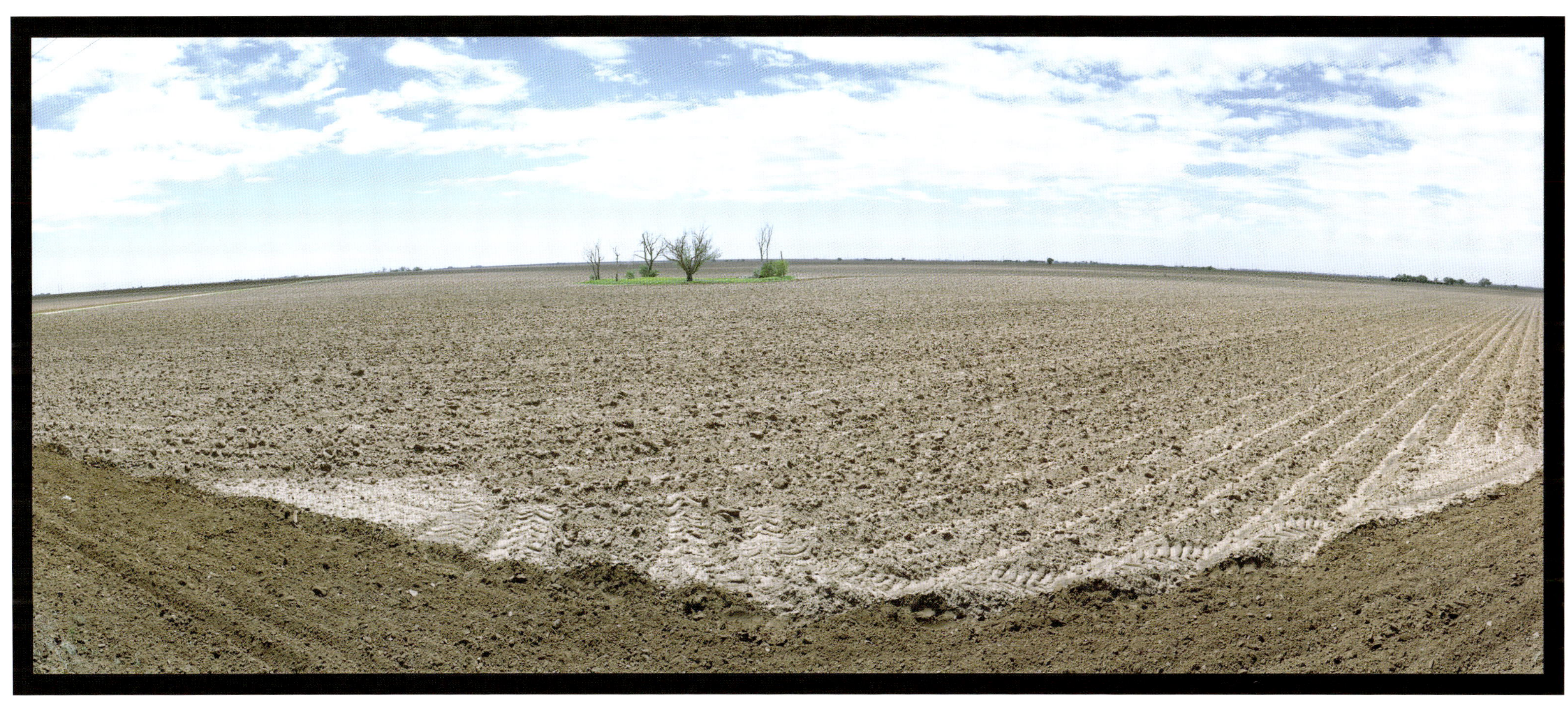

Old home place in a plowed field, Posey, Texas, 2004–2006

Lamesa's "Rainmaker Rocket," now in Big Spring, Texas, 2004–2006

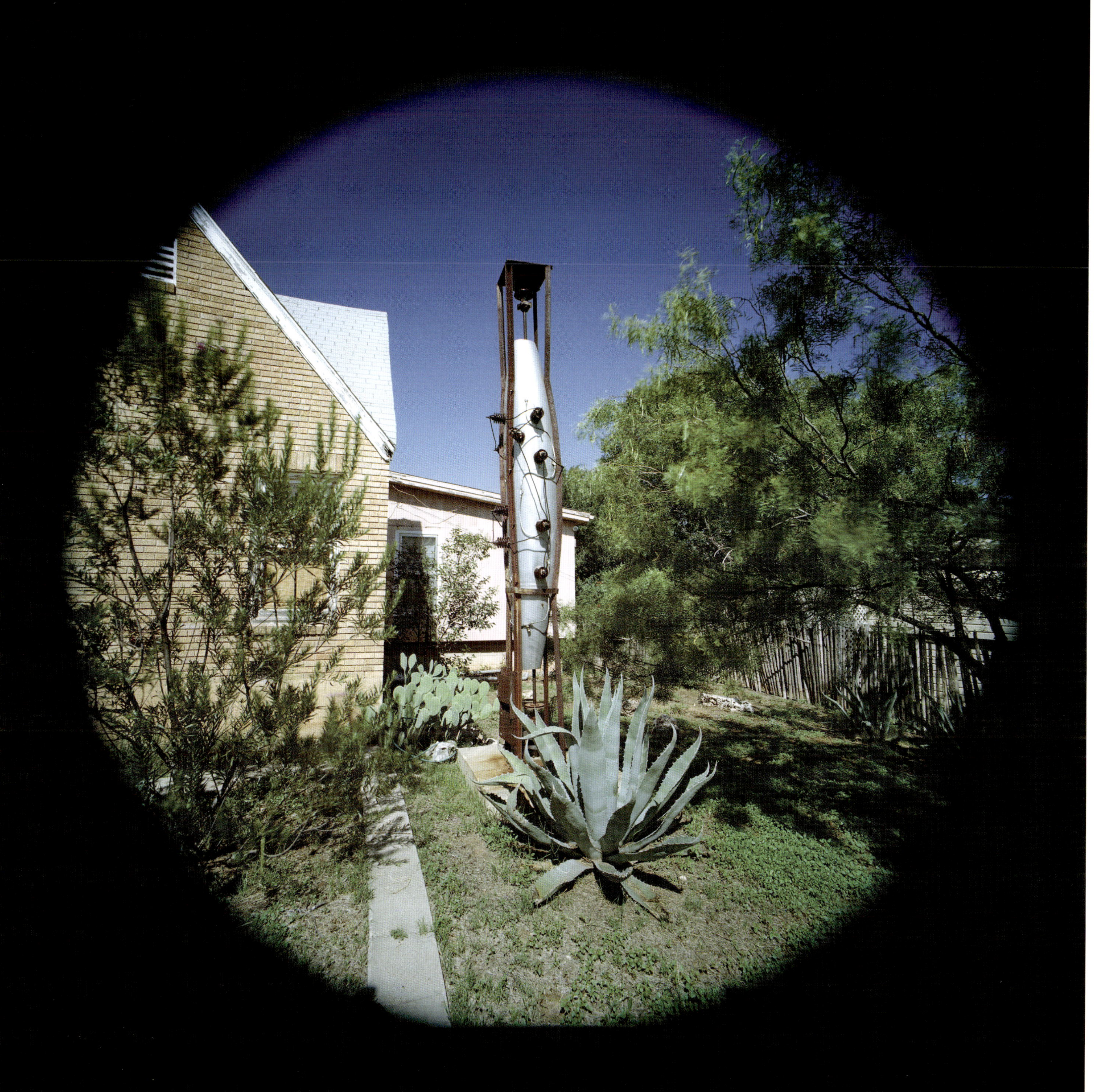

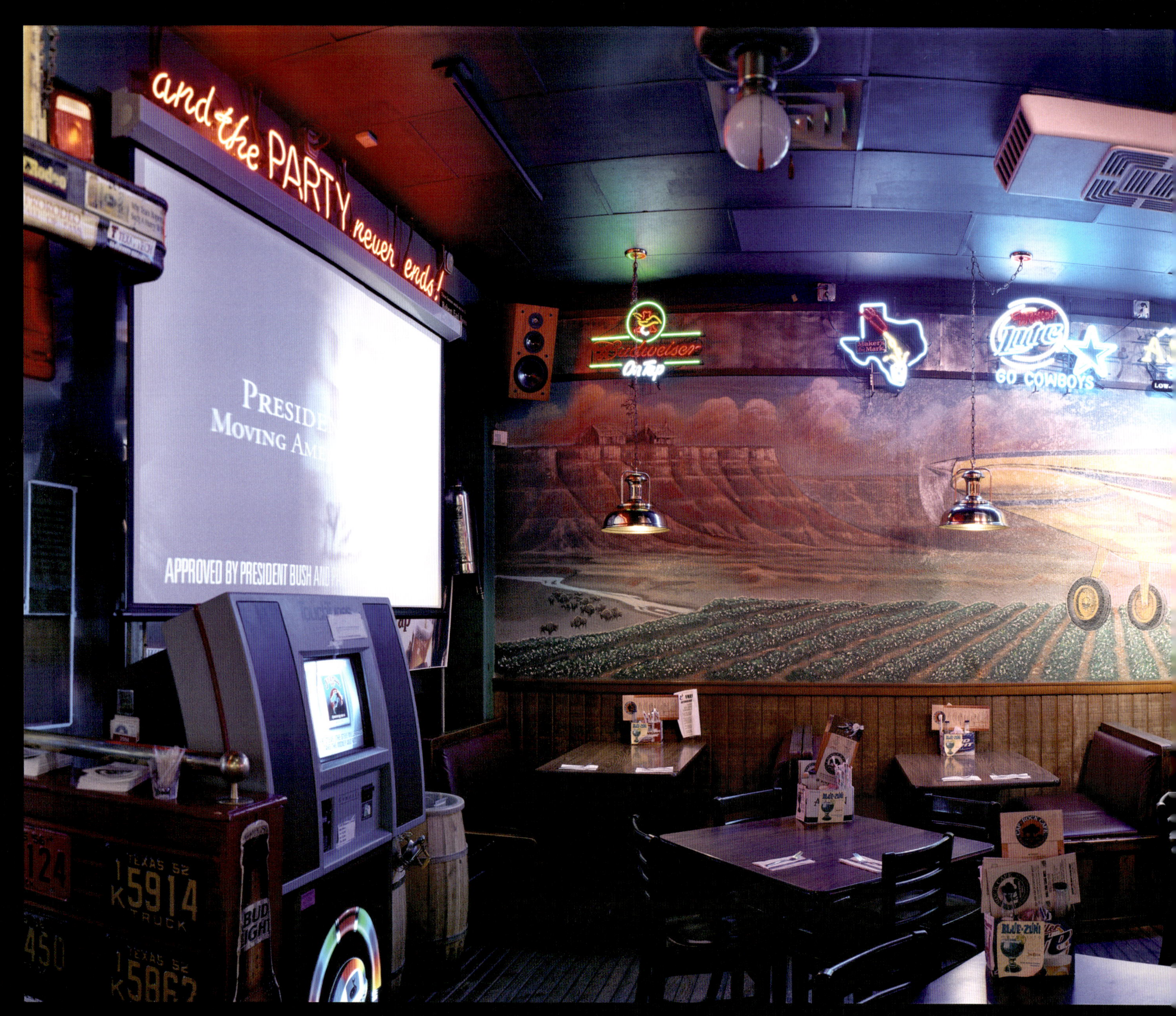
and the PARTY never ends!
APPROVED BY PRESIDENT BUSH AND
Budweiser
On Tap
GO COWBOYS
TEXAS 52
K5914
TRUCK
BUD LIGHT

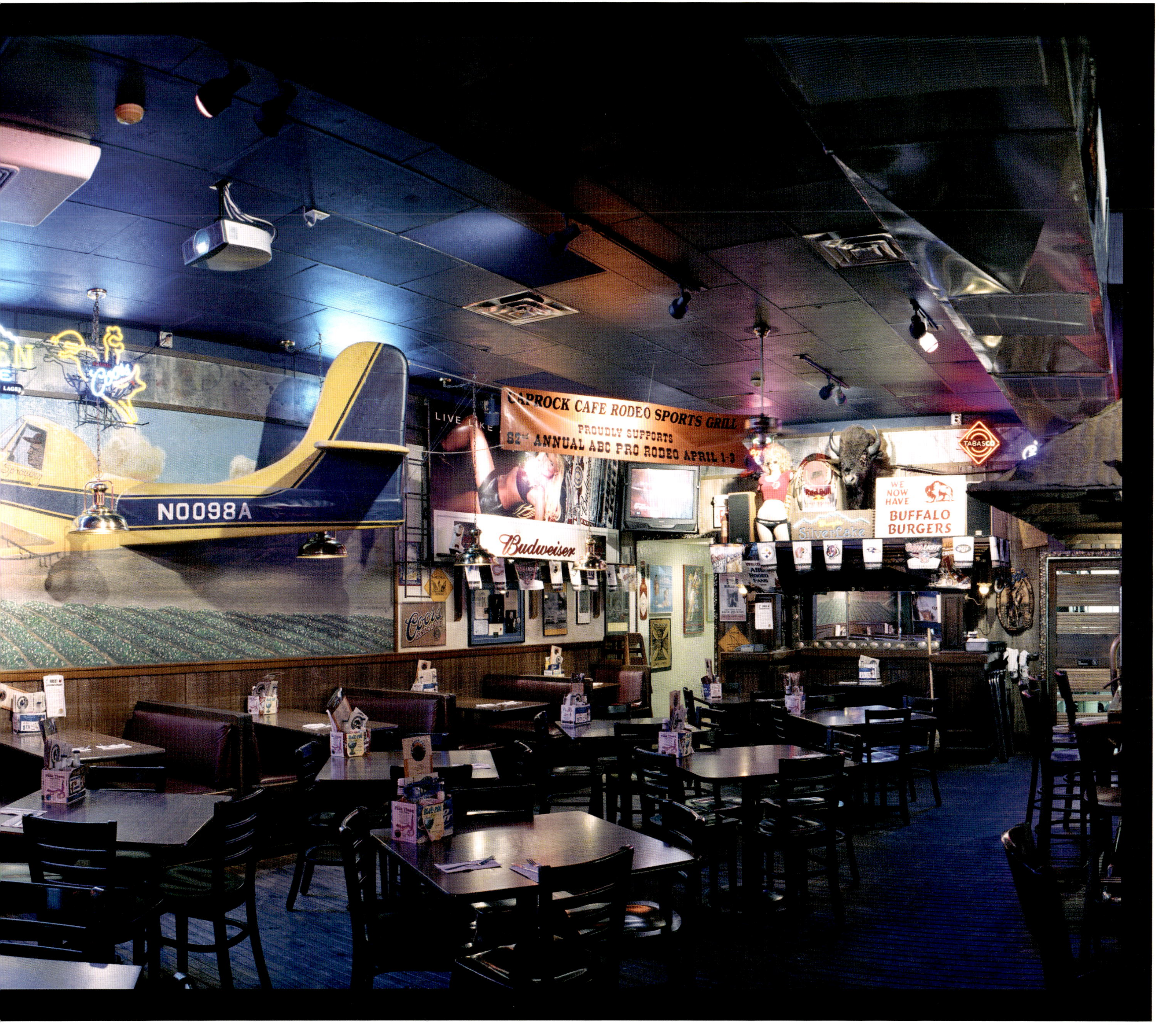

Crop duster mural, Caprock Café, Lubbock, Texas, 2005–2006

Once and Never—
The Plains of Imagination

ANNICK SMITH

HOL VOLT, HOL NEM VOLT are words that begin every Hungarian fairy tale. Loosely translated, the phrase means *There was, and there was not* or *There is, and there is not*; or, closer to the English tradition, *Once upon a time . . . and never.* The storyteller is putting the listener on notice that what follows is both true and not true. That the story to be told exists in some real world, and in no real world—at the same time.

I am Hungarian on both sides of my family, and have been educated in this double-think mode.

So it is no surprise that my Llano Estacado does not exist primarily in West Texas. Of course I know there is a there there. I have seen its Caprock rim rising pale and forbidding three hundred feet above the red Permian plains. I have driven across its slightly slanted, horizon-bound mesa, a tabletop as level as the isthmus of Florida. "Remember," a guide once told me as he poled our flatboat out toward open waters through a literal sea of grass, "you can't drown in these Everglades cuz the water's only three feet deep. Florida is flat, flat, flat." It is a place where land and sea, swamps and mangrove islands flow tepidly from one state of solidity to another like gumbo soup poured into a dinner plate.

On these Texas flatlands it is soil, not water, that moves in the ever-present currents of wind. I have been stung by blowing topsoil in this country, and I have walked dusty pathways, but I did not see the prairie I had traveled so far to see—the great high grassy plain that comes alive for me when I speak its evocative, musical, almost magical name—*lla-no es-ta-ca-do.*

Before I ever stepped onto what Francisco Vasquez de Coronado called the palisaded plains, I had read about his expedition riding into West Texas in 1541, when, having found no golden cities of Cibola, the conquistadores ascended a rimrock formation that looked to them like palisades. "I reached some plains so vast, that I did not find their limit anywhere I went," wrote Coronado, "although I traveled over them for more than 300 leagues." Failing to find a more fitting metaphor, he compared this expanse of high dry grasslands to a limitless sweep of undulating waters. It was, he wrote, as if his company had been "swallowed up by the sea."

That was the image that stuck in my mind after reading about Coronado's explorations. I was a freshman at Cornell University at the time and had never traveled across the southern plains, had never been to Texas, had never seen what some have called the "island in the sky." So it was easy to imagine horseback knights enveloped in tall grass like the grasses of Kansas—which I had seen—and the once-upon-a-time prairies of Illinois, where I had been raised on stories of pioneers in sod houses and Midwestern tribes in a jungle of grass. I pictured the plumed helmets of conquistadores rising above head-high big bluestem, horses racing in circles, no roads, no paths, no nothing to guide their riders except the sun and the stars.

Later, after I had crisscrossed the Great Plains on journeys to and from Montana, I realized my daydream was foolish. There could be no tall grasses in the semiarid climate of those southern plains, so I envisioned shin-high blue grama and buffalo grasses, green and ruffled in spring like the shortgrass prairies of the northern Rockies, which I actually knew and loved. In this fantasy, I was not off base. Varieties of these short-grasses once dominated the West Texas plains, but the ground there has been so overgrazed or plowed under for farms and agribusiness that native grasses have become as rare as the great herds of bison that once roamed what my friend the historian Dan Flores calls the "horizontal yellow."

The Llano Estacado was yellow most seasons. It was the perfect secret hideout, harboring gold Coronado could not see—grasses that supported birds and bison, wolves and prairie dogs, hunters and gatherers, as well as the late-coming horse herds and Comanche warriors who raised and rode them. The old island in the sky, it seemed to those travelers, would always be a garden for nomads, a huge and wealthy landscape painted by nature in colors of the sun. But "always" is a dangerous notion. Now that the garden's native grasses are mostly gone, the plains have been turned upside down, scorched brown and gray and ochre from attempts to tame and reap them by invasions of Anglo cattlemen, farmer sons of ex-Confederates, and hardcore settlers looking for freedom. They came to find free homesteads, religious freedom, freedom of expression for fringe political groups, and freedom from zealous law enforcement for Mexican migrants as well as for outlaws of one kind or another.

Coronado's small but fateful excursion connected in my free-associating mind with stories of horseback invaders entering the Hungarian plains—plains that were home to my mother and her mother's family. I recalled Mother's stories of Magyar tribes, of Huns and Mongol hordes, and later the Ottoman Turks whipping their horses across the *puszta*—that fabled "uninhabited" or "deserted" grassland that occupies half of my family's homeland and more than half of its identity stories. I often wonder if my attraction to the plains of the American West and its native inhabitants is rooted in those childhood fantasies of a lost prairie homeland, if there is some pre-conscious thread that weaves me tight to a prairie mentality: a love of space, of oceans and grasslands and deserts; of running horses, herds of bison, wild animals such as antelope, elk, wolves and grizzlies; or the roaming ways of cowboys, Indians, gypsies, naturalists, and every kind of explorer.

The history of Hungary holds so many invasions by so many peoples for so many years that it makes my head swirl in a confusion of names and dates. But the most significant early settlers in the Carpathian Bowl were Indo-Europeans who arrived from the East about seven thousand years ago. They were, primarily, a farming people whose culture of agriculture had originated in Iraq and southern Turkey and at the foot of the Caucasuses. Banished by natural forces, they fled their Eden when glaciers melted at the end of the Ice Age, flooding the fertile basin that had supported them—and transforming it eventually into the Black Sea. Those ancient farming Caucasian tribes drove out the Cro-Magnon hunting and gathering people who had lived for eons along Hungary's great rivers, the Danube and the Tisza. They brought technologies of the Bronze Age to a Stone-Age land: cattle and horses, and a domesticated grass we know as wheat. It was an invasion that changed the history of the world.

The staked plain of West Texas had its own tribes, and its own history of invaders, but its history is different from the history of the European steppes because not so long ago—less than two hundred years back—the Llano Estacado ran with wild bison. Bison had fed and clothed local prehistoric peoples who hunted them on foot. Later, Apachean tribes drove out the hunter-gatherers and held hegemony on the Southern Plains. The Apache, in turn, were expelled from their heartland by an aggressive, horse-breeding, well armed and organized Comanche confederation seeking empire from the central Great Plains all the way south into Mexico. With the arrival of the Comanche, horses became the key to power. Horses offered mobility and made bison hunting not only a source of food but of wealth. Horses in their thousands were good for trade, for fighting enemies, stealing arms and slaves, and for war. Their presence on the plains created a technological revolution that would transform the American West.

It seems ironic to me that the horses that empowered the Comanche were descended from horses let loose in the New World by Spanish invaders who followed Columbus, perhaps including mounts that Coronado's men had lost on the Llano Estacado in the sixteenth century. Although the Comanche empire was a hundred years briefer than Spain's, both went down because they were beset by forces beyond their control, compounded by conditions set up by their own greed. This is a warning to all empire-seekers!

For the Comanche, the uncontrollable condition was drought, which burned up the grasslands and caused competition between the over-hunted bison herds they depended on for food and the burgeoning horse herds they depended on for power. The Comanche in their last days were starving. Holdout bands refused to live on reservations in Oklahoma. They hid in canyons deep in the high plains of their homeland, where they had always gone to find shelter and water. But U.S. cavalry forces allowed for the systematic destruction of the last herd of bison, then searched out and destroyed the Comanche holdouts. Following their final battle, on September 28, 1874 in the peach- and pumpkin-striped badlands of Palo Duro Canyon, U.S. Army soldiers gathered up the approximately 1,100 remaining Comanche horses and led them to nearby Tule Canyon, where they were destroyed in a screaming, thrashing, tragic bloodbath. Only a few Comanche were killed, but the bands of survivors were stripped of their will to fight or endure.

This vivid history is all I knew about the Llano Estacado before I stepped onto it. And I also knew the story that came next, about ranchers and cowboys and hundreds of thousands of cattle grazing the short-grasses that only recently fed bison in their millions. It had been easy to imagine conquistadores and Comanche, the U.S. Cavalry and ranchers such as Charlie Goodnight on the Llano Estacado. The staked plains of my imagination were a once-and-never storyland of wild open spaces where anything could happen and often did. They were part of the great American drama of conquest—a story about American identity—a microcosm of the myths of the American West.

So, it is not hard to understand my discomfort at discovering an actual, hard-scrabble country of plowed ground in irrigated rows radiating to the horizon; and straight roads bisecting the dun-colored fields like white crosses on evangelical storefront churches. I had not envisioned farm worker shanties and dusty towns called Tulia and Plainview and Brownfield. I had not imagined windmills and silos and gigantic, stinking feedlots at the edges of urban sprawl. Invasive species like sunflowers and tumbleweed were not alien to my fantasies, but I never dreamed of cotton fields.

After the big ranches had overgrazed the native grasses on the staked plains and run their great herds of cattle north and west to Montana, after drought and wind had transformed the plowed topsoil of former grasslands into what was accurately called the Dust Bowl—farmers discovered they could use gasoline and electric pumps to bring water up from the Ogallala Aquifer to irrigate crops. Today, the best lands on the palisaded plains are worked by agribusiness. Cotton is king around Lubbock. But cotton demands lots of water, as well as the hot sunshine of West Texas. And just as the Comanche could not continue to hold sway on their sky island without horses, the corporations cannot keep farming the high, dry plains without water. And the aquifer is being pumped toward dry. To make the situation more dire, our climate is warming. The "semi" part of the semiarid plains might soon be replaced by pure "arid." Without a steady source of water, what will come next?

What I imagine, and what is surely beginning, is another technological revolution. The technologies of renewable energy may not be as transformative as the technologies of farming and domestication that Indo-Europeans brought to the Hungarian *puszta* seven thousand years ago, or as devastating to local peoples as the mass killing of bison on the Great Plains, or as myth-making as cowboys versus Indians. But life-changing, nevertheless.

Today we see gigantic new stakes on the Llano Estacado—huge high-stemmed windmills that define horizons, their gleaming propellers churning the dusty air. There will be more. And I can imagine solar power plants spread across what used to be cotton fields gleaning the energy of the sun, a source of relatively clean, renewable power to replace the derricks and pumps of depleted Texas oilfields. In the story I have made up for myself, the once-and-never future will bring new empires and new emperors, a grid to help fuel the nation. And to make these changes possible, there must be cities on the plains. I envision energized communities scattered where the straight-line roads meet, replenishing the deserted and declining towns of today. My vision includes green houses and green laboratories to shelter scientists and train technicians. I see work for willing hands, shiny factories, and good schools to support new industries and keep the children at home. And on the depleted lands that surround these communities, I see more wildlife preserves; the replanting of native flora; museums and libraries to tell the stories of the past and enrich future generations.

It's not as pretty a picture as the once-upon-a-time sea of native grasses that Coronado rode into. There will be no more black clumps of bison shadowed by packs of wolves, no more blanketed tribes pulling their goods on dog-drawn travois. Conquistadores in armor, horseback Comanche, and Texas cowboys driving herds of longhorns will never again ride the horizontal yellow, but they will continue to exist in our myths and imaginations.

The Llano Estacado does not care. Like its famous mirages that make far seem near and near seem larger than life, the huge flat wind-blown plateau still holds promises of treasures and is rife with illusions. It rises from red bottomlands like an island in the sky—a deceptive, secretive, and crevassed plain dominated by blue northers, clouds floating like dreams, and the everlasting sun.

Andrew John Liccardo

THE LLANO ESTACADO region of West Texas and eastern New Mexico, like a lot of good places, is simple and maddeningly complex at the same time. Out on the Western Plains, environmental and economic issues (which are often not unrelated) have, in many places, produced steady depopulation. In Texas, New Mexico, and Oklahoma, Kansas, Colorado, and Nebraska, managed depletion of the Ogallala Aquifer makes farming possible on otherwise unproductive land. As a result, the future of a significant region of the Great Plains appears to be in serious jeopardy. Most of the communities on the Llano are losing their children to urban centers miles and miles away. The Llano Estacado is emptying out, drying up, and slowly dying.

At the same time, though, it is a beautiful and strangely uplifting place. Much of what happens out there, which often can't be comprehended with a quick glance, is a logical extension of the current realities intersecting with historic tendencies. On the Llano, you are quickly and directly confronted with its vastness. It looks sparse and it feels sparse. It is sparsely populated, sparsely watered, sparsely adorned, and sparsely acknowledged. That is its real strength. It is a piece of geography that gives you space and time and quiet, and it demands you deal with it on those terms. Although sparseness defines it visually, the Llano derives its central character from its contradictions. It appears perfectly flat as you drive across it, but is actually a huge plateau rising above the surrounding plains (hence the term "the flattest mountain"). It is a place that requires that you get to know it a bit before you can begin to understand where you are. As in all good places, you can learn a lot about where you are, and why, from the place names: New Deal, New Home, Levelland, Goodland, Grassland, Muleshoe, White Deer, Nazareth, Happy, Wayside, Halfway, Needmore, Progress, Plainview, Shallowater, Sweetwater, Blackwater, Cotton Center, Justiceburg.

I see in the landscapes of the Llano Estacado a reflection of the character of the people who occupy it. I want my Llano pictures to talk about a place I love and miss, and I hope that they in some way accurately describe the value of these kinds of places. For the wider community, I want these images to articulate how the Llano functions as an intersection of the physical place and the people, past and present, who occupy it. In the future, I think, places like this, now largely ignored and seen as vast wastelands, will be seen as places where we overlooked some things; where we missed some opportunities. I want a few of those to be in my pictures.

Rangeland near Friona, Texas, 2004

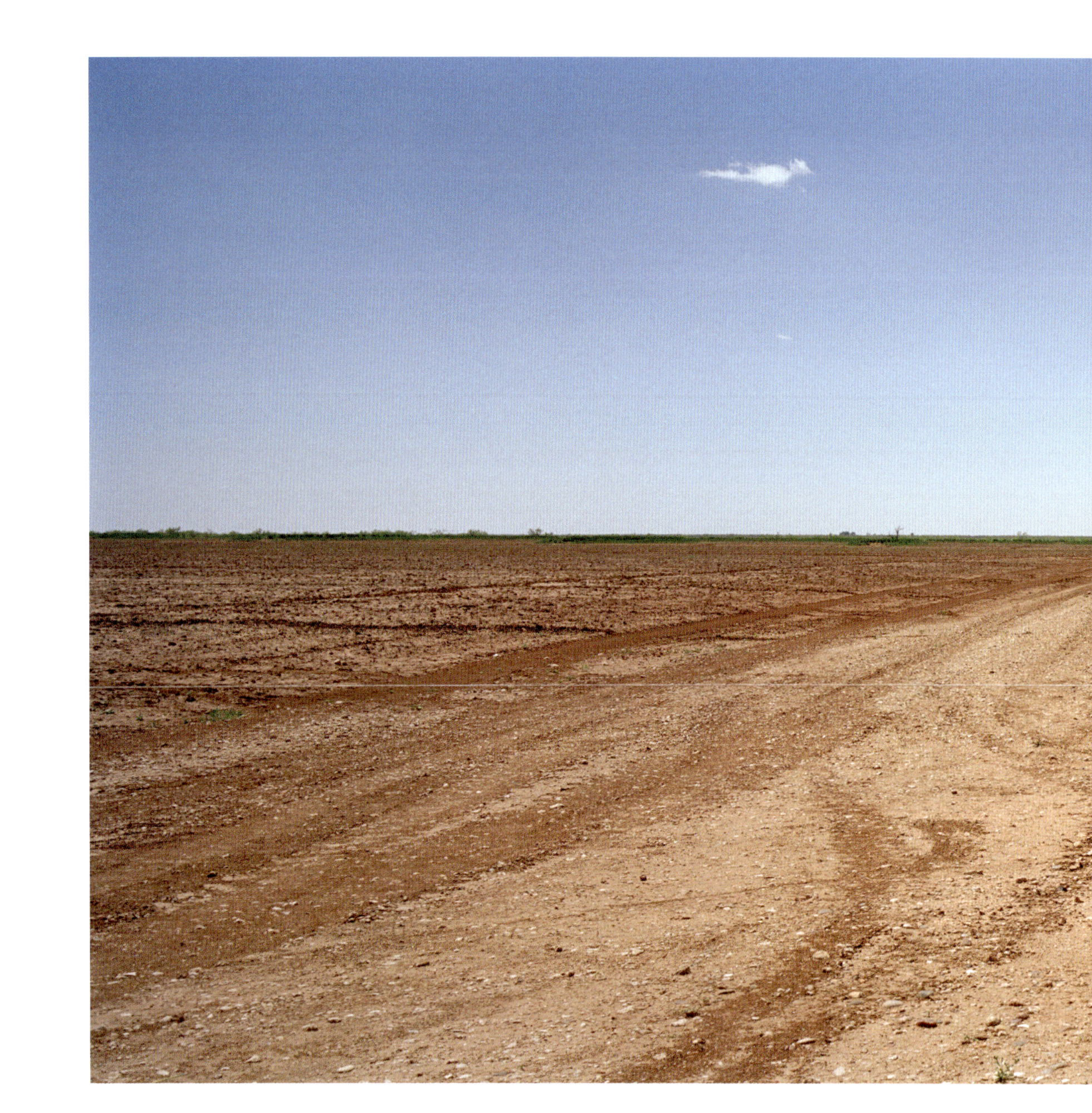

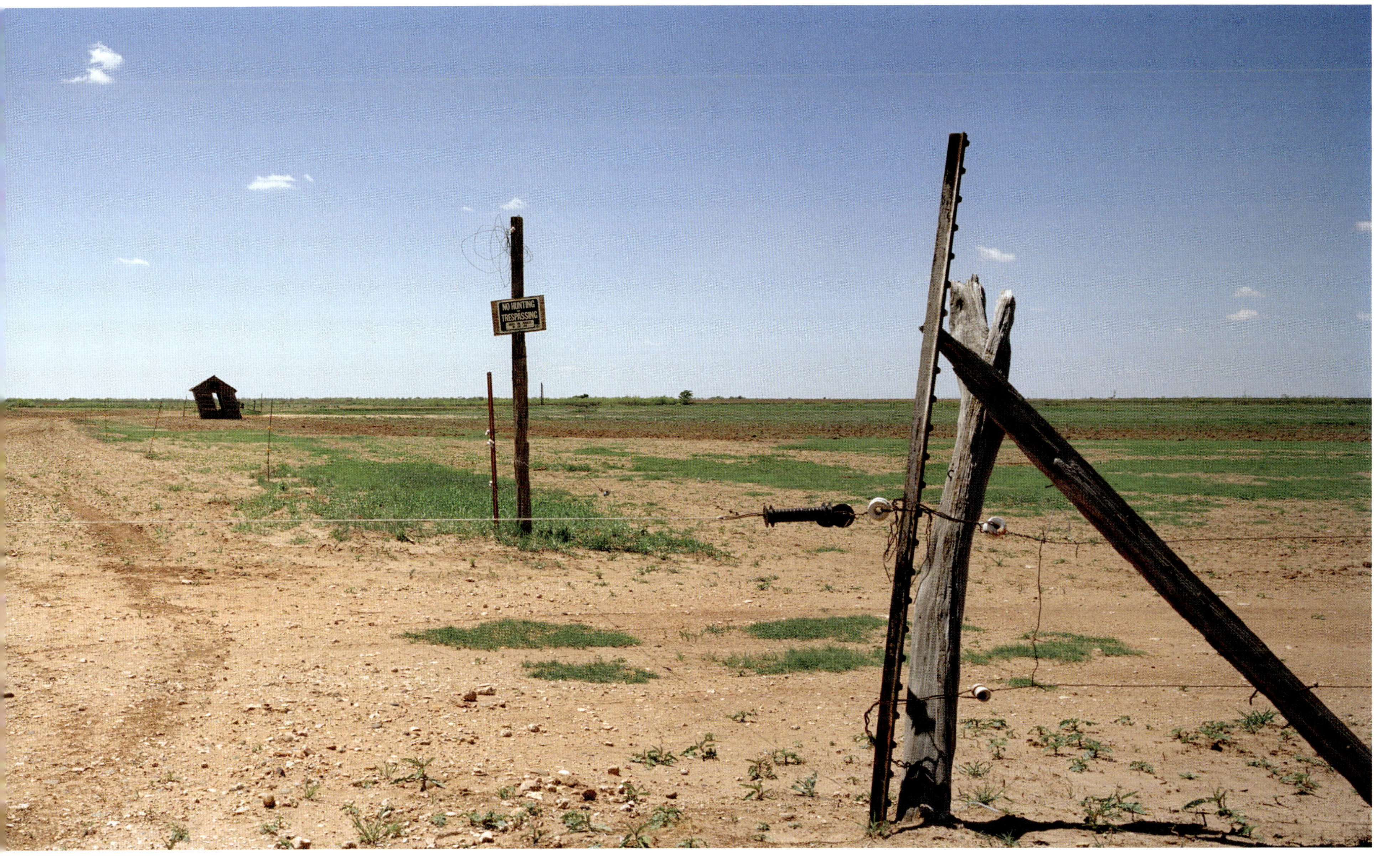
NO HUNTING
TRESPASSING

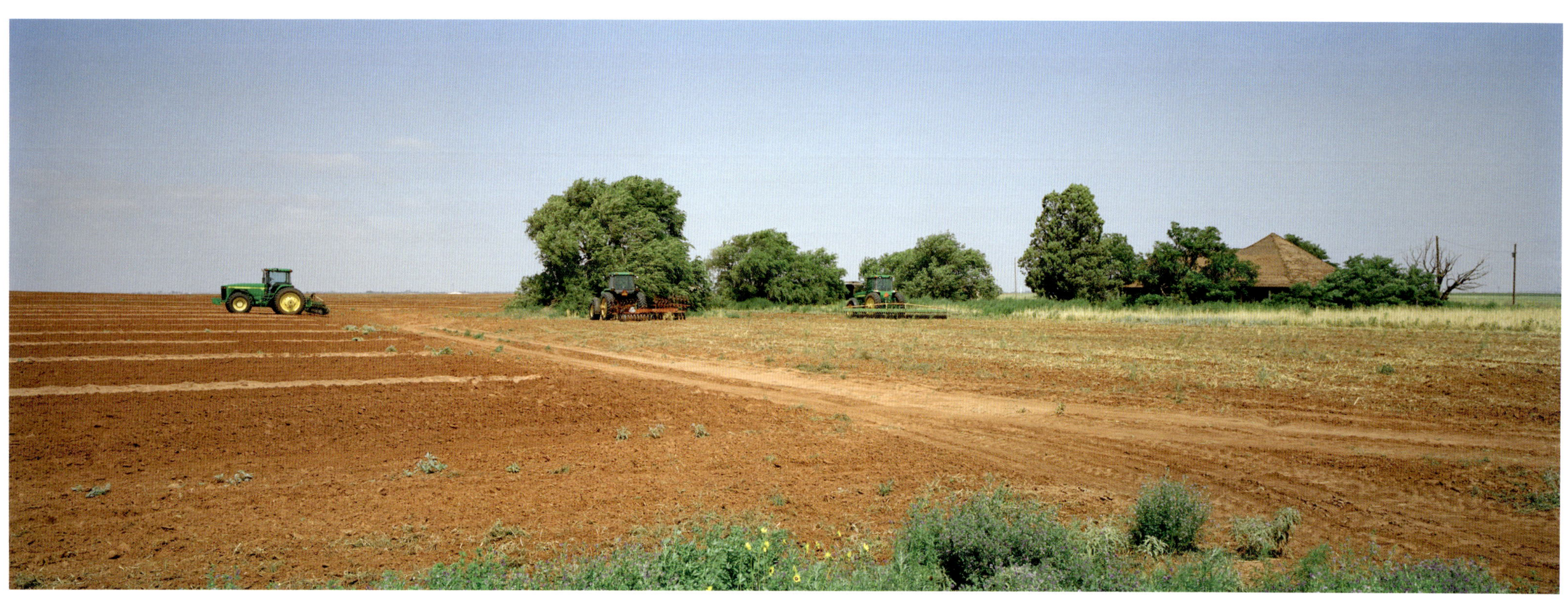

Abandoned homestead near Meadow, Texas, 2004

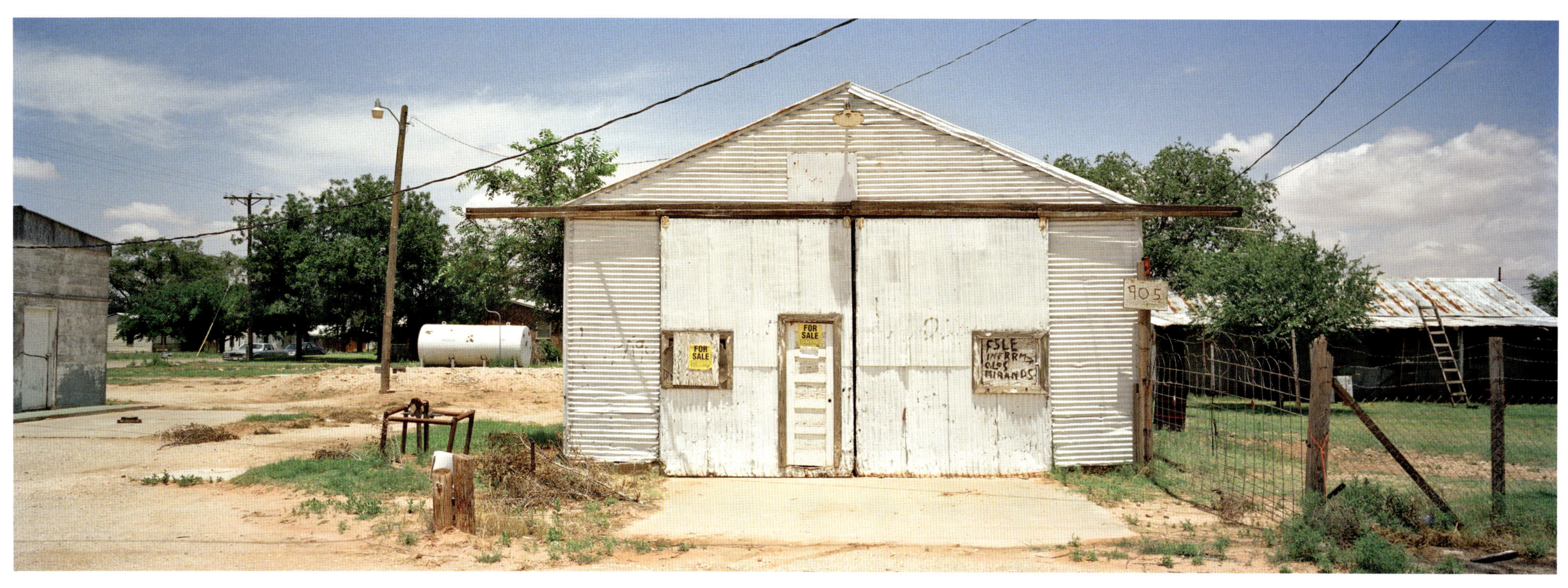

Building for sale, Loop, Texas, 2004

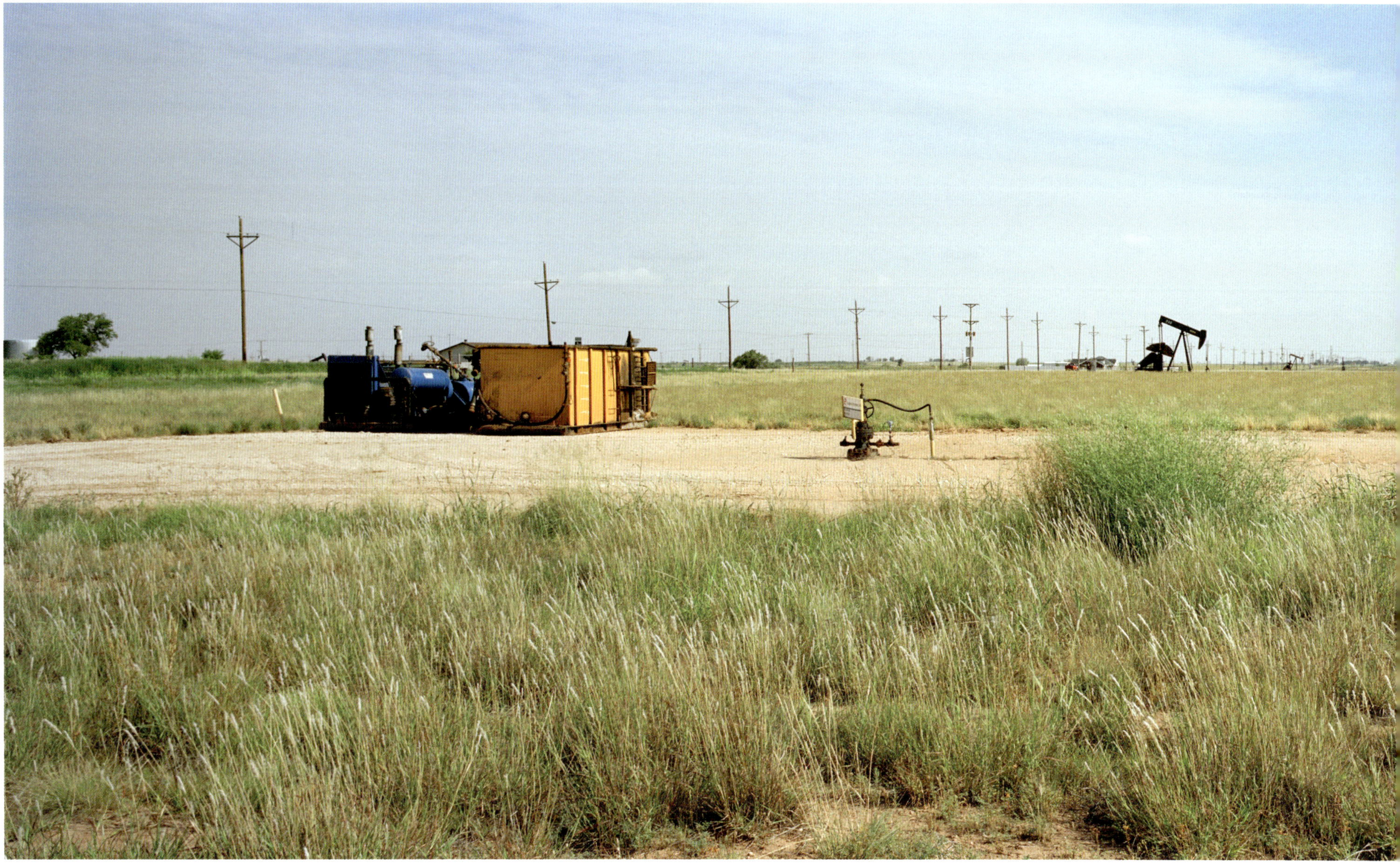

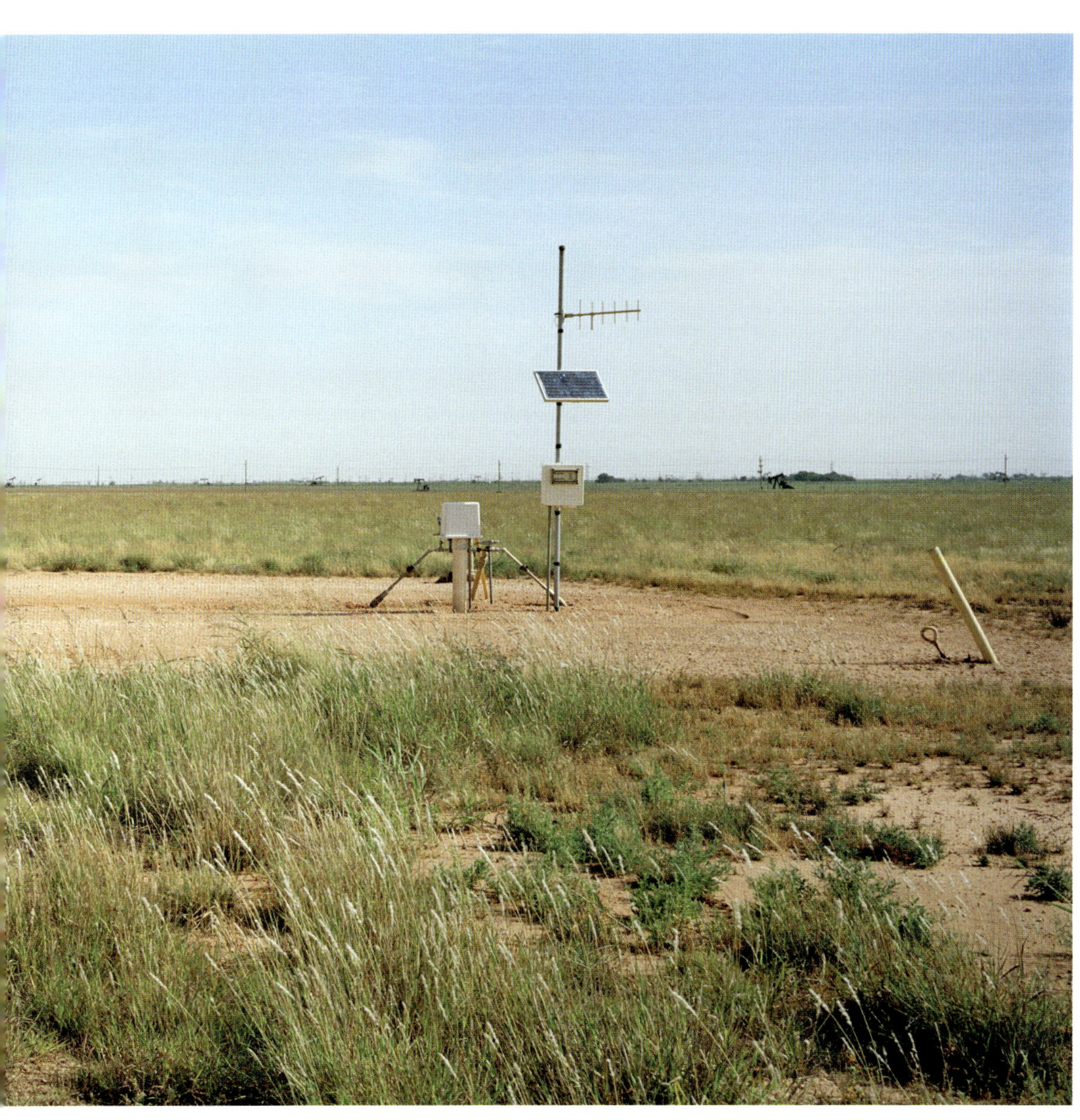

Solar power panel and pump jack outside Sundown, Texas, 2004

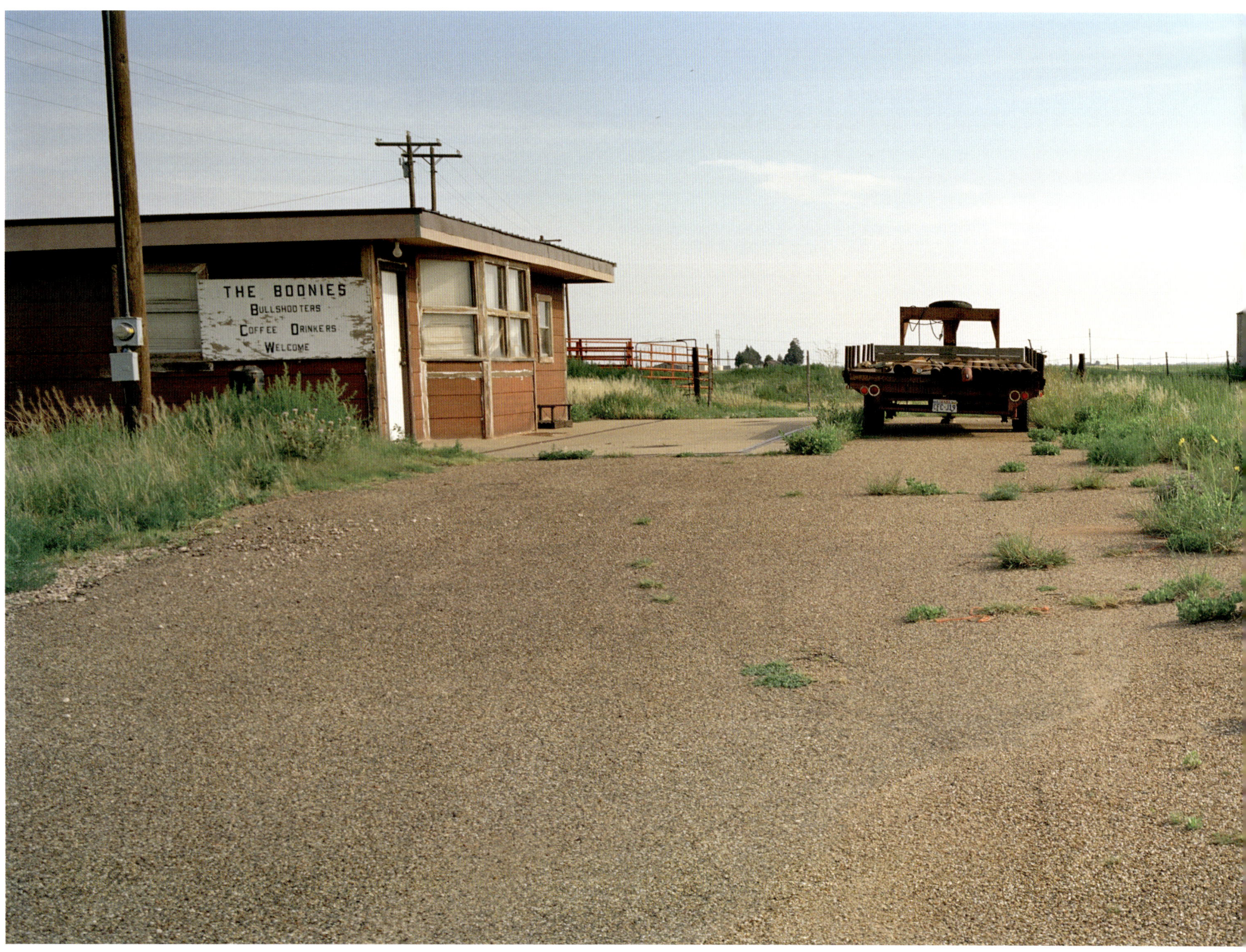
THE BOONIES
BULLSHOOTERS
COFFEE DRINKERS
WELCOME

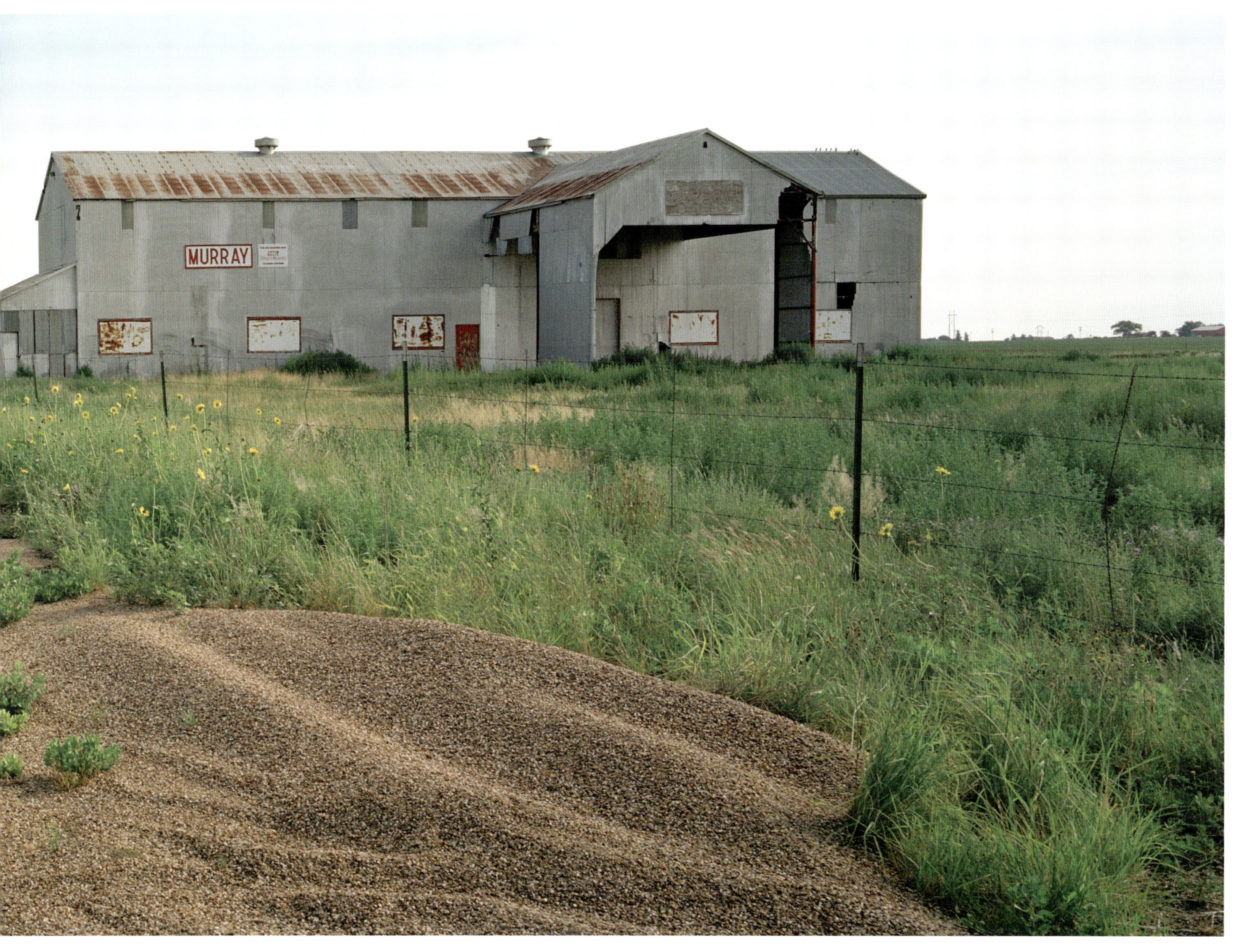

Restaurant and cotton gin outside Levelland, Texas, 2004

Police station, Lockney, Texas, 2004

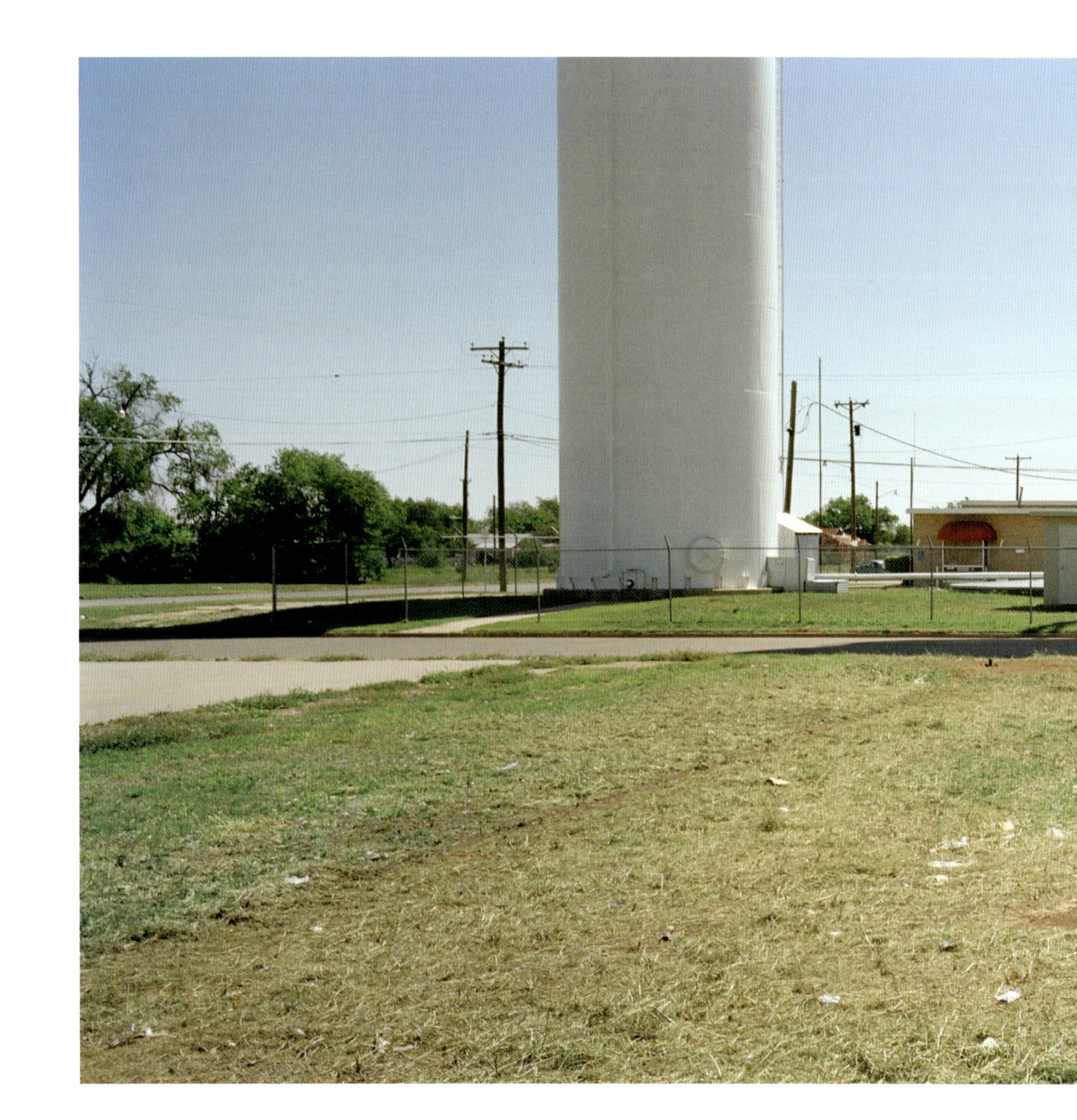

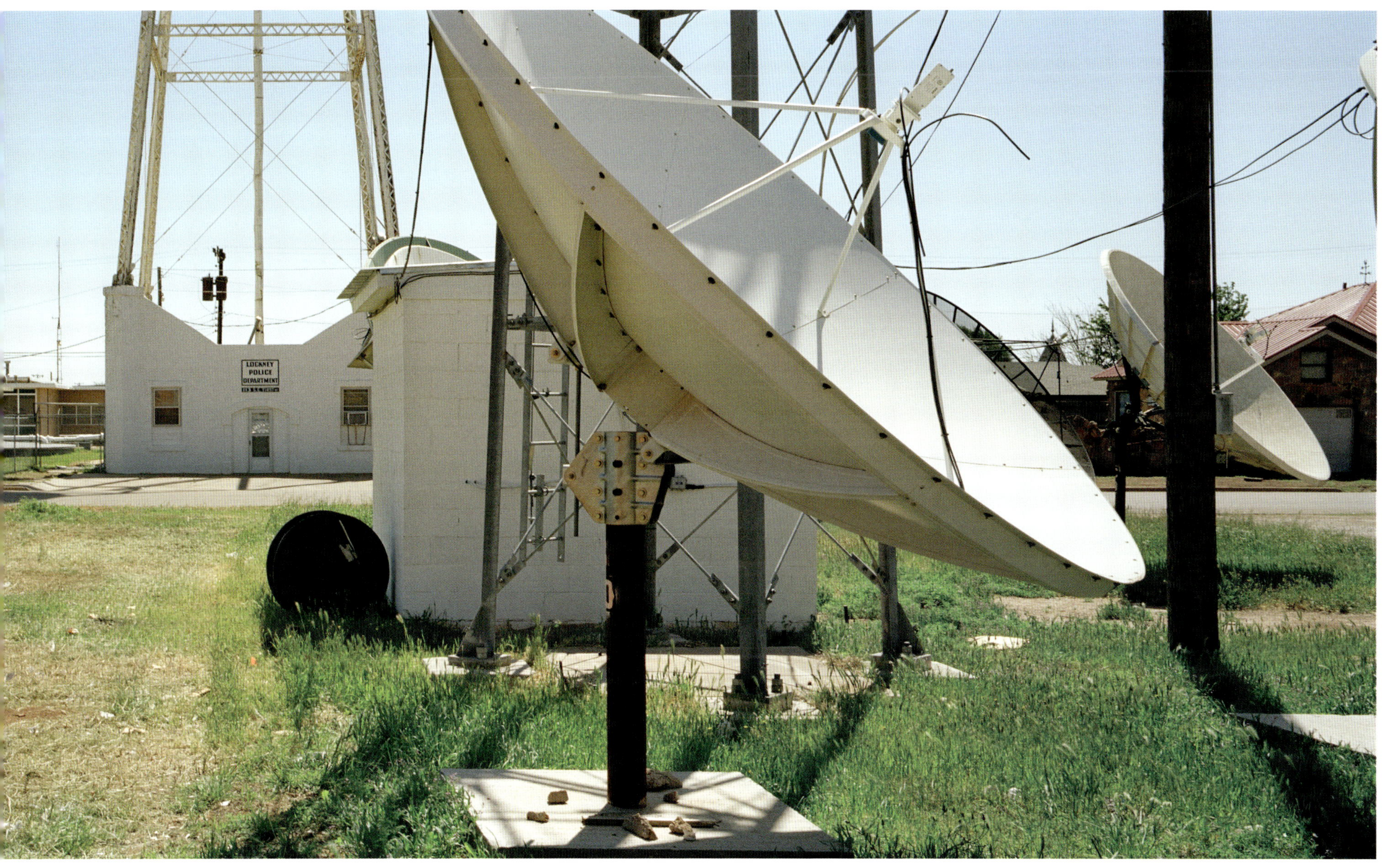
LOCKNEY
POLICE
DEPARTMENT

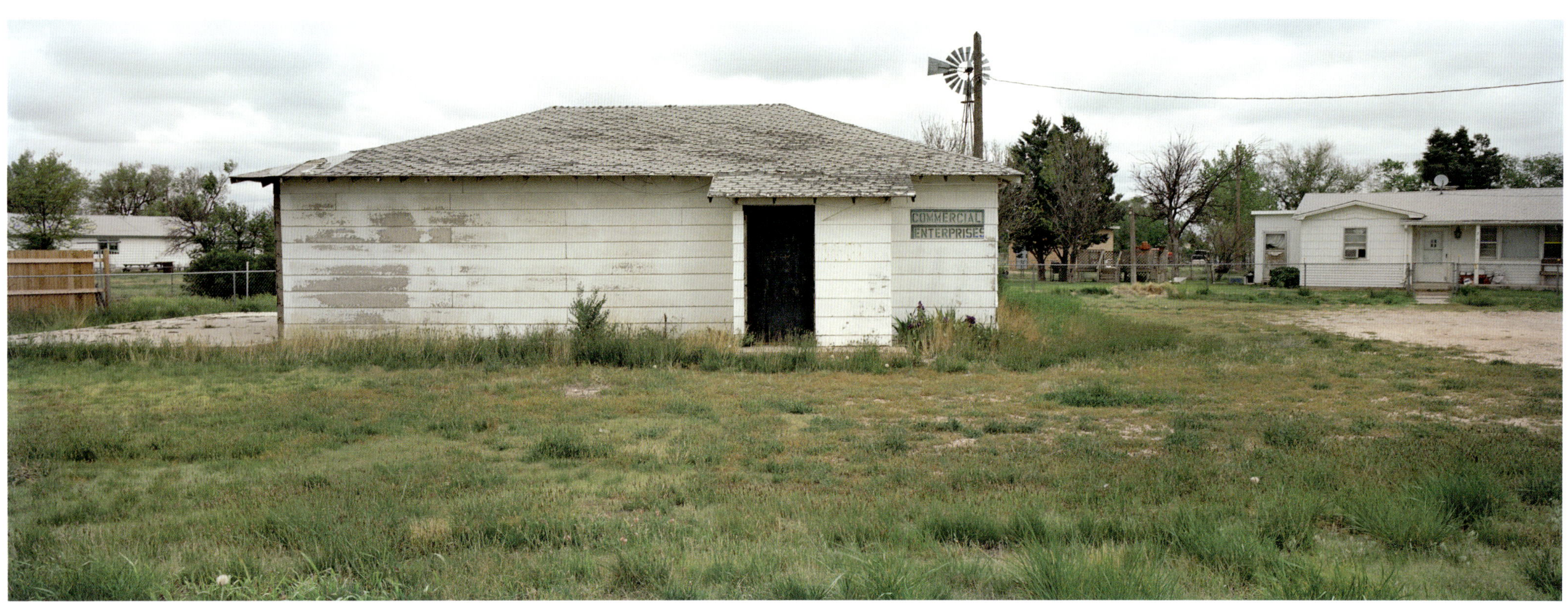

Commercial Enterprises Building, Silverton, Texas, 2004

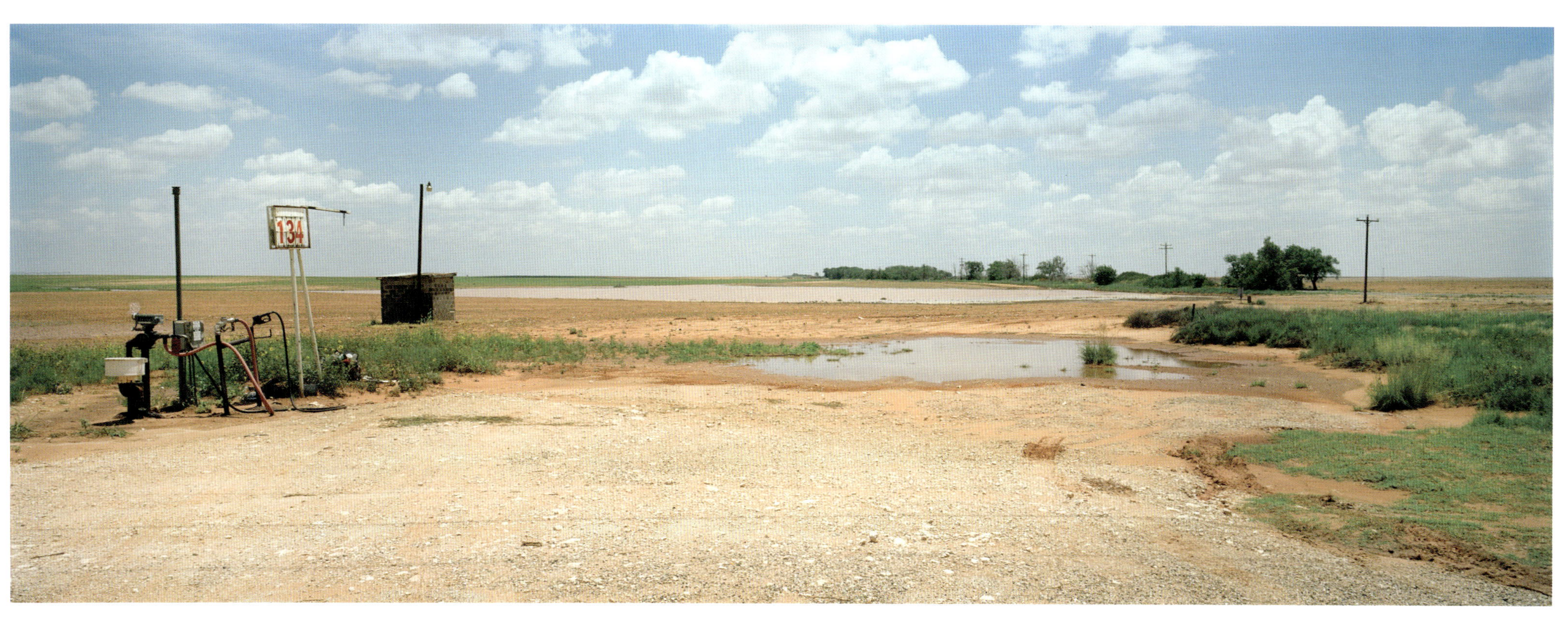

Abandoned gas station and plowed-up playa lake near Seagraves, Texas, 2004

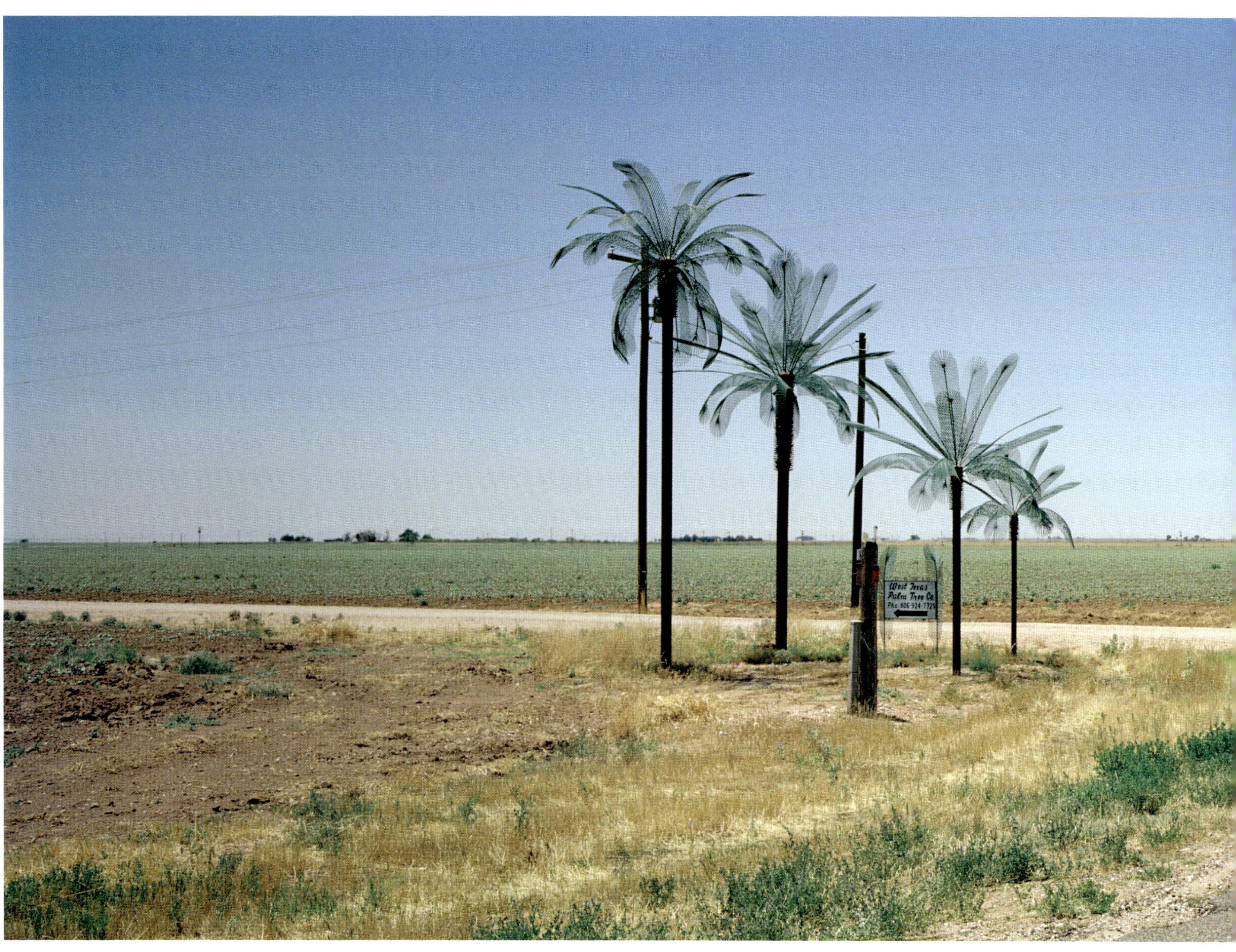
West Texas
Palm Tree Co.
Pho. 806-924-7725

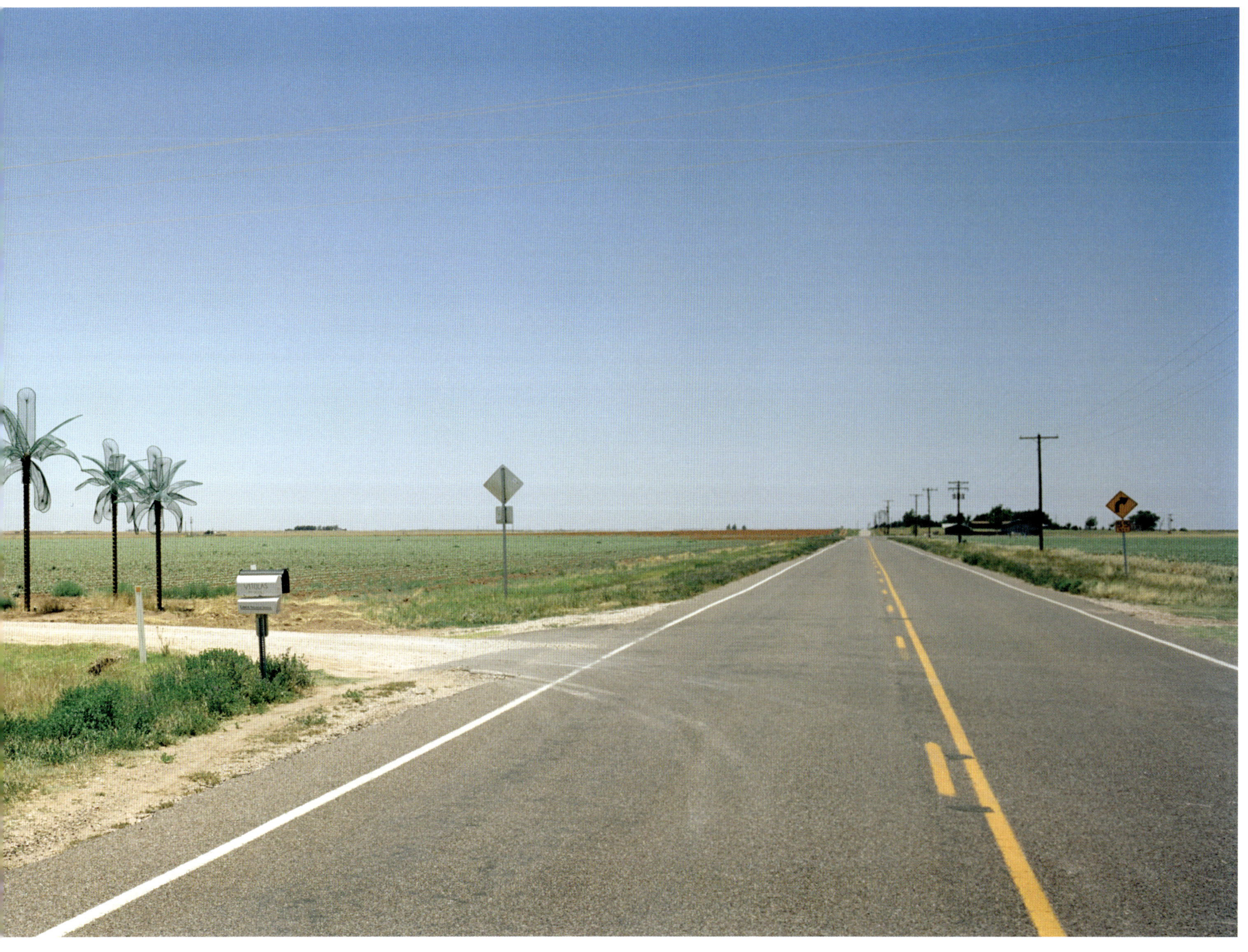

Plastic palm trees at the entrance to the West Texas Palm Tree Company, New Home, Texas, 2004

Cone elevator and center pivot irrigation
near New Deal, Texas, 2004

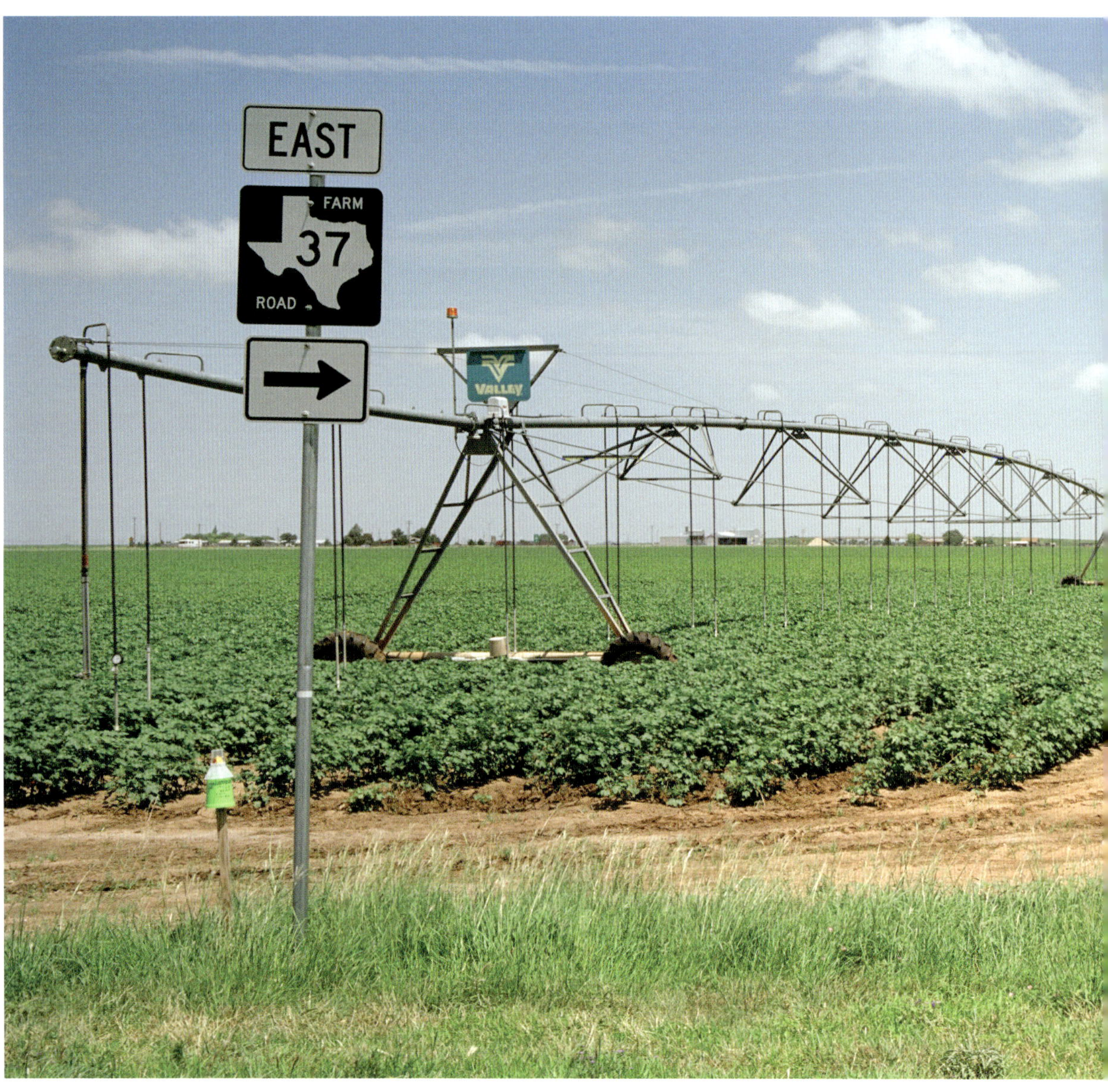

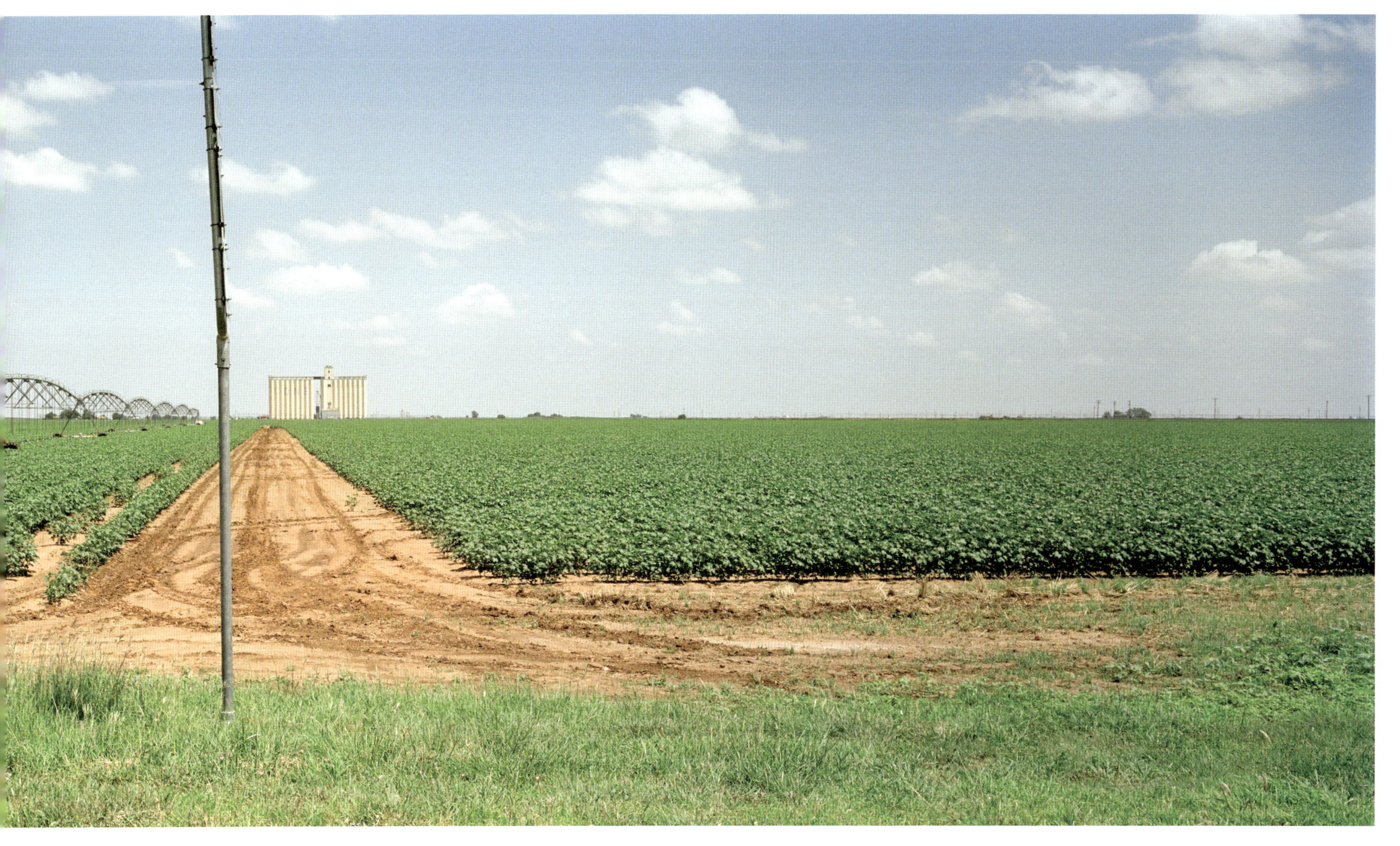

The Llano Estacado: An Island in the Sky

STEPHEN BOGENER

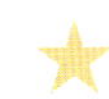

THE LLANO ESTACADO, 32,000 square miles of sun, grass, and sky, is larger than New England, taking up a good portion of northwestern Texas and eastern New Mexico. The southern extension of the High Plains, the Llano is part of what was long known as the Great American Desert, a high semi-arid mesa sloping ten feet per mile toward the southeast, one of the largest tablelands in North America. Though canyon badlands cut through this endless horizon of yellow grass supporting blue sky, 85 percent of what the human eye registers on the Llano Estacado is sky. Denizens of the region have long squinted keenly for something vertical in the sun-drenched grassland that makes up the other 15 percent. The perceived sameness of the country can blind the casual observer to the secrets of the land, the subtleties of its culture and history.

The Llano offers not only unexpected geophysical features like sand dunes, draws, and canyons amidst a sea of grass, but a paradoxical cultural milieu as well. Naturally, West Texas natives, whose roots here may go back two or three generations, resolutely defend the region's politics, religion, culture, land, and people, even as they admit to some striking paradoxes in a land newly settled by their great-grandparents. What strikes many about this land above the Caprock, the yellow-white band of caliche marking the edge of the Llano, is that the contradictions of the place—much like the scattered draws and canyons rising up in front of an unwary horseman at full gallop—are hidden in plain sight. The Llano stands out as a place under-appreciated for these subtleties, and for the stories etched across the land and faces of the people who settled here.

The name "Llano Estacado" is ensconced in the Spanish mystery and lore of Francisco Vasquez de Coronado's 1540 *entrada* across the American Southwest. Pedro de Castañeda, who chronicled Coronado's chimerical search for the fabled land of Quivira and the Seven Cities of Cibola, described two of the expedition's campsites with intriguing detail. For one hundred years, historians, geographers, and archaeologists have tried to interpret what Castañeda meant when he described Cona, a land of lush *barrancas*, or canyons, slicing through the Llano, a land where Spaniards and their Indian guides experienced a violent hailstorm but also found abundant spring water, wild grapes, and nearby herds of bison.

Sixteenth-century Spaniards approaching the Llano's Mescalero Escarpment from the West likened the Caprock, the uppermost geologic feature of the Llano, to "palisades, ramparts, or stockades," like those witnessed in Europe. Approaching the Llano from the north and east as well, travelers encountered steep escarpments caused by erosion of softer beds underlying the resistant Caprock. Others have surmised that the name "Llano Estacado" is a reference to yucca stalks which periodically broke the linearity of the grass plain above the Caprock. Still others claim that the name derived from the practice of staking one's mount on the grassland to prevent the animals from vanishing into the horizon, or to keep one's route marked by a continuous column of stakes planted to mark the trail homeward.

The Llano perimeter is marked on the north by the southern escarpment of the Canadian River Valley and on the east by the edge of the Caprock escarpment. The southern stretches of the Llano are not so obvious, gradually sloping into the Edwards Plateau near Big Spring. To the west, the Mescalero Escarpment east of New Mexico's Pecos River Valley stands as historic sentinel to the caravans of human activity passing this way.

In a letter to the king of Spain on October 20, 1541, Coronado wrote about the island of grass he found after climbing the Mescalero: "I reached some plains so vast, that I did not find their limit anywhere I went, although I travelled over them for more than 300 leagues . . . with no more landmarks than if we had been swallowed up by the sea . . ." One of Coronado's soldiers was equally amazed, describing what he saw as "country . . . like a bowl, [where] when a man sits down the horizon surrounds him at the distance of a musket shot. There are no groves of trees except at the rivers . . . In traversing eight hundred miles, [no] mountain range was seen, nor a hill nor a hillock three times as high as a man." Spaniards were terrified of the open grassland, especially at midday when the sun bleached even subtle differences in perspective and color. Coronado lost a few men who went out hunting and failed to come back. At night the Spaniards took a count of who was missing, hoping to lead them back to camp by building enormous bonfires, firing guns, blowing trumpets, and beating drums. Some came back after wandering aimlessly for hours or days. Some had ventured too far to ever return.

More than three hundred years later, United States Army Captain Randolph B. Marcy, seeking the headwaters of the Canadian and Red Rivers, concurred with Coronado's assessment when he described the smooth and seemingly level Llano as a region "without tree, shrub, or any other herbage to intercept the vision." In deference to Navajo descriptions of the place, historian Dan Flores calls the sea of yellow grasses of the Llano and near Southwest "horizontal yellow." For those enamored of tall trees, running rivers, and taller grasses farther east, the Llano Estacado can look awfully flat and vacant, but as Coronado and subsequent explorers would discover, the Llano is not nearly as flat, featureless, or empty as it first appears.

From a bio-regional perspective, until the twentieth century, the Llano Estacado of West Texas and eastern New Mexico was far from empty, harboring an extensive variety of species both plant and animal. Prior to the twentieth century, shortgrass prairies dominated by blue grama, hairy grama, buffalo grass, and dozens of other shortgrasses and forbs blanketed the area. Three-foot-tall western wheat grass often covered buffalo wallows, canyons housed sand sage and frequent stands of side oats grama, and sweet blue stem graced the prairie. In the sixteenth century, according to Spanish accounts, a variety of wild grape thrived within these canyons. Sage, cat claw, and covered-spike dropseed occurred in the most drought-prone, sandy areas of the Llano. More recently, overgrazing and plowing have favored exotic species such as sunflowers and tumbleweed.

Like many areas of North America, the Llano Estacado is a story of resource extraction and exploitation. The most glaring example is the destruction of the vast herds of bison, a commodity sought for its hide and meat—food, tools, and shelter on the hoof—which had sustained Plains peoples for centuries. Wagon trains in the early nineteenth century encountered the shaggy creatures almost constantly between the Missouri River and Rocky Mountain foothills, stalling progress for days at a time. Even as late as the mid-1870s, military expeditions observed herds fifty miles long. Estimates for the number of bison roaming the North American continent prior to European arrival range as high as seventy million. By the 1880s, thanks in part to the policy of the U.S. military to destroy the herds, few of the animals remained on the Llano Estacado or elsewhere across the plains.

At one time, the Llano was also home to widespread colonies of prairie dogs, grey wolves, cougars, bobcats, black-footed ferrets, sharp-tailed grouse, coyotes, and jaguars, most of which are now extinct or threatened. With the replacement of bison by cattle in the 1870s and 80s, ranchers made elimination of *Canis lupus* a priority. Llano cowboys, for fifty years beginning in the 1870s, supplemented their meager incomes by killing grey wolves for bounties. By 1926, the State of Texas stopped reporting grey wolf populations, as they had declined to a point where numbers were negligible. Between the 1870s and 1920s, cattle operators killed 34,000 of them. An apocryphal story told by numerous ranchers at the time has it that the last of the grey wolves left the Llano en masse between 1877 and 1880. Wolf packs numbering in the thousands, sometimes twenty abreast and trailing for several miles, reportedly migrated through Yellow House Canyon to escape the onslaught of early settlers. Although this supposed event contradicts everything practiced observers know about wolf behavior, the story persists.

Settlers killed the few jaguars on the Southern Plains for their pelts, and by 1905, only four were left. The Predator and Rodent Control Act of 1931 targeted prairie dogs and dozens of other species, nearly devastating coyote, rabbit, fox, and several bird populations throughout the Great Plains and American West. Settlement on the Llano has destroyed some 45 percent of the grama-buffalo grass and 65 percent of the bluestem-grama prairies. With the exception of the national grasslands in the far northwest corner of the state, little pristine grassland exists in the twenty-first century, and many characteristic species are gone.

Beyond the wholesale elimination of ecosystems, introduced species such as cattle and sheep have affected plant growth and their evolution. Cattle and sheep, grazing on the buds of shrubs and young trees, have created bushier, hedge-like shinnery instead of taller plants in the draws and canyons. With better concealment for nesting sites and more insects, the process has encouraged bird populations, but native plants susceptible to grazing have decreased or disappeared altogether.

Some species have adapted at least partially to agricultural transformations. Sandhill cranes, near extinction in the early twentieth century, now thrive by roosting among the larger playa lakes of the region and feeding on grain and cottonseed from harvested fields. The Muleshoe and Buffalo Lake National Wildlife Refuges provide niche habitats for the cranes and other species like rattlesnakes, jackrabbits, owls, prairie dogs, and cottontails which formerly populated the Llano in great numbers. Soils exposed to wind and water as a result of intense cotton farming and trampling by cattle are highly eroded, affording new homes for rock wrens, rough-winged swallows, and barn owls, but reducing habitats for meadowlarks, which require taller grasses for nesting.

Before settlement began in earnest in the early years of the twentieth century, the Llano Estacado boasted a complex grassland ecosystem. Within two or three generations, ranchers and farmers had greatly reduced or eliminated natural grasses and varmints that interfered with the emerging agricultural economy of the region. By the 1940s, pump technology allowed farmers to irrigate their fields by harnessing ancient groundwater from the Ogallala Aquifer. The subsequent lowering of the water table dried up numerous springs in draws and canyons. Despite its relatively scanty population, the Llano's fragile grassland and the dogged determination of farmers and ranchers to make it produce led to perhaps the most altered landscape of flora and fauna in North America. In the twenty-first century, despite a one-hundred-year history of human alteration, the Llano still offers up a vast sense of enchanted emptiness, a place yet to be fully explored, one of the last rural frontiers of North America to be settled.

The freedom experienced here on crisp November days, looking across an open expanse of cotton-patch brown and blue near Lubbock, is offset by the realization that the landscape was once a continuous sea of yellow grasses interrupted only by canyons and draws naturally meandering from northwest to southeast. Far back in geologic history, rivers from the Rocky Mountains flowed through the canyons, until the Pecos River began intersecting the streams and stealing their waters.

In between the canyons where the ancient rivers flowed, lands today planted in cotton, especially in the two dozen counties surrounding Lubbock, leave little hint of the natural grasses which once fed millions of buffalo. Grasses subsidized by the federal government's Conservation Reserve

Program (CRP) serve as wildlife habitat and as a means of keeping the soil from blowing away as it did in the 1930s. Without the CRP's establishment of the new grasslands, and water from the Ogallala Aquifer, conditions in the fifties might have mimicked those of the Dust Bowl. Early in the program, the government recommended a seed mixture including non-native species to hold the soil in place. Today CRP lands more closely reflect the native species which once proliferated across the Llano Estacado, with a new element added to the landscape. Bands of renegade elm trees, the descendants of a fast-growing variety imported by homesteaders, dot the new grasslands.

On top of the Llano Estacado, the winds still blow, especially in the spring. The average annual wind speeds for Lubbock and Amarillo respectively are 12.4 and 13.5 miles per hour, making them windier on average than Chicago, which gained its moniker not through wind speeds, but rather through the bluster of its promoters. The National Weather Service defines breezy conditions as winds between fifteen and twenty-five miles per hour, and windy as sustained winds of twenty to thirty miles per hour. Lubbock and Amarillo often experience wind gusts exceeding thirty or forty miles per hour, but their duration is limited and usually associated with thunderstorms or approaching cold fronts. Anything above that can loosen shingles and cause tumbleweeds to bound across empty winter fields or chase your truck down a caliche road.

Local chambers of commerce do not advertise the winds of March or April. Such thinking may be a latter-day response to Dorothy Scarborough's classic novel, *The Wind*, set in Sweetwater, Texas, in the 1880s, about a heroine driven to insanity and murder by wind and drought. One of the last of the great silent films, *The Wind*, starring Lillian Gish and Lars Hansen, came to theaters just two years after the novel's publication in 1925. As a child, Scarborough lived in Sweetwater from 1882 to 1887. Her family, like many others, moved to arid West Texas to improve her mother's health. The sojourn west and the drought of the 1880s had a lasting impact on the author, much to the dismay of area boosters in the 1920s.

Contrary to the popular view of visitors in March or April, the wind does not always blow in West Texas, but when it does, the sand and dirt from the next county etch an imprint on the human psyche. In the late nineteenth century, white newcomers to the High Plains found the stark, treeless landscape at once beautiful and frightening. Without trees to reckon distance or space, earlier travelers saw the Llano as a sea of grass not unlike the ocean swells of the Gulf of Mexico. Not a few settlers enamored of the landscape east of the 100th meridian turned back. Some turned melancholy, and some, like Scarborough's character Letty, went crazy listening to the wind as it bent the grass sideways on its way to nowhere.

In the middle of the summer, days are long and the ground is often cracked from drought. The wind blows hot out of the southwest, and the sweat on a man's back dries quickly. In the winter, "blue northers"—what West Texans call the low gray-blue formations that rapidly drop temperatures as much as fifty degrees or more—approach from the north and northwest; meanwhile, the wind whistles past while it does its endless work, carving canyons and lifting topsoil high into the sky to be deposited miles away.

The winds here have helped shape the built environment as well. Early resident Paris Cox and cattleman Charles Goodnight built earthen dugouts well before railroads carried lumber to the region. These cave-like dwellings, often dug out of a slight hill, were crude but effective living quarters against the elements. It is no accident that western Comanche bands located their winter camps within the Llano's miles of canyons, out of the howling wind and close to water. By the 1890s, the few wooden frame houses and windmills stood as the tallest features of the plain, defiantly erect in contrast

STEPHEN BOGENER

to the yellow grasses surrounding them. In the 1940s, two air bases for training pilots were located here, and Lubbock became a military town. One of them, South Plains Army Air Field, was the site of glider training during World War II. Military officials reckoned, if pilots could manage the winds over the Llano Estacado, they could fly over anything, including the beaches at Normandy. For millennia before glider pilots soared over the High Plains, the wind and water had carved out this land-locked island in the sky—a landscape waiting for the last in a long line of Americans seeking land, refuge, and God.

Rising 100 to 800 feet above the surrounding countryside, the Llano Estacado stretches for 250 miles north to south, two hundred miles east to west, and is culturally and geographically an island. A Lubbockite who has lived in the region most of his life portrays the Llano as a "city on a hill." That religious metaphor makes sense. Braced with the never-say-die convictions of the old Confederacy and the evangelical Calvinist rhetoric of Methodist, Baptist, and Church of Christ ministers ringing in their ears, settlers once or twice removed from the Old South slowly made their way west and up the Caprock, the final ascent to the promised land.

However, Yankees paved the way. Seeking a place to establish a Quaker colony in the late 1870s, Paris Cox obtained railroad land in western Crosby and eastern Lubbock Counties in exchange for his Indiana sawmill. In 1878, Quakers from Indiana arrived on the Southern Plains, led by Cox. Cox arranged for a German immigrant, adventurer and businessman to break some land and help establish the new Quaker community of Marietta, later called Estacado. A severe winter spent in tents convinced many of these first families to leave the colony by springtime. Immigrant Heinrich Schmitt had changed his name to Henry Clay "Hank" Smith, a patriotically American name, and made the most of opportunities presented him on the High Plains.

A former surveyor in Nebraska, a teamster and gold seeker in California, New Mexico and Arizona, Smith had also served as muleteer for Texas Forts Quitman and Bliss; by the age of forty-two he had been a cattle hand, a Confederate soldier, a buffalo hunter, a scout, and a hotelier. First settling east of the Llano in the Flat, the notorious frontier community near present-day Albany, Smith built the Occidental Hotel, often called the finest hotel west of Fort Worth. Springing up below Government Hill and Fort Griffin, the Flat saw its share of western characters at the height of the buffalo hunting era. Smith encountered the likes of John Henry "Doc" Holiday, Patrick F. (Pat) Garrett, William H. Bonney (a.k.a. Billy the Kid), Wyatt Earp, Lottie Deno, John Wesley Hardin, Judge Roy Bean and Christopher "Kit" Carson. Here, Smith also met and married a Scottish immigrant, Elizabeth Boyle, or Aunt Hank, as she was affectionately known.

In 1876, Smith headed west, climbed the Caprock, and became one of a handful of white men since Coronado, the Mexican buffalo hunters, and Indian traders to witness the high island of grass called the Llano Estacado. Like those before him, Smith found the Llano torn along its eastern edge by canyons running northwest. Like the Spanish explorers, Apache, Comanche, *ciboleros* and Comancheros, he found water and protection in one of these canyons.

Smith might never have become the historical fixture that he is if not for Philadelphian Charles Tasker and his Irish partner "Lord" Jamieson. The partners hired Smith to find an appropriate location to headquarter a large cattle operation on the Llano. In 1876, following Ranald Mackenzie's 1872 military trail across the Llano, he reached Mount Blanco, a prominent rise within the canyon of the same name. Following Smith's recommendation, Tasker chose the location for his new ranch headquarters, Hacienda Glorieta. In the summer of 1877, Smith drove 500 to 600 head of cattle into the area, and in early 1878 he began construction on the

Rock House, a formidable two-story structure with two-foot stone walls quarried from Blanco Canyon. When Tasker and Jamieson encountered financial difficulties, the partners abandoned their cattle business and Smith, who had lent Tasker $11,000, took over the house and ranch as payment on the debt and his labor. In the fall of 1878, Smith moved his family from the Fort Griffin area to their new homestead in Blanco Canyon, the first permanent homestead on the southern portion of the Llano Estacado. Smith was the first to establish a post office, break and farm land, and run a general store on the Southern High Plains. In retrospect, Smith was a latecomer to the Llano. More than 300 years before the arrival of Smith, a more famous adventurer traversed the country in search of Quivira, a fabled land of riches.

While many Llano localities lay claim to Francisco Vasquez de Coronado's early presence on the High Plains, it is almost certain that one of his camps was in Blanco Canyon. At one point, after seeing nothing but "buffalo and sky," Coronado's scribe, or *chronista*, Pedro de Castañeda, recorded the discovery by the expedition's advance guard of an Indian village in the bottom of a large ravine. According to Castañeda's account, the natives were familiar with Alvar Nuñez de Cabeza de Vaca and his fellow castaways who washed ashore at Galveston Island in 1528. Stories of their legendary journey across the Southwest and their exalted status as shamans and healers had spread across the land in the twelve years since their passage. Upon seeing Coronado's reconnaissance party, the villagers had assembled a large pile of tanned skins and "a tent as big as a house." The Indians expected Coronado's men, like Cabeza de Vaca, to bless the skins, but left tearfully when the conquistadores plundered the pile in less than fifteen minutes.

Almost as a foreshadowing of the plunder and desecration of the Indian encampment at Blanco Canyon, the Spaniards had experienced a wicked storm that developed out of nowhere a few days before. The storm delivered heavy winds and "hailstones as big as bowls or bigger . . . [falling] as thick as raindrops." Protecting their horses with shields and sea nets, the Spaniards watched in amazement as the hailstorm ripped through tents, dented helmets, wounded horses, and shattered all of the expedition's crockery. It is this last bit of recorded information that fueled archaeological speculation more than 400 years later. Where were the remains of this crockery, definitive markers for the Coronado *entrada* and a second campsite? Perhaps the remains had washed away, or perhaps the mysterious canyon in the midst of Castañeda's Cona is yet to be discovered.

In the 1950s, four hundred years after Coronado's adventure across the plains, and years after Hank Smith departed this earth, a farmer was plowing along the edge of Blanco Canyon a few miles northwest of his pioneer homestead. Visible in the newly turned soil was a metal glove, a gauntlet to be exact. Confirmed as belonging to a Spanish soldier, most probably one from Coronado's 1540 expedition, the metal artifact led to further archaeological discoveries in the canyon, many by Jimmy Owens, amateur historian, rock hound, and archaeologist. His passion for finding artifacts buried in the canyon by using a metal detector led him to find an assortment of copper arrow points, nails, and other relics, the site of which is named in his honor. With a passion rivaling Coronado's, teams led by Wichita State University archaeologist Donald Blakeslee continue to scour the canyons of the Llano in search of buried evidence. Scholars have long known Coronado's route through Mexico, Arizona, New Mexico, Oklahoma, and Kansas, but the trek across the Llano Estacado has been sketchy. In 1995, Blakeslee's discovery of a sixteenth-century horseshoe and copper boltheads led him to conclude that the Owens site in Blanco is the second of two camps Coronado established on the Llano. Blakeslee believes Blanco Canyon is the point where the explorer likely left the bulk of his army to hunt bison while continuing to Kansas with a smaller detachment.

Blakeslee continues his quest for Coronado's trail and the elusive first campsite, theorizing that Coronado entered the Llano Estacado from New Mexico through a gap in the Caprock long known among locals as *el Puerto de los Rivajenos*, or the Door to the High Plains, just inside the Texas line in Deaf Smith County. He believes Coronado returned from South-Central Kansas to Santa Fe, New Mexico, on three early Native American trails referred to as the Fort Dodge–Fort Supply Trail, the Dodge City–Tascosa Trail and the Fort Smith–Santa Fe Trail, all of which were later used by military expeditions, traders, and early settlers.

Blakeslee's proposed route for Coronado is based on the detailed 1790s journal of Frenchman Pedro Vial, who journeyed from Santa Fe to St. Louis, Missouri, taking an alternative route on his return. Blakeslee has plotted Vial's route and, comparing it to the journal entries compiled by Coronado's expedition, believes Coronado followed the same route. The search continues for the elusive first campsite canyon. Kicking in the dirt of Blanco Canyon, unearthing the occasional copper point or arrowhead, Hank Smith may also have pondered those who came to the Llano long before his arrival. Unlike Smith, who prospered here, the nearby Indiana Quakers soon had their fill of the wide-open spaces and opted to join their brothers and sisters in more hospitable climes. Like many towns above the Caprock slowly turning into ghost towns, the Quaker town of Estacado eventually disappeared. Although Paleo-Indian large game hunters such as the Apache and Comanche made vital use of its resources, to Europeans and later Americans the Llano has often been a transitory place, something to cross to get to someplace else.

Those who have most recently called the lands of the Llano their home were all latecomers. The Apache wandered the High Plains a couple hundred years before Columbus arrived in the Caribbean, and well before them, ancient Clovis peoples hunted the area. The Lubbock Lake Landmark northwest of Lubbock, and Blackwater Draw near Portales, New Mexico, show periodic occupation going back ten thousand years. In the Panhandle along the Canadian River, Antelope Creek Phase peoples thrived between AD 1200 and AD 1500 and had ties to Pueblo cultures near the Rio Grande.

The Shoshone peoples who mastered the Llano Estacado came in the early eighteenth century from the Rocky Mountain foothills of Wyoming, moving southward onto the plains to avoid conflict with the powerful Blackfeet. The Comanche discovered the horse and it transformed them. Ranging from the Arkansas River headwaters south across the Llano Estacado into Mexico for almost two hundred years, the Comanche ruled the High Plains. As historians have pointed out, the Comanche created a vast empire based on reciprocal trade agreements, military alliances, and their possession and mastery of the horse. Their reign ended scarcely more than a century ago.

At their peak, the Comanche numbered forty thousand, and their horse populations exceeded one hundred thousand, making them pivotal middlemen in an expanding network of trade and dominance on the Southern Plains. Following the 1846 Mexican-American War, increasing pressures descended on the Comanche from various sources—from the Texas Rangers and encroaching Texas settlement into Comanchería, from the United States military, and from immigrants carrying cholera and smallpox epidemics to the West. Unprecedented drought and overgrazing by Comanche horse herds deprived bison of traditional forested river valleys in the winter. Neighboring Indian nations took advantage of the Comanche's weakened state, overhunting the shaggy creatures. New policies governing the conduct and trade of New Mexican Comancheros combined with hunger and internal dissent to unravel the Comanche Nation long before the concerted effort of the U.S. military to subdue them.

Despite the Comanche's cultural renaissance and adaptation to these pressures in the 1860s, the United States military silenced the restructured tribe during the Red River campaigns of 1874 and 1875. Finally subdued by a hard-core professional soldier from New York named Ranald Slidell Mackenzie, the Comanche bands one by one surrendered their nomadic existence in return for forced government dependency and reservation life in southwestern Oklahoma. The Comanche presence lingers still in the canyons and draws that carve their way through the Llano and across the flatlands above. Salt Creek, Adobe Walls, Tahoka Lake, Tule, Blanco, and Palo Duro Canyons conjure images of a people desperate to retain their land and way of life. Less than a decade after eliminating Comanche and Kiowa resistance on the High Plains, Mackenzie went crazy. Suffering from "paralysis of the insane," in December of 1883, he was escorted to New York City and placed in Bloomingdale Asylum.

For thousands of years before Mackenzie and the subsequent arrival of Anglo settlers in the 1880s, the wide-open spaces of the Llano Estacado served as a prime grazing land for millions of bison, providing a way of life for a succession of Indians, Spanish, and Mexican buffalo hunters. These *ciboleros*, who made their way east from Taos and the Mora Valley in New Mexico, charted the place names of the Llano and nearby breaks off the Caprock: Mescalero, Tule, Blanco, Las Lenguas, Casas Amarillas, Aguas Corriente, Brazos, Cita, Frio, Tierra Blanca, Palo Duro, Muchaque. And they traded with the Comanche everything from Taos Lightning, or *aguardiente*, to horses and human captives in places like Cañon del Rescate, today's Ransom Canyon just east of present-day Lubbock; at Coyote Lake, one of the largest natural salt lakes on the High Plains, ten miles southwest of Muleshoe; at Silver Lake, or Laguna Plata, located in the northwest corner of Hockley County where an historic spring provided waters for Casas Amarillas, or Yellow House Draw. Northeast of Silver Lake and due north of Yellow and Illusion Lakes in the Yellow House drainage, present-day Bull Lake was also a popular rendezvous site for Comanchero and Comanche traders. Historically a deep lake relative to most surface waters in West Texas, Bull Lake now resembles a near-waterless salt flat. A hundred miles north, along the eastern Llano escarpment where Cottonwood and Los Lingos Creeks come together near Quitaque, lies Valles de las Lagrimas, or the Valley of Tears. It was a popular rendezvous site for the exchange of captives well into the nineteenth century. In the early twenty-first century, a remnant of the great southern bison herd lives nearby at Caprock Canyons State Park.

One hundred thirty years earlier, the huge mesa yielded up tons of buffalo hides to clothe easterners and Europeans in fashionable robes. Phillip Sheridan, the great Yankee Civil War general and practitioner of total war, dramatically quashed a bill before the Texas Legislature in 1876 that would have saved the quickly vanishing southern bison herd from extinction. Sheridan advocated the extermination of the Indians' storehouse as a means of advancing white civilization. Although provisions of the Medicine Lodge Treaty of 1867 held the Army responsible for protecting the hunting grounds of the Comanche and other tribes south of the Arkansas River, the military simply looked the other way as hundreds of white buffalo hunters invaded the territory in the 1870s. Furthermore, the military actively supported the destruction of the buffalo by providing protection and ammunition to sharpshooters who sometimes killed a hundred or more animals in a single day.

The near extinction of *Bison Americus* opened the Llano Estacado and its flanks to thousands of cattle and far-flung ranches, often controlled by European investors. Stephen Long's government-sponsored 1823 trek across the plains of eastern Colorado during an exceptional drought led the explorer to label the region the Great American Desert. More observant opportunists like Charles Goodnight and Oliver Loving began trailing cattle to New Mexico and Colorado by skirting the vast Comanchería, including the Llano Estacado, in the 1860s. Following Loving's death, the establishment of a ranch in Colorado, and the removal of the Comanche, Goodnight in 1885 established the JA Ranch in the watered Palo Duro country of the Texas Panhandle. Named for John Adair,

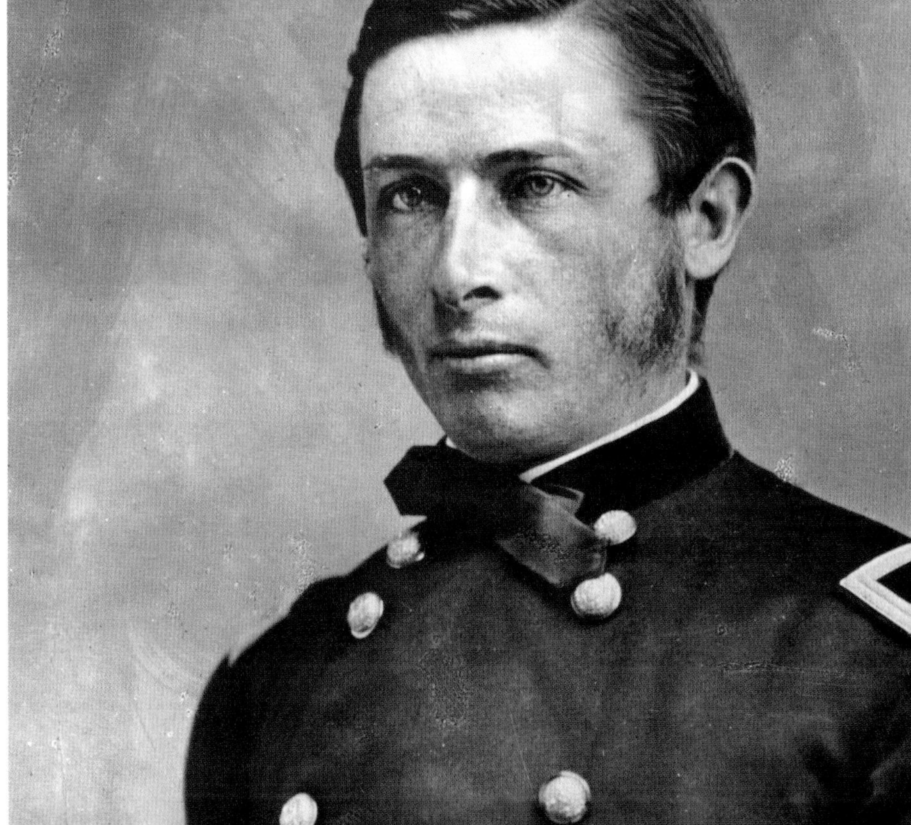

Ranald Slidell Mackenzie.

In September 1874, Mackenzie, under command of Lt. Gen. Philip H. Sheridan, destroyed five Indian villages in Palo Duro Canyon as part of the Red River Campaign. These losses, along with Mackenzie's destruction of the Indians' horses, eliminated resistance on the Llano Estacado. Mackenzie later served with distinction in various Indian campaigns across the American West. By the end of 1883, Mackenzie was suffering from "paralysis of the insane," and was placed in New York City's Bloomingdale Asylum. Southwest Collection, Texas Tech University, SWCPC 418-246, National Archives, 111-B-2735.

Goodnight's newfound Scottish business partner and provider of capital, the ranch eventually encompassed 1,385,000 acres of land in Randall, Armstrong, Donley, Briscoe, and Swisher Counties.

The long-held perception of the High Plains as the Great American Desert was changing rapidly by the 1880s as foreign investors flocked to opportunities available on the Llano's huge island of grass. The storied Espuela (Spur), Matador, and JA ranches encompassed huge portions of unsettled land. But the largest, the XIT, dwarfed all others, covering three million acres and extending 220 miles north to south along the eastern New Mexico border. In exchange for this vast rangeland of virgin grass, Chicago and London investors ponied up cash for the construction of the Texas State Capitol building in Austin to replace the one that burned in 1881. Completed in 1888, the massive building cost the Chicago investment syndicate $3.75 million. Investors paid slightly more than one dollar per acre for the largest ranch in the world.

The next latecomers to the High Plains, those who followed the military, Quakers, and mega-ranchers, brought with them a strong will to survive in what seemed a harsh and unforgiving environment. Proud, stubborn dirt farmers also brought along a religious conviction that they were destined to succeed on the Llano where they might have failed in the past. A land-grant law in 1876, and Texas's unabashed courting of railroads, opened up the vast lands of the Llano Estacado to these lean, hard "nesters," as cowpunchers and cattlemen derisively called them.

The large investment ranching syndicates headquartered in Illinois, England, and Scotland, successful enterprises in the 1870s and early '80s, had lost their places to the nesters by the end of the nineteenth century. Barbed wire, overgrazing, a glut in the cattle market, range wars, an unprecedented drought, winter storms, political pressure, and the coming of railroads—all combined to reduce the size of High Plains ranches like the XIT, Matador, Slaughter, and Spur controlled by "foreign" investors from Chicago, London, and Edinburgh.

Instead of making money from meat on the hoof, the ranches sold huge chunks of territory to a generation of rancher-cum-land developers who organized companies specifically to sell land to farmers. Fencing off some of the best pastures for cattle, second-generation ranchers like George Littlefield resigned themselves to putting up with the nesters and small-time ranchers in their midst.

After some lean years as a storekeeper and farmer near Gonzales, Texas, the former Confederate Major's fortunes changed when he got into the cattle-trailing business in 1871. In 1877, Littlefield established the LIT Ranch, purchasing water rights along the Canadian River near the rambunctious town of Tascosa, and four years later sold the property for $248,000. After securing water rights in New Mexico east of the Pecos River between Ft. Sumner and Roswell, Littlefield controlled four million acres of land. He later developed ranch and farming interests in the Texas Hill Country counties of Mason, Kimble, and Menard. When XIT Ranch officials began withdrawing from the cattle business in 1901, Littlefield emerged as a major force in events unfolding on the Llano when he purchased the 312,000-acre Yellow House (southern) Division of the XIT in Lamb and Hockley counties. Erecting the world's tallest windmill 130 feet above the escarpment of his Yellow House Draw headquarters, Littlefield established the Littlefield Lands Company to sell more than 60,000 acres to farmers a decade later. The newcomers brought families, and the trappings of civilization soon followed. The W. P. Soash Land Company enticed Midwesterners with tales of Eden in a country which blooms with bright promise during wet years, but more closely reflects western deserts during dry ones. The key issue then, as it is today, was water.

Water, like religion and the wind, has always been an issue on the High Plains. In West Texas and elsewhere, controlling the land meant controlling the scant available surface water. It was not by accident, then, that the Comanche, and the Spanish and Mexican traders who all followed the draws, canyons, and playa lakes that ensured water, and provided access to the

Bailey County, Texas, circa 1913.

In 1902, E. K. Warren of Michigan purchased 85,000 acres from the XIT Ranch and established the Y. L. Ranch near the present-day town of Muleshoe. Warren, a successful manufacturer of corset stays and buggy whips, also owned ranches in New Mexico, Colorado, and Chihuahua, Mexico. This image shows the transition from cattle country to farming as farmers began to plow under the cattle trails of previous days. Southwest Collection, Texas Tech University, SWCPC 57(Z)-E27.1

According to historian Walter Prescott Webb, barbed wire, windmills and the six-shooter were largely responsible for settling the West. By the end of the nineteenth century, the open range of the cattle-drive era had come to an end. Southwest Collection, Texas Tech University, SWCPC 410-D-E1

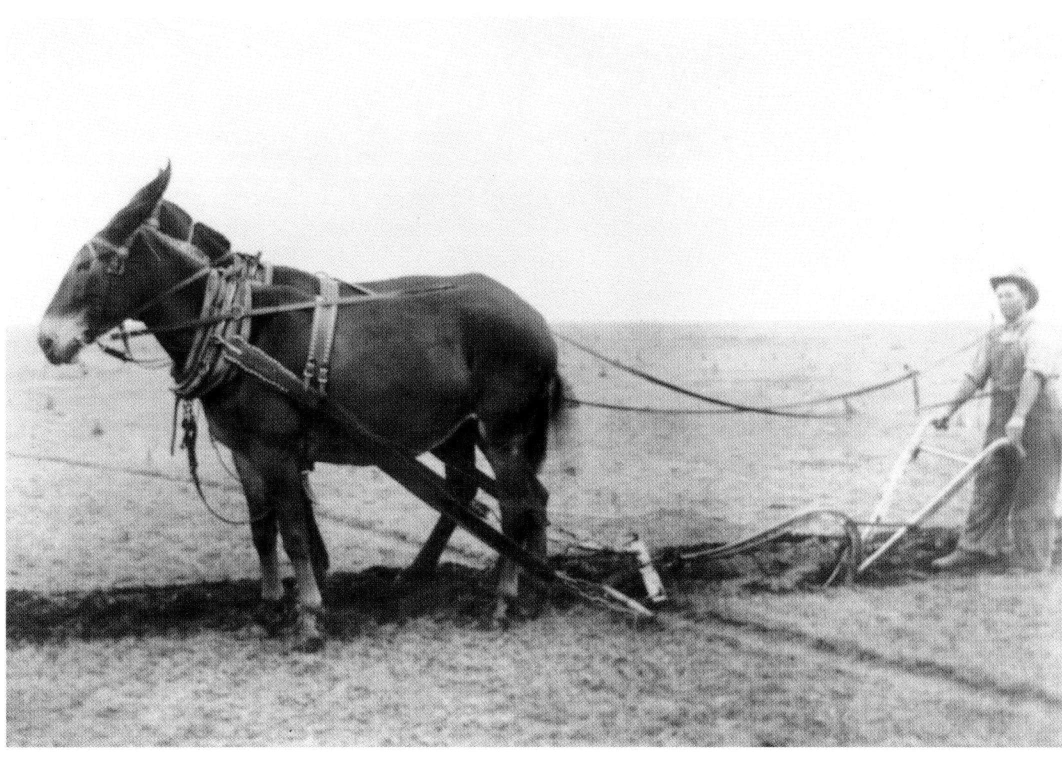

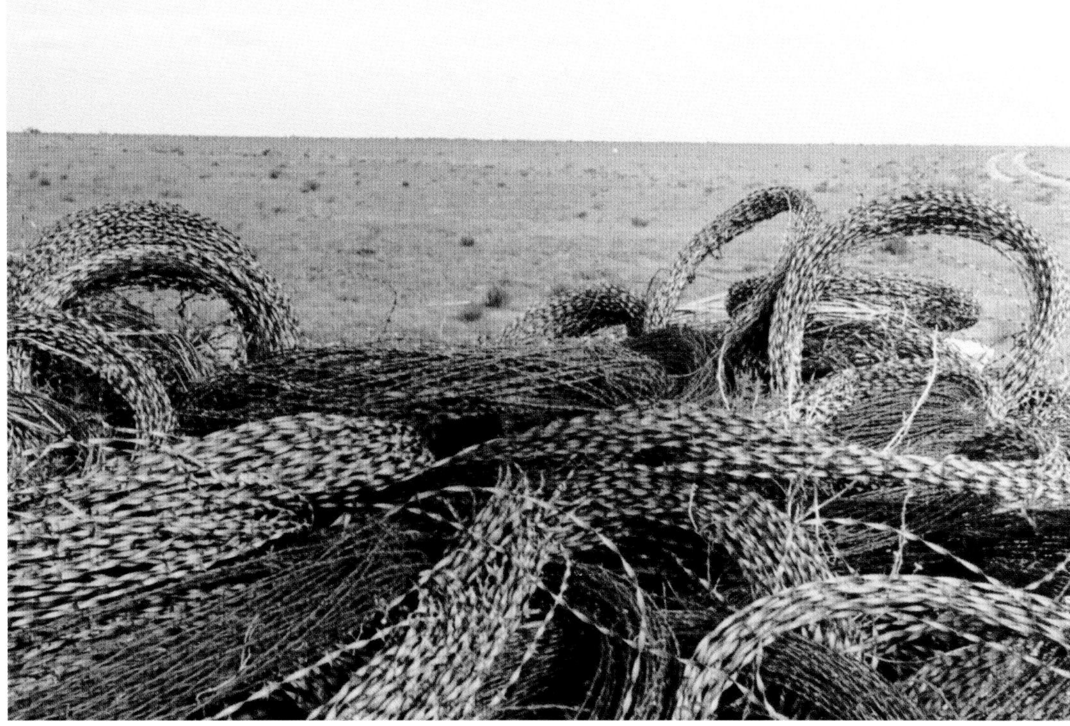

Llano's great store of bison and Comanche trade goods. To get caught up the Caprock without water meant trouble. In July 1877, twenty buffalo soldiers along with twenty-two buffalo hunters gave chase across the Llano after a band of Comanche who left the reservation in Oklahoma and killed buffalo hunter John Sharp near Double Mountain, southwest of present day Aspermont. The next morning the Indians raided Rath City, a buffalo hunter's camp in present-day Stonewall County, and stole almost all of the horses there. Failing to fill their canteens with water, the party soon found itself in dire straits. The hunters went northwest and found water at the Casas Amarillas, but the soldiers were without the precious liquid for eighty-six hours, and resorted to drinking horse's blood and urine to survive. Some of them did not.

Ironically, the black buffalo soldiers, who were themselves members of a people long subjugated by the bonds of slavery, were pursuing another group of Americans who had temporarily interrupted white dreams of manifest destiny. Known through the prism of racism as the "Lost Nigger Expedition," these mounted black cavalry soldiers under command of Captain Nicholas Nolan, a white man, pursued the last Comanche raiders in Texas.

Anglos who started trekking up the Caprock in the late nineteenth century chose watered canyons in which to live, but those who came later had no choice but to brave the elements out on the open plain above. Windmills helped. The advent of windmills allowed ranchers to fence their lands and water their cattle from earthen, wooden, and later, steel tanks. Small towns like Lubbock and Amarillo sprang up in the middle of cow pastures, and preachers baptized the faithful in these stock tanks or playa lakes, if they held enough water. But farmers needed more, especially on the southern portion of the plains where cotton became the main crop by the 1920s. As springs were tapped out, farmers discovered what one writer has called "the land of underground rain," an aquifer stretching from the High Plains of Texas north to the Dakotas. The Ogallala Aquifer was a godsend to former dryland

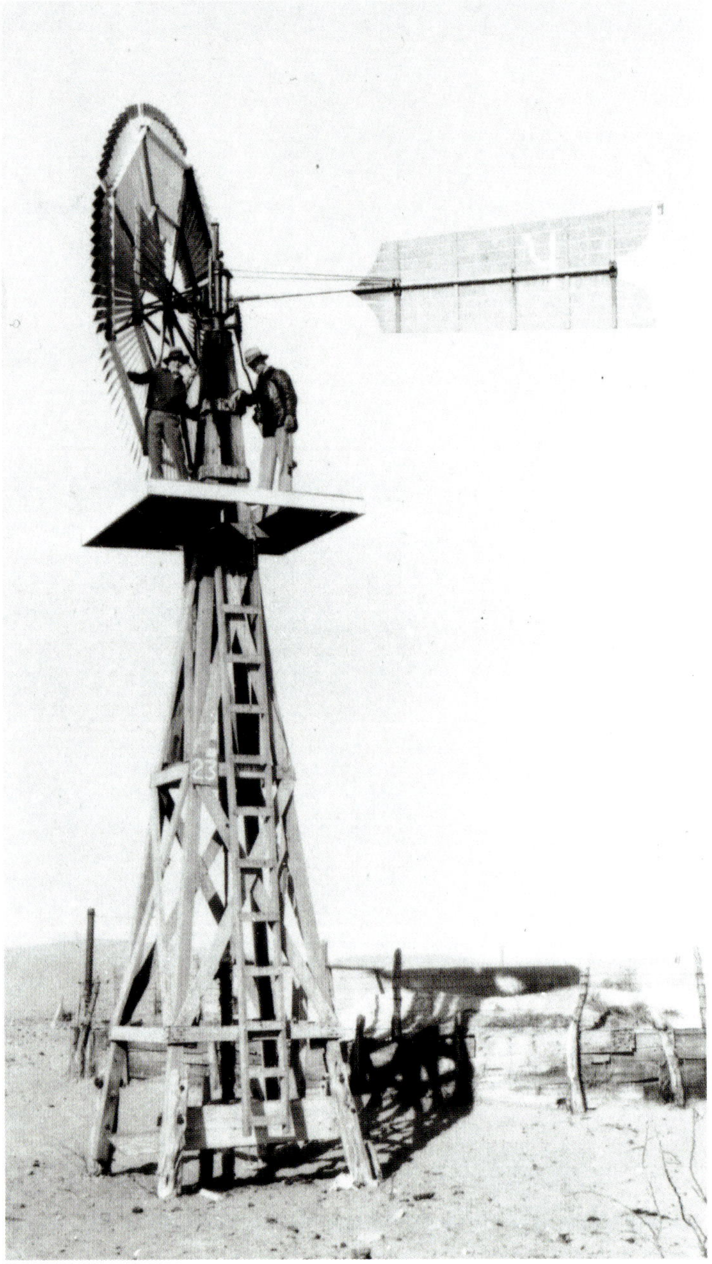

Windmills provided water in a dry land and became vital once the watering holes of the open range had been fenced in. The earliest windmills were made of wood and provided a bird's-eye view across the Llano for miles in any direction. Southwest Collection, Texas Tech University, SWCPC 665-E2-283

farmers, especially since state law allowed them to pump as much water as they wanted from beneath their land.

Although innovative pioneers like B. O. McWhorter, who came to Lubbock in 1887, tapped wells bearing appreciable streams of gushing water in the early 1900s, the artesian nature of the early wells soon diminished. During the "dirty thirties," when they could have used it most, farmers had to wait for a time when reliable pump technology and financing were both at hand. Beginning in the 1940s with reliable technology, farmers flooded their fields with the ancient elixir. By the 1950s, when much of Texas was again afflicted by cyclical drought, and again in the 1970s, the proliferation of deep underground drilling led to bumper crops, the rising affluence of farmers, and an appreciable lowering of the Ogallala's water table.

Unlike early assessments of the Ogallala as a deep inexhaustible "underground lake, " it is more accurately described as a huge underground sponge with varying degrees of saturation. Stretching from the Llano Estacado at its southern edge into the Dakotas, the Ogallala is the largest repository of fossil waters in the United States. Along this southern edge of the sponge in Texas, saturation is diminishing rapidly. Today, as the aquifer is becoming depleted, farmers, who consume some 95 percent of the water used on the Llano, continue to suck ancient rainwater deposited long ago, using electricity instead of wind or gasoline to pull it to the surface.

Anticipating the future growth of major Texas metropolitan areas, enterprising entrepreneurs like T. Boone Pickens have more in mind than just watering cotton. Former oil tycoon Pickens is chairman and chief operating officer of Mesa Water Inc. With Texas regularly suffering drought, the demand for water is urgent. Pickens' acquisition of the water rights to tens of thousands of acres in the Panhandle's Gray and Roberts Counties, including his own 24,000 acre ranch, was part and parcel of a plan (now abandoned) to pipe groundwater more than six hundred miles from the

Panhandle to thirsty cities like Dallas and San Antonio. El Paso, Phoenix, and Lubbock, anticipating their own needs, have secured water rights in the area.

Portraying himself as a friend of the environment, Pickens also put into motion a plan for harvesting the ever-present winds above those same West Texas counties that sold him their water rights. The plan would create North America's largest wind energy farm. Pickens is not alone in his commitment to harvesting energy from the wind. Across the Llano Estacado and into far west Texas, energy companies have seized upon these winds of change, investing in miles of electric transmission lines and erecting hundreds of ivory turbines that scratch the sky. Wind and solar power offer viable sources of energy and economic development for West Texas, but water is still the key to living here.

To be sure, cotton backed with water from inside the earth, government subsidies, crop insurance, and layers of chemical fertilizers, pesticides, and herbicides generates $10 billion each year for the South Plains around Lubbock, but at a cost to the environment and to taxpayers. Farmers in the region have also jumped at the chance to cash in on government supports and the latest market for biofuels. With plants built for converting vegetable matter into ethanol before the economic bust of 2009, farmers signed lucrative contracts, committing themselves to producing tall stands of corn watered by efficient center-pivot irrigation systems. Except for the circular shape of the stands, cornfields near Nazareth, Olton, and Lazbuddie make the area look more like Iowa than the semi-arid grasslands of the Llano Estacado.

In the Panhandle, the proliferation of cattle feedlots has generated additional billions of dollars and employment for the region. To many folks who need jobs, the stench of thousands of cattle milling about in close quarters is not so much a nuisance as the smell of money. Many of these cattle-feeding factories are located directly in the middle of draws and creeks like Tierra Blanca, whose waters once fed the wildlife oasis of Buffalo Lake, eight miles east of present-day Canyon. While the site once attracted locals who enjoyed water skiing, swimming, fishing, and sailing, the lake is no longer safe for human activities.

The scant rainfall that falls on the Llano slowly percolates through the recharge of as many as twenty thousand playa lakes dotting the landscape like so many craters on the moon. Some day, because of cost, scarcity, or the absence of government support, the underground rain will stop coming to the surface of the Llano Estacado. Feedlots may disappear. Irrigated cotton and corn will vanish along with the remnants of towns already in decline due to consolidation of family farms into "agribusiness," and opportunities in bigger towns like Amarillo and Lubbock.

But for now, Amarillo, at the northern end of the Llano, is the center of the largest cattle-feeding region of the country. Oprah Winfrey's pleas notwithstanding, beef production and its attendant use of growth hormones and feedlot "finishing" reign supreme in the Texas Panhandle. Lubbock, long called the "Hub of the Plains" by the local Chamber of Commerce, sits in the middle of the largest cotton patch in the United States and represents 25 percent of the nation's production. More than half of the cotton produced in Texas comes from a twenty-five county area surrounding Lubbock. In 1928, the region planted 1,666,500 acres of cotton; at its peak in 1981, farmers devoted more than 4.5 million acres to the white fiber. In the first decade of the twenty-first century, farmers planted between 3.52 and 3.89 million acres. Chances are good that the cotton used to make your favorite pair of blue jeans originated here.

In the spring now, air-conditioned, digital stereo- and GPS-equipped John Deere tractors roam across dormant cotton fields like so many green giants carving up the soil. Standing on the edge of such a field, it is hard to fathom that it was scarcely more than one hundred years ago that farmers ripped open the virgin soil that overlay the Caprock for the first time.

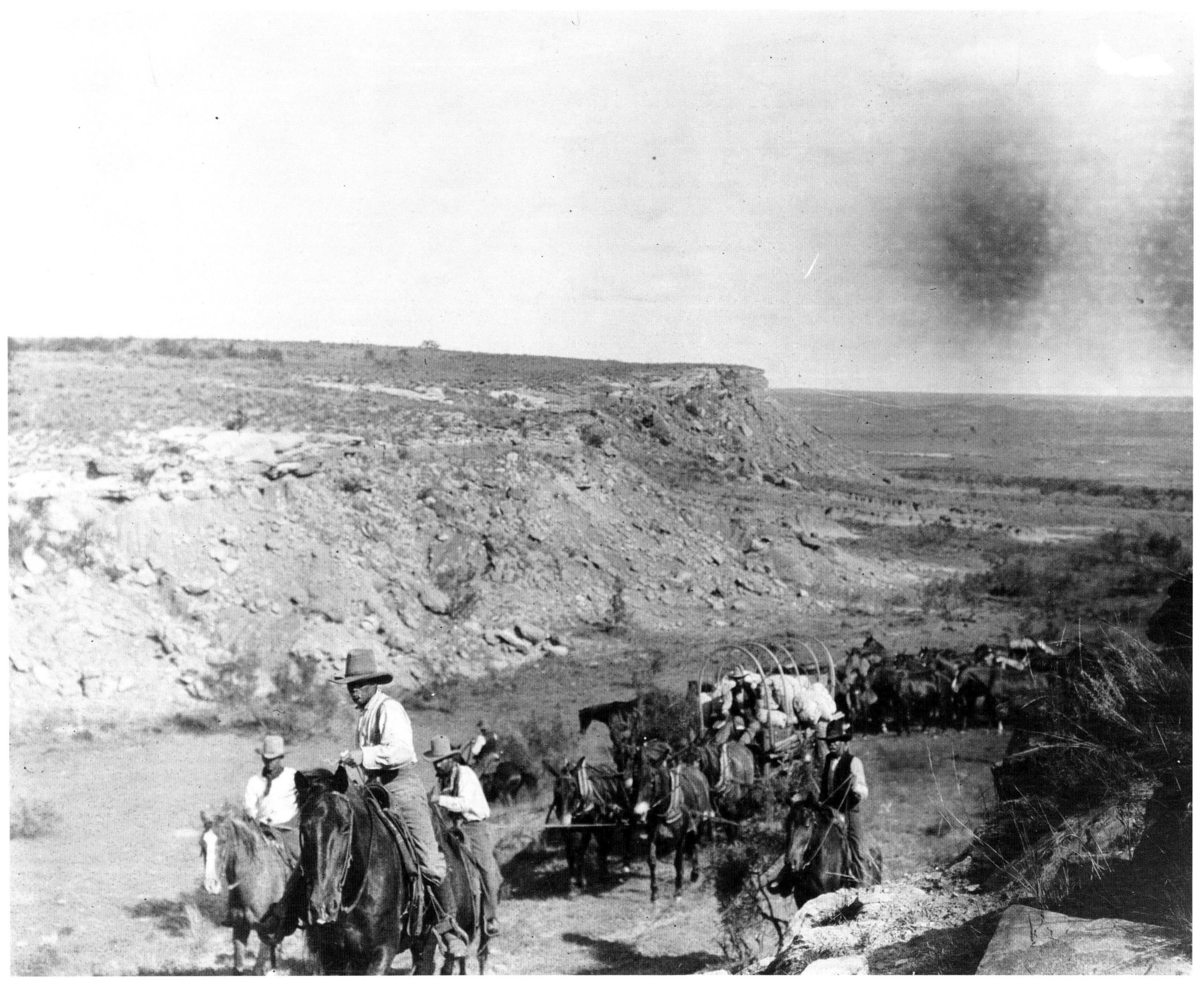

Spur Ranch horsemen ascending the Caprock, circa 1900.

Southwest Collection, Texas Tech University, SWCPC 418-245

The Llano Estacado: An Island in the Sky

STEPHEN BOGENER

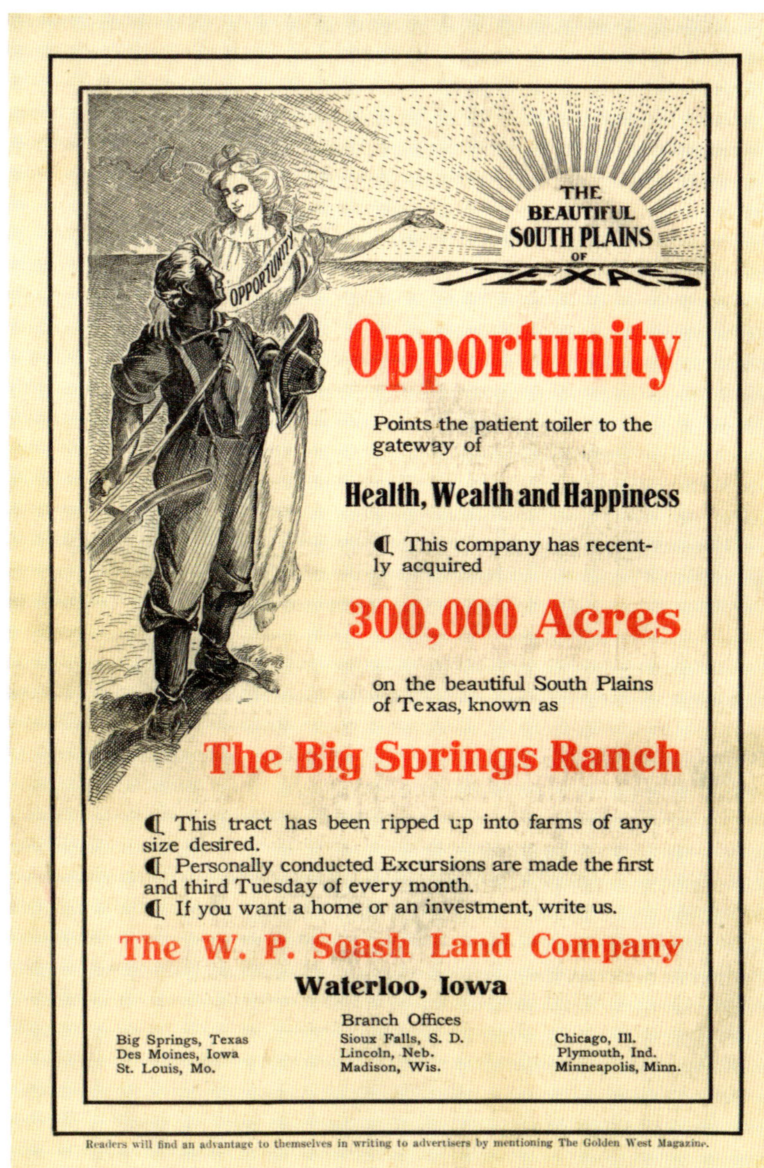

In 1905, Iowan William Pulver Soash founded the W. P. Soash Land Company, acquiring a 30,000-acre tract in the Texas Panhandle from the Capitol Freehold Land and Investment Company and Christopher Columbus Slaughter's 100,000-acre Running Water Ranch on the South Plains. Soash utilized new advertising techniques, including The Golden West company magazine and excursion trains, to deliver prospective parties across the High Plains to see the lands onsite. Southwest Collection, Texas Tech University, William Pulver Soash Manuscript Collection

Second-wave settlers came to the Llano in the 1920s and early '30s from the worn-out cotton fields of places like Erath and Wise counties, part of the Rolling Plains and Cross Timbers regions of Texas, a few generations removed from roots in the Deep South of the Carolinas or Tennessee. They struggled up the Caprock in wagons piled with earthly possessions. The outcropping of rock that defines the outline of the Llano Estacado marked a cultural as well as a geographical frontier for those who finally reached the top and set about breaking the soil.

As historical geographer Terry Jordan discovered, the folks who settled the Llano came, by and large, from portions of Texas whose residents could trace their lineage directly to the Confederacy. Early Lubbock included several defenders of the Southern Cause, with roots deep in Arkansas, Alabama, and Tennessee. This southern cultural hegemony was tempered increasingly in the early twentieth century by land and railroad promoters plying their trade as far away as Iowa and Illinois. Until the propaganda of promoters like Soash and Littlefield, when choice lands with more rainfall had already been settled, the Southern High Plains had remained, except for a few ranchers, largely *tierra despoplado*.

The arrival of farm families was gradual. From worn-out farmlands further east and north came those looking for cheap land, people wanting to believe the exaggerated claims of corn and other crops growing above a man's head in a dry land receiving less than twenty inches of rain in a year. It was an ongoing journey of tired souls and tired bodies heading for the promised land. There were many who got here late, the same kind of folk depicted in the imagery of Dorothea Lange, Russell Lee, Arthur Rothstein, and John Steinbeck from the 1930s. Some came later still. Part of the acreage now contributing to the white monoculture of farmland surrounding Lubbock was not broken out until the 1940s.

Second- and third-generation High Plains farmers—those who descended from the tough, wind-bitten pioneers—were

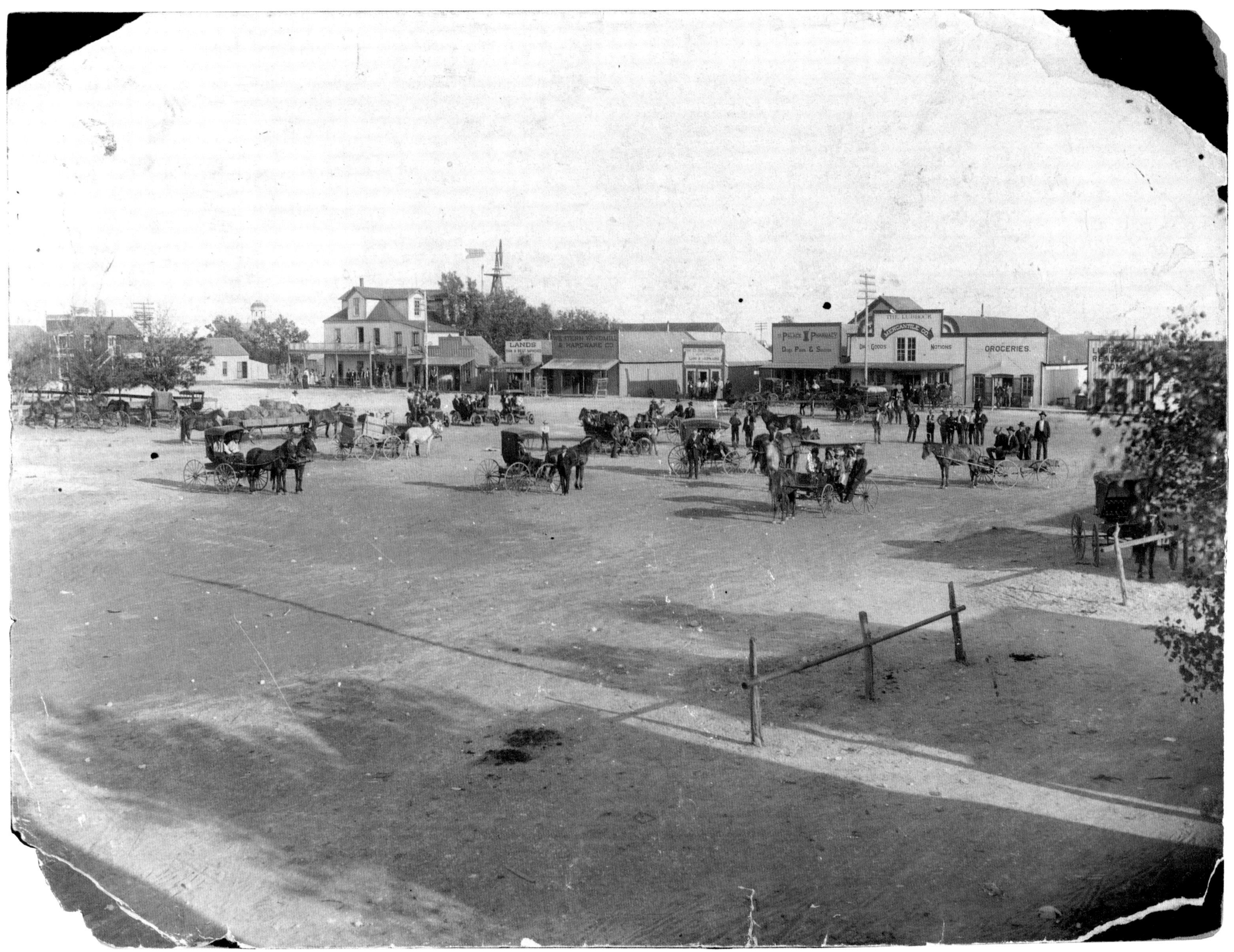

Lubbock, Texas, first decade of the twentieth century.

From a postcard, "A street in Lubbock, Tex., where everybody [has it] easy, has a good time, and makes a lot of money. Come to Lubbock, the lately developed summer health resort." Lubbock and other areas of the West were seen as havens for those suffering from tuberculosis or other ailments. Southwest Collection, Texas Tech University, MPC 42-4-12C

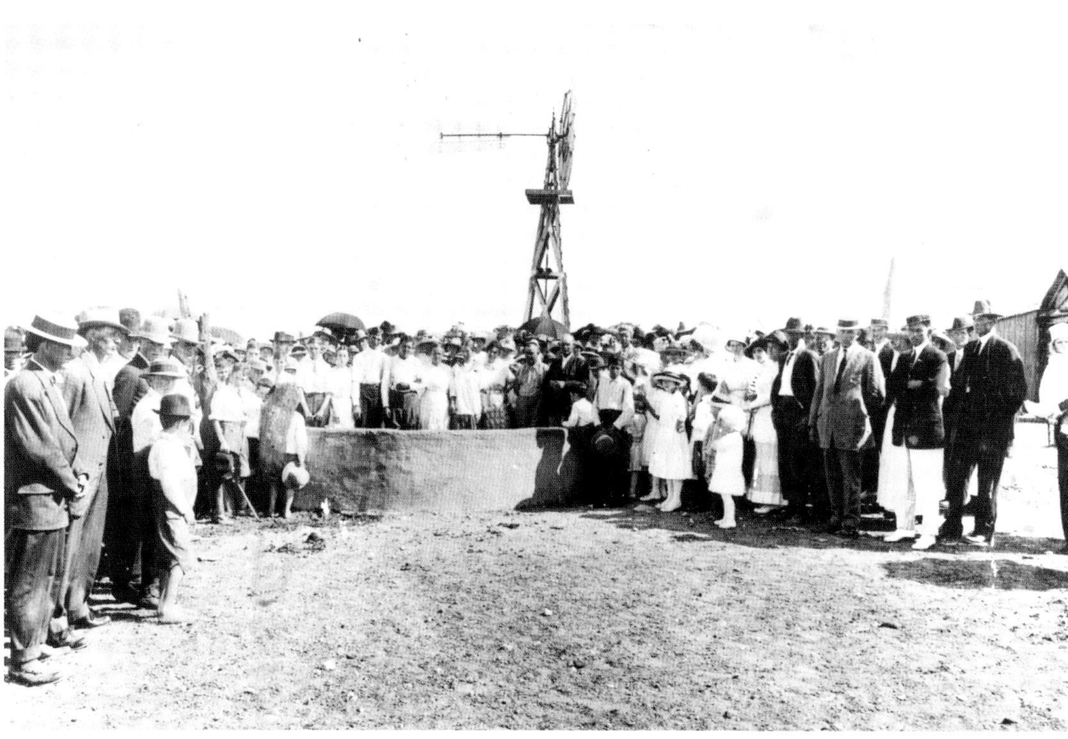

Baptism at first windmill west of Lubbock, 1920s.

Southwest Collection, Texas Tech University, SWCPC (57)T-E6.1.

moving towards a progressively easier lifestyle with the widespread use of gasoline tractors in the 1920s. These new metal machines, along with abundant rainfall and high commodity prices on the tail-end of World War I, created the illusion that the High Plains were one big productive sandbox to dig up and plant.

In the Panhandle, farmers gassed up their tractors, hooked up their plows, and plowed under just about every square inch of native bluestem and grama grass, replacing it with wheat called Turkey Red from the steppes of Russia. Day and night they churned up topsoil that had taken natural forces thousands of years to create. The earliest settlers walked behind draft animals and a breaking plow that tortured limbs and back, plowing only three acres a day. The new machine-driven contraptions could eat through one hundred acres, or— more if they ran twenty-four hours a day.

In 1931, the High Plains began to experience one of the cyclical droughts that had afflicted the region for millennia. Over the ensuing decade, farmers hoping to reap the benefits of a wheat bonanza reaped only dust. Marginal lands in parts of five states—Kansas, Colorado, Oklahoma, New Mexico, and Texas—started to blow away. A journalist traveling the region in the thirties christened the region the Dust Bowl. Recent evidence suggests that factors influencing the drought in the Dust Bowl states were compounded by unique weather patterns in the 1930s. But more importantly, the topsoil held intact for eons by a blanket of grasses now turned into huge clouds of dirt that stretched for miles across the sky blocking out the sun. And still some farmers, confident that the rains would soon return, continued to plow up what remained of the southern plains. As dust storms continued, many residents thought the end of the world was at hand, and prepared to die. Others succumbed to dust pneumonia. At one point in the middle of the decade, the wind and dust howled for twenty-seven days and nights without stopping, the color of the clouds indicating whether the dust came from Kansas, Oklahoma, or from some place more sinister. Some, convinced that the Apocalypse was at hand, seriously considered infanticide to spare their children the cataclysm to come.

Areas considered at-best marginal for planting lost all their topsoil. Fence rows disappeared under a torrent of dust that clung to anything in its path. What plants the dust did not destroy, static electricity carried by billions of dust particles did, turning living green plants to brown and black. Jackrabbits, scrounging for food, came out of the low hills and appeared from a distance like a vast army of ants moving across the barren earth. Hungry settlers joined together and drove the long-eared creatures into makeshift corrals where they clubbed them to death and divvied up the spoils. Many likened the plaintive cries of the rabbits to the cries of infants. Today, you can still find jackrabbits darting across the sand dunes deposited by dustbowl winds more than half a century ago. In the 1950s, after the collective memory of West Texas farmers had been bathed in the relative prosperity and rainfall of the postwar 1940s, they did it all again.

Lured by an abundance of available creature comforts such as new tractors, automobiles, and modern housing, many farmers chased high prices for cotton by significantly increasing the acreage devoted to the plant. When another "drouth" hit in the 1950s, farmers who could afford it sank more holes into the Ogallala and pulled the water to the surface. Dryland farmers relied on more dubious methods.

Julie Boatright, rummaging through West Texas junk emporiums and talking to "old timers" in the 1990s, uncovered the story of the "rainmaker rocket," a throwback to the Great Depression and the pseudoscience of human "rainmaker" Tex Thornton, an itinerant explosives expert. Thornton, like cereal king C. W. Post before him, used dynamite to disturb the clouds above the Texas Plains. Boatright discovered the story of the Rainmaker Rocket while talking to locals at what passes today for the local diner—the Lamesa Dairy Queen. The rocket, which now proudly rests on a Big Springs lawn, in the 1950s was mounted to the ground and plugged into an

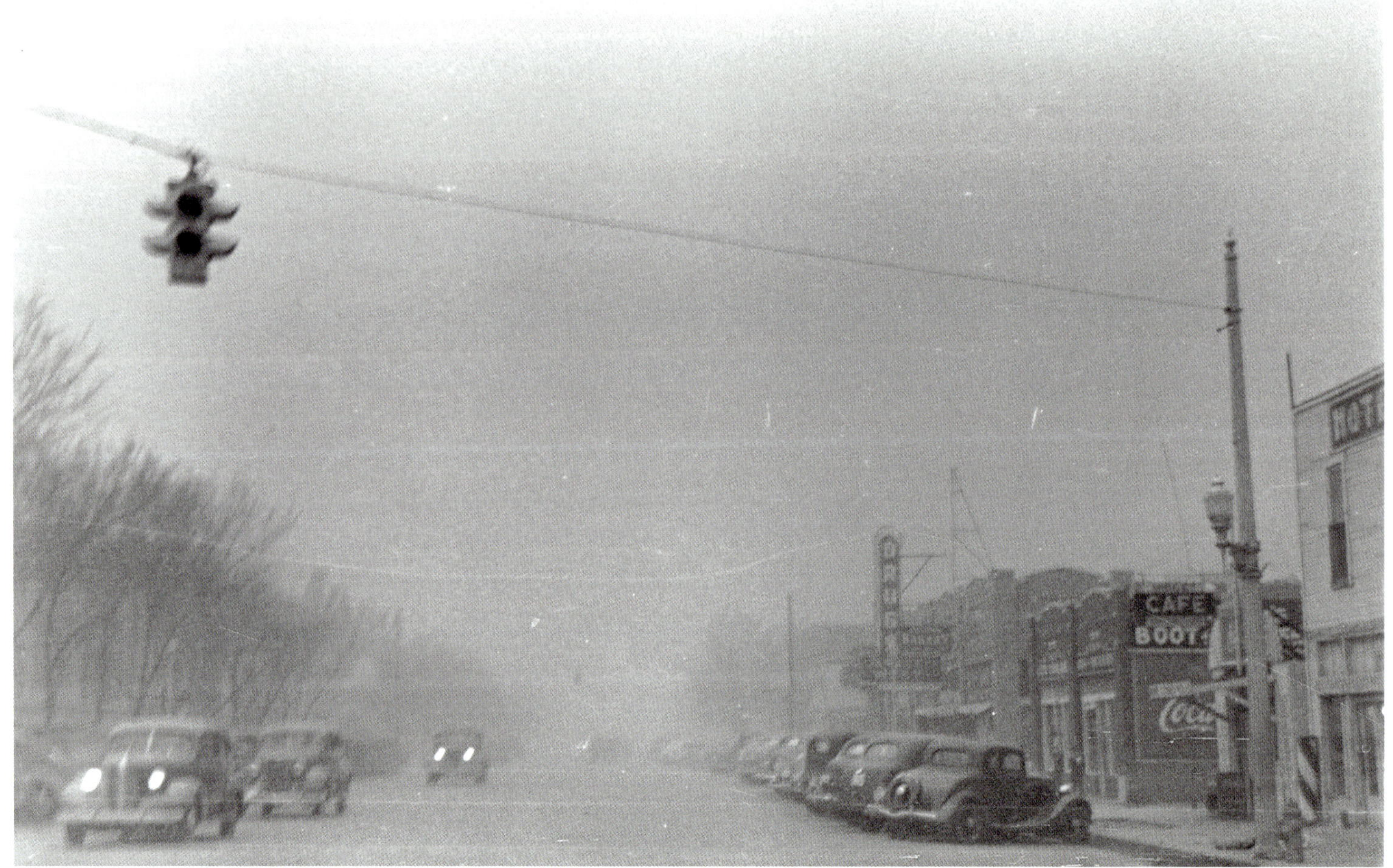

Lubbock during the Dirty Thirties of the Great Depression.

Southwest Collection, Texas Tech University, SWCPC 57(X)-E4-27

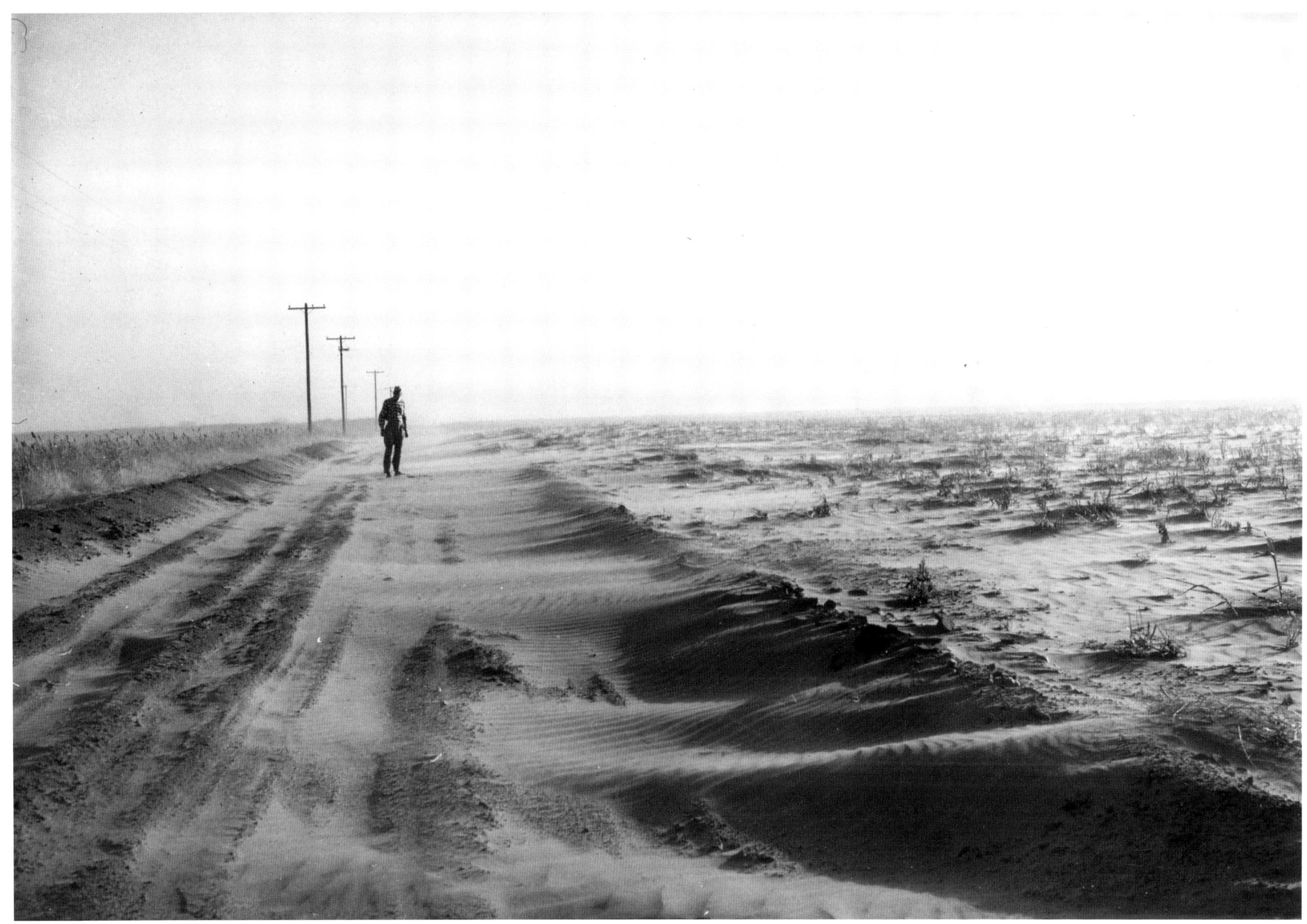

Wind-blown soil accumulates along county road near Lamesa, Texas, December 4, 1950.

Southwest Collection, Texas Tech University, SWCPC 413-D-E1

electrical source at a Lamesa cotton gin. When operating, the machine emitted puffs of mist from its top. Folks were generally evenly split over the more or less spectacular effectiveness of the contraption. While many were embarrassed by the story forty years after it took place, it nonetheless paints a picture of desperation, hope, and a willingness to try anything to make it rain. Not so quick to judge it a failure, supporters point to the equivalent of the rocket, the practice of seeding storm clouds with silver iodide crystals by air. In Lubbock, church and civic leaders regularly meet and pray for rain.

A few years ago, Darryl Birkenfeld, at the time a priest in the Texas Panhandle, started the Promised Land Network, which advocates sustainable agriculture and land-use ethics. Birkenfeld believes the basis of prosperity is the land; that how people treat the land and how they live on it have a strong correlation with spirituality and justice. Many farmers on the Llano fail to see the merit in such thinking. When confronted by the notion of returning a portion of the High Plains to a buffalo commons as suggested in 1987 by Frank and Deborah Popper, farmers and those who grew up as "hands" working the cotton patch are universally astounded at the notion of returning vast portions of the Llano to grass, although this has already occurred on large sections of the northern Llano. With stone-sober faces, many reply that Texas is a property rights state where a farmer "can use or abuse the land any way he sees fit." And so it goes.

For the settlers who started trickling into the territory in the last decades of the nineteenth century, the vast wilderness of grass on the Llano Estacado represented a last chance to obtain cheap land and make it produce. From Amarillo southwest to Portales, New Mexico, to Lubbock, perched along Yellowhouse and Blackwater Draws, and south towards Mustang Draw and Midland-Odessa, buildings tell the story of a newly settled land. In the early days of the twentieth century, settlers found themselves eking out a meager existence fighting wind, drought, and tough sod, living in dugouts, the sod equivalent of caves carved into a hill. Soon after the beginning of the twentieth century, rail lines provided lumber and tools for construction of wood frame houses. When the post World War I agricultural downturn slid into the general economic malaise of the 1930s, few farmers on the South Plains could afford both the cost of land and housing. Land promoters like the Littlefield Land Company offered 177 acres or more of prime pasture ready for the plow. To attain a home as well as land, building crews readily offered 800-square-foot frame houses sheathed in the popular stucco facade popular at the time. Builders erected houses across the Llano with a mechanic's lien for all building materials attached to the property until the purchaser secured a loan to pay for the structure. Structures raised in the 1920s and early '30s before arrival of the dust and Depression stand in stark contrast to the ranch-style homes favored in the 1950s and '60s. White farmers, anxious to show their prosperity, abandoned the earlier yellow-cream stucco of harder times. Earlier decades represent a time when the practicality of using Spanish and Mexican architectural styles outweighed the later (perceived) need for the ostentation of brick and mortar.

Anyone traveling the region's blue highways today can readily see the remnants of that early settlement period through the planted windbreaks and little yellow stucco dwellings slowly sinking into the earth amidst wind, sun, and desolation. Though most are abandoned and falling into the earth, those left standing have frequently served as dwellings for farm hands, often Mexican nationals who were counted upon to do much of the manual labor on lands owned by the "farmer," a corporate enterprise, or someone who inherited sizeable acreage and lived in the brick house down the road from the stucco house where his grandparents used to live.

The Spanish, Mexican, and Mexican-American presence on the Llano is a long one, owing to the ties between the *ciboleros*, Comancheros, and *pastores* who came here seasonally from their homeland in northern New Mexico. Much later,

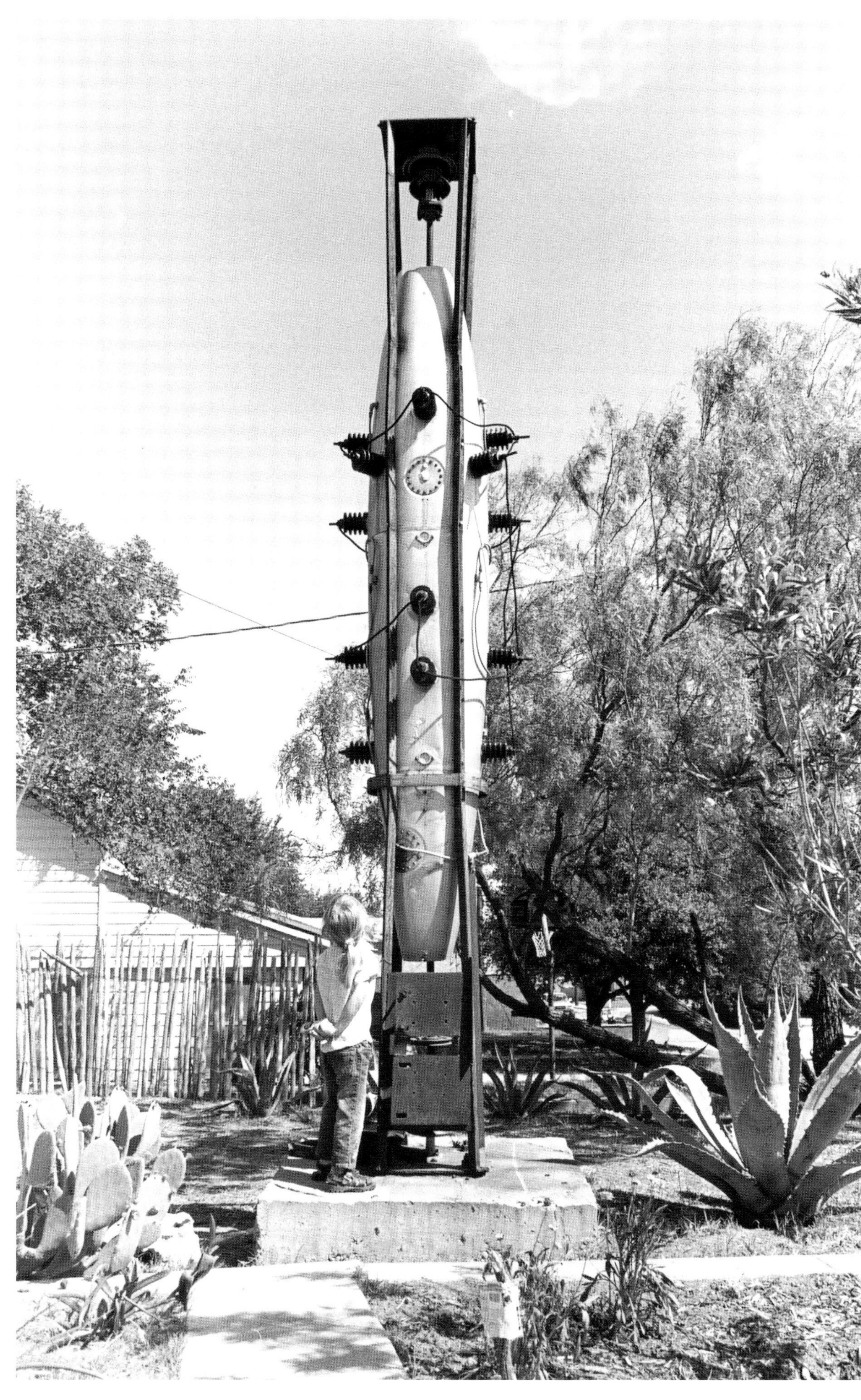

Untitled, The Rainmaker Rocket, 2003.

Southwest Collection, Texas Tech University, Millennial Collection 283, © Julie Boatright

due to the increasing need for manual labor on Texas farms and ranches, and for the building of railroads, Texans actively recruited workers from south of the Rio Grande. In 1942, the United States government initiated the Bracero program, which allowed Mexican nationals to contract for temporary agricultural jobs in the United States. Over the course of 22 years, four and a half million Mexican workers took jobs at low wages that most Americans considered beneath them. Across the American Southwest including Texas, New Mexico, and the Llano Estacado, the influx of Bracero immigrants contributed significantly to agribusiness and culture.

Besides Mexican Americans, a large number of Mennonites also found work in the cotton and peanut fields of the Llano. Settling near Seminole, Texas, beginning in 1977, two groups purchased more than seven thousand acres of land in Andrews and Gaines Counties after leaving their homes in Canada and Chihuahua, Mexico. Following an attempt by the Immigration and Naturalization Service to deport the Mennonites as illegal aliens, a highly publicized 1980 effort to give them citizenship finally won the day, although they lost most of their land. Today, Mennonites live in and around Seminole and across West Texas, where they work long hours making other people's lands—and increasingly their own lands—productive.

The farmer's move from simple stucco to brick and shingles represents a symbolic cultural construct of the most recent arrivals to the High Plains. It poses the question of who were the real pioneers of the Llano. Finally able to profit from an unforgiving land, High Plains farmers wanted to show they had made it. With water and chemicals to help them out, former hardscrabble plow-boys joined the rest of America in the post-war boom, distancing themselves from architecture which they associated with hard times and an alien culture. In Lubbock, despite the advantages of building with adobe, the ancient method of house building in the arid Southwest, visitors seldom see such construction anywhere in the city except for two or three early examples in the oldest parts of town, or newer faux adobe structures outside the city limits. Perhaps local building contractors and lumber suppliers lacked the knowledge to build with mud and straw. Because adobe was cheap, readily available, and possessed of a high insulation efficiency, it threatened to cut into their trade; so, in the 1930s, builders banded together and convinced the Lubbock City Council to ban further adobe construction in town. Perhaps, too, there was more than a little racial bias reflected in a decision which mirrored closely the thinking of Anglos in other parts of the American Southwest who disdained the "excremental" appearance of adobe. Despite following on the heels of countless other peoples who had adapted well to the Llano using the natural tools afforded them, the cultural baggage of these latecomers to the Plains helped mold the recent cultural characteristics of the built environment.

The Mexican presence on the Texas High Plains began early. Mexican sheep herders, or *pastores*, got here in the mid-1870s, and a few undoubtedly ventured here earlier than that, well before the Anglo latecomers. In Oldham County, along the Canadian River, one can still view the crumbling shelter remains of these wanderers. Spanish law and custom had established the principle of the commons in New Mexico. Spanish villages were surrounded by fields watered by *acequias*, or irrigation ditches, with water allotted to individual families. Cattle roamed the adjacent lands, including forests that also served as a commons for cutting timber and firewood. But large flocks of sheep required moving the animals across the meadows or *vegas* of northern New Mexico and along the watered passageways leading to, and cutting through, the Llano Estacado. Common, or *ejido*, pastures in New Mexico were not sufficient to support large flocks, so Mexican sheepherders followed the ancient practice of transhumance, the practice of moving sheep and cattle from high mountain meadows to grazing areas at lower elevations. The grasslands of the Llano offered the pastores lush, nutrient-rich pastures to feed

STEPHEN BOGENER

their herds of sheep and goats. Like their buffalo-hunting and Comanchero ancestors, these shepherds of the nineteenth century worked out an accommodation and seasonal accord with the Llano until Anglo latecomers forced them back into New Mexico. Despite the politically drawn western boundary of Texas, the Llano's western edge juts out across that line towards Clovis, Roswell, and Tucumcari, geographically, culturally, and historically drawing together Texas and the Spanish and Mexican heritage of New Mexico. Isolated in the extreme, both geographically and culturally, from their Anglo cousins further east, late-arriving Anglo citizens of the Southern Plains nonetheless soon rejected nearby New Mexican culture—at least its presence in the midst of prime grazing and farm lands.

Today, the large influx of Tejanos from other parts of the state, from both old and New Mexico into the Panhandle will influence Llano culture yet again. In places like Cactus, Texas, not far from Nazareth, thirteen miles north of Dumas, an entire village from Old Mexico and Guatemala brought the transplanted Hispanic culture full circle, returning to the Texas Panhandle. Residents worked in the growing feedlot, meat packing, and agribusiness trades. In 2007, in the midst of public outrage over illegal immigrants, the Immigration and Naturalization Service engineered raids in Minnesota, Iowa, and Texas, leading to the deportation of many illegal immigrants, including a substantial portion of Cactus's population. Farther south, many among the Mexican American communities of Lubbock and Amarillo can trace their High Plains ancestry to migrant labor and railroad construction camps. At the beginning of the twenty-first century, the Mexican American population of Lubbock made up 27.5 percent of the total population. One hundred miles north in Amarillo, the percentage was 21.9.

Although friendly without exception to their fellow plainsmen, Anglos tended to regard those from beyond the island of the Llano as foreigners. For many years, the words *damn* and *Yankee*, and *damn* and *Mexican* were inseparable, used by South Plains locals to describe anyone from north of Pampa, in the first instance, and anyone with brown skin in the second.

South Plains is a designation widely used by those living in the counties south of an east-west latitudinal line near the community of Plainview, not quite halfway between Lubbock and Amarillo. Not coincidentally, this line marks the traditional boundary between farmers' ability to grow cotton profitably to the south, and north of the line where wheat, sorghum, feed crops, and cattle predominate. The twenty-six counties north of the Plainview line, anchored to Amarillo, refer to themselves collectively as the Panhandle. South of the line, residents prefer to use the term *South Plains* to describe the southern part of the Llano Estacado. As Amarillo and Lubbock grew to become the centers of their respective economies on the northern and southern portions of the Llano, the rivalry and distinctions grew as well.

Because the beginnings of Anglo settlement on the High Plains were precarious, the isolated settlers' penchant for looking to themselves for answers created highly localized means for establishing agricultural economies, homesteads, governments, and schools well beyond the concept of states' rights. Based on agreements made at the time of the Lone Star Republic's annexation in 1845, Texas, unlike other states, has the right to divide into as many as five separate states. West Texans, more than once, have clamored for their independence from Austin. Living in what was truly one of the last American frontiers, people who settled the Llano Estacado often feel neglected by legislators in the capital, a city in a part of the state seemingly disconnected from the High Plains. If for nothing other than distance and the marked increase in aridity, the two parts of the state seem worlds apart.

Likewise, although the Llano historically has as much in common with lands to the west as to those east of the 100th meridian, observers will be hard pressed to find any acknowledgement by Llano residents to these historical links. Red River and Ruidoso notwithstanding, people of the Llano tend to see themselves as separate from everywhere else. When folks from the Llano venture away from the island in the sky and are asked where they live, the response, more often than not, is unhesitatingly, *West Texas*, not *Texas*, as if the region were its own state. In many ways it is. The resulting insularity of the Llano was born also of a stubborn desire—and a final chance for many—to make this hard land not only livable but also profitable on their own terms, regardless of what anyone outside the island in the sky may have thought about it.

By the 1930s, in the midst of the Great Depression, the proud, wind-scarred, and weather-beaten people of the High Plains found it difficult and distasteful to succumb to the necessity of relying on Roosevelt's New Deal. Encouraged first by the federal government to plant more wheat for the war effort, new Llano farmers were only too happy to comply, especially during the rainy years of the 1920s. By the 1930s, however, a cycle of drought had returned, and wheat prices had plummeted. Now Roosevelt implemented emergency measures calling for the elimination of surplus cattle and crops. Finally moved to action by Agriculture Secretary Hugh Bennett's proposals for sound, environmentally friendly farming methods, Llano farmers took their time in adopting such practices. Shelterbelts, contour plowing, and planting drought-resistant grasses on marginal soils met with little success until the government started offering a dollar an acre as an inducement.

Circulating documentaries like *The Plow that Broke the Plains* did nothing to endear the government to Dust Bowl residents. The movie, released in 1936, portrayed Bam White, a real-life down-on-his-luck cowboy, in the pivotal role of the sturdy pioneer who first broke the virgin soil of the Panhandle. In real life, White was moving his family from southeast Colorado to Littlefield, Texas to secure farmland, when he broke down near Dalhart smack in the middle of the dust disaster. For his portrayal in the film, White earned some twenty dollars for a couple of hours' work, a small fortune in those days. Farmers reluctantly joined government work crews in rehabilitating blown-out, abandoned farms and on New Deal projects hauling caliche and building roads. Only as a last resort, however, did farmers place their names on the list for receiving government assistance for their families. Many families resorted to canning tumbleweeds for survival, and some came close to starvation.

The creation of towns with names like New Deal, Roosevelt, and the re-settlement community of Ropesville, however, bear witness to Washington's ambitious plans. Fifty years after the dust had supposedly settled on the Llano, locals were just as adamant as they had been in the 1930s about wanting Washington, or for that matter those in Austin, to stay home. In the mid-1990s, the Environmental Protection Agency visited the High Plains during one of the springtime's frequent days of what local meteorologists refer to as "patchy areas of blowing dust." Cotton farmers use "sand fighters," contraptions used specifically to break up the crust that forms on top of the soil. Through minimum cultivation, the sand fighter kicks up moister soil which is too heavy to blow away. Despite these measures, the EPA declared the air in Lubbock, Texas, and the surrounding area unfit for breathing. Hard-bitten cotton farmers, many the descendants of High Plains pioneers, turned their heads sideways and spat a mixture of grit and bile from between their teeth. Obviously the foreigners from Washington should mind their own business.

This attitude prevailed despite the fact that the farm industry beginning in the 1930s became so dependent on the government trough of subsidies, crop insurance, and disaster relief that they would never be independent in the way their proud fathers and grandfathers had been. In 2001, Congress passed the largest farm bill in United States history, with billions of dollars aimed at propping up falling corn and cotton prices through ambitious subsidies. In the rougher times of the 1930s, self-reliance increasingly gave in to the desire to feed their families. Lean rawboned figures depicted in the photographs of Dorothea Lange and Russell Lee literally dug themselves out from the dunes of dirt encasing their homes and accepted government aid. Some joined local support groups like Dalhart's "Last Man's Club," whose members promised never to give up on the Plains while watching their neighbors load up belongings in rickety pickup trucks and head west to California. In the end, only 25 percent of Dust Bowl residents left the region. The creaking of doors of abandoned homes, churches, and schools across the Llano during the 1930s only intensified the resolve of those who stayed here to wait out the storm.

Intensely religious—if religious means God-fearing—the people who stayed on this windy, dusty island in the sky looked for support and a sense of community to churches which had not yet closed their doors. Just as they had before the dust, handfuls of settlers built churches and schools in short order. Football games, livestock shows, and county fairs also continued to serve the cultural needs of communities on top of the Caprock.

The trend of church building and community continues across what some have described as "the buckle of the Bible belt." Today, there are more churches per capita in Lubbock, Texas, than in any city of comparable size in the country. More than two hundred thousand people call Lubbock home, and a good portion of them can be found in church on Sunday mornings and Wednesday evenings.

Politically, the people of the Texas High Plains have always been a conservative lot—hard working, God-fearing, and traditionally insular. In surveys, Lubbock has been ranked second behind Salt Lake City as the most conservative city in the United States. In 2008, Llano voters overwhelmingly endorsed John McCain over Barack Obama. The Llano has consistently been a bastion of conservatism despite the influence of half a dozen colleges and universities.

Religion and politics on the High Plains are akin to the way the roads were laid out—very straight with lots of right angles. In dozens of West Texas towns and counties, the streets are wide like the lands of the Llano, arranged in perfect order, creating a grid of lines parallel and perpendicular to each other. Lubbock grew up with the automobile. An automobile town almost from its inception, Lubbock is typical of what J. B. Jackson, a critic of artificial modernism, described as a twenty-first-century automobile city, and reflects the culture of the people that live there. Some city streets have eight lanes, designed to help ferry folks from residential quadrants of the city to glittering shopping meccas or to a mall built over what was once a sprawling playa lake.

There are eighteen large playa lakes in Lubbock and hundreds of smaller ones in and around the city, a sizeable representation of the almost 20,000 across the Llano. An ambitious drainage project drains the lakes one to another from west to east until excess rainwater is diverted into Yellowhouse Canyon and finally into the Brazos River. The automobile, a sacred animal revered in a land of far-flung outposts, and high-brow developments built in natural drainages, were thought to be safe from the occasional downpour. In 2008, Lubbock received more than eight inches of rain in twenty-four hours. The hundred-year flood inundated business, closed schools and universities, and brought the Hub City to a standstill.

Farmers carving roads in nearby counties never bothered to go around the many playas which dot the cotton country, as if that might destroy the perfect linearity of the farm roads. When it rains in such places, it becomes painfully obvious to the unseasoned traveler wading through the muck that these roads were built right through the middle of lakes harboring wildlife and millions of birds traveling one of the great flyways of North America.

Once the home of wolves, antelope, deer, wild horses, mountain lions, and bear, Lubbock and a huge swath of territory stretching to San Angelo have the historical distinction of serving as the home to perhaps the world's largest colony of black-tailed prairie dogs. Infatuated with their human characteristics, Lewis and Clark sent one of the animals from the Dakota prairie back to Thomas Jefferson in Washington. Although sound science has supported their usefulness to the prairie ecosystem, prairie dogs were all but eradicated in the last century by ranchers and farmers who claimed that cattle and horses kept stepping into the critters' holes and breaking their legs. That did not stop the Lubbock Chamber of Commerce from adopting this furry sociable animal as a poster boy for promoting the Hub City. For years, Prairie Dog Pete was perhaps the most visible symbol of Lubbock, Texas. Today, a small remnant of Pete's colony thrives in Mackenzie Park (named after the subduer of the Comanche) under the close supervision of groundskeepers at the well-manicured golf course across the road.

In 2002, another colony of prairie dogs brought attention to Lubbock. The Texas Commission on Environmental Quality in the state capital determined early in the year that prairie dogs burrowing on land used by the city as a wastewater application farm (a place where the city also grazed cattle), had increased nitrate levels in the soil, threatening Lubbock's groundwater. The TCEQ demanded action by city officials, who prepared a narrow list of solutions mostly limited to eradication of the furry rodents by poisoning them, a method long championed by locals. A quiet yet effective groundswell of petitions and letters to the editor, along with protests from state and national environmental groups, led the TCEQ to reexamine the issue. The folks from Austin soon realized they were on the horns of a dilemma. Further study showed that the prairie dogs were probably no more responsible for increased nitrate levels in the groundwater than were City Council members for letting their favorite bird dogs urinate on fire hydrants.

Local musician and colleague Andy Wilkinson, an astute observer of the Llano Estacado and the grandnephew of legendary cowman Charles Goodnight, has emphasized that Lubbock is the largest city on the High Plains, which stretches all the way to Canada. Yet Lubbock never quite feels like a big city. As far as most large American cities go, Lubbock is a new town and wants to keep it that way.

Local real estate developer Delbert McDougal re-invented one of the oldest sections of town, not with a facelift but by leveling it and starting over. Touted as the largest urban renewal project of its kind in the country, the project changed the face of Lubbock forever. In 1907, when the city was a few years old, a frontier physician from Kentucky named M. C. Overton bought a 640-acre plot of land just west of the original Lubbock townsite and named the property Overton Addition. Founded in 1923, Texas Tech University grew up adjacent to Overton. The addition was the first subdivision of the new town, and until 2002, housed some of the oldest residences in the city, including the house where musician Buddy Holly grew up. Redevelopment leveled the northern half of Overton's neighborhood, some 325 acres. Replacing the neighborhood, which had fallen on hard times over the last thirty years and was referred to by locals as the Tech Ghetto, are upscale residential housing, condos, a five-star hotel and conference center, and commercial sites. Much of the initial phase of development took place under the administration of Mayor Marc McDougal, the developer's son. Under the senior McDougal's direction, contractors moved out most of the oldest houses and those with unique architecture, or razed them entirely to make way for the new development. Lubbock remains at heart and in fact a frontier city on the High Plains.

Like the McDougal family fortune, most of the money made here has been made in one or two generations. There is really no "old" money here, and the town tends to be

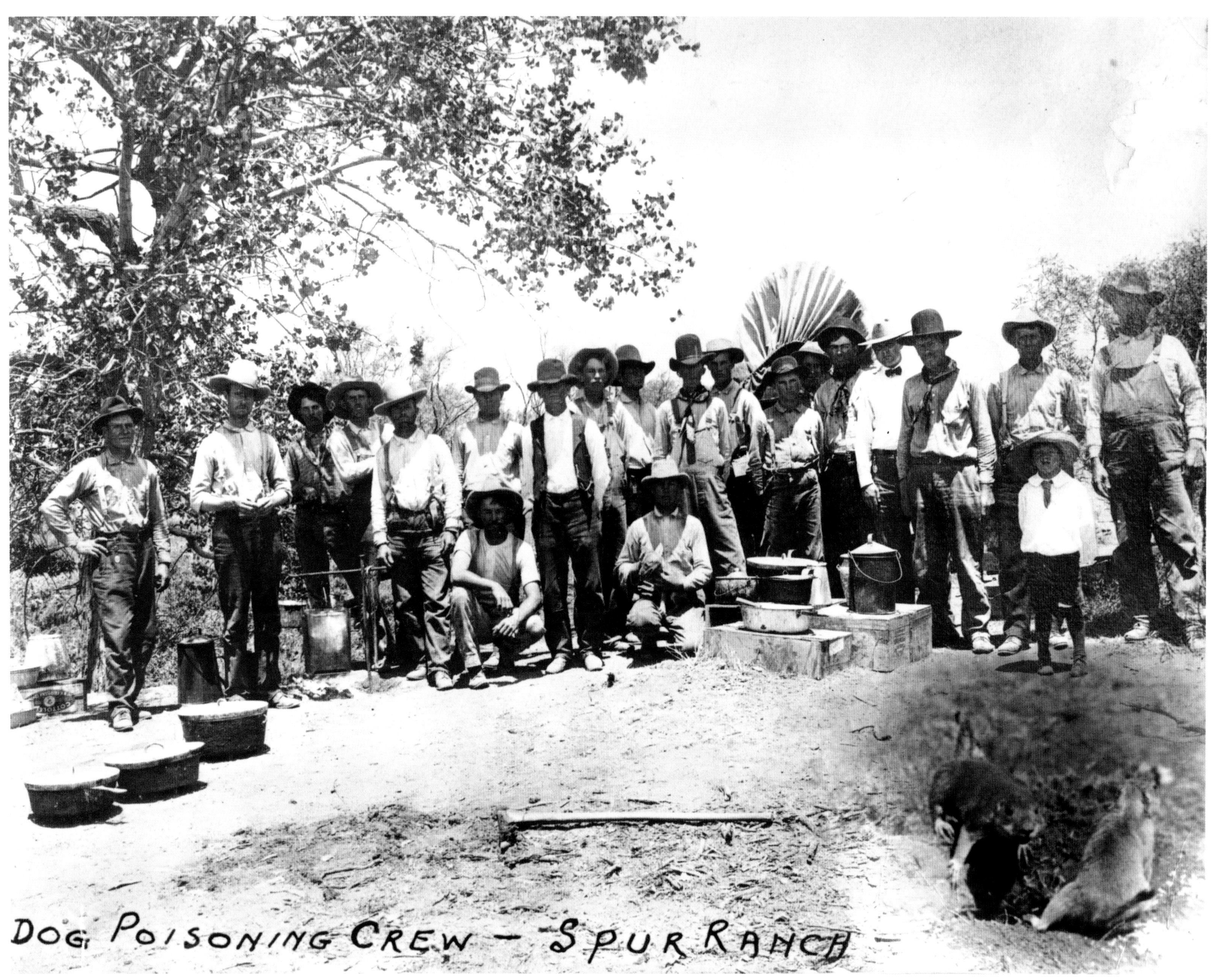

Prairie dog poisoning crew on the Espuela Land and Cattle Company (Spur) Ranch, circa 1900. Southwest Collection, Texas Tech University, MPC 55-130-2

egalitarian in many respects. The driver sitting next to you at the traffic light might be a millionaire, but he drives the same model pickup truck as the other 80 percent of the city. Pickups are a throwback to riding high and surveying the land, much like riding horseback. And while a horse was often more than a form of transportation, allowing rider to mend fences and chase cattle, the modern-day equivalent is used less to ride the range than to convey folks to their favorite church, restaurant, bar, or cockfight.

Lubbock has almost as many restaurants per capita as it has churches, which may or may not be a coincidence given the close proximity of one to the other. As the new millennium began, Lubbockites spent something on the average of $1500 a year eating out. It is uncertain how much they might spend on gambling or cockfights, which are illegal in Texas, or dog fights, which are equally against the law, but all forms of entertainment exist on the High Plains. It is not the kind of thing publicized by the Chamber of Commerce.

The Chamber and the local school district do publicize the success of area schools, and for good reason: local schools have consistently been cited for excellence. In 2002, Lubbock High School won the State Academic Decathlon. However, following the lead of Lubbock residents and clergy, much like the hubbub created by a local university professor's teaching of evolutionary theory in the 1930s, school officials do not condone the teaching of sex education in the classroom. In recent years, along with reaping state-wide acclaim for academics, Lubbock has frequently led the state in the proliferation of sexually transmitted diseases. The Lubbock Independent School District, however, following the lead of former Governor George W. Bush and the Texas legislature in 1995, adheres to a policy of abstinence-only regarding sex education in the schools. In 2001, Shelby Knox, a high-school student in Lubbock, advocated a comprehensive sex education program by the district. Her highly publicized crusade led to a PBS documentary film, *The Education of Shelby Knox,* highlighting the power of local clergy and parent groups to prevent sex education in Lubbock schools despite the prevalence of STDs. Superintendent Jack Clemmons dutifully upheld school policy, not only standing firm against comprehensive sex education, but also banning a student gay-straight alliance group at Lubbock High. While the superintendent was barring all things sex-related in the district, he was, according to the Lubbock *Avalanche-Journal,* conducting an extramarital affair with an employee on school property. The school district quietly paid its superintendent his remaining salary and released him from district service. In 2009, Lubbock residents were said by *Men's Health Magazine* to be the second most in need of Viagra among metropolitan areas in the U.S. (That is, men in Lubbock have more of the health problems that can lead to a need for Viagra, such as diabetes and high blood pressure; the number of actual prescriptions is much lower, by the magazine's own figures.)

The writer and cultural critic Molly Ivins once claimed, perhaps tongue-in-cheek, that Lubbock was her favorite place in Texas. Ivins went on to say that people in Lubbock have a real good understanding of what sin is, and therefore they can go right out and enjoy it. In a column for *Texas Monthly*, Ivins called Lubbock the seat of rebellion, a place where "you don't have to waste time trying to figure out what the rules are; you can go right ahead and break 'em and see what happens." Sometimes, despite compliance with the rules, the long arm of conservative values exercises its muscle under the guise of law and order. In 2007, after assurances from city officials that he was in compliance with local ordinances, a local nightclub owner arranged for a show featuring the Chippendales male revue dancers, and hundreds of customers came to enjoy the show; then local law enforcement arrived on the scene and shut the revue down in the middle of their act because a dancer allegedly "simulated a sexual act." Singer Butch Hancock, a Lubbock native, once said, "Living in Lubbock taught me two things: One is that God loves you and you're going to burn in hell; the other is that sex is the most awful, filthy thing on earth and you should save it for someone you love." Outside the city limits on the other side of town, women continued to gyrate onstage for male patrons in one of the area's more popular male entertainment venues.

Ivins was on to something else. Lubbock is one of those places where creativity has always been a part of the local fabric. While preachers railed at teenagers in the 1950s for listening to the Devil's music, Buddy Holly and Waylon Jennings broke the rules anyway. For whatever reason—some have suggested it is because of the wind, the dirt, the wide-open spaces, the majestic sunsets, or just plain isolation and boredom—this area has turned out more musicians and artists than its population would suggest. Woody Guthrie, Bob Wills, Buddy Holly, Waylon Jennings, Roy Orbison, Tanya Tucker, Bobby Keys of the Rolling Stones, Mac Davis, opera singers Mary Jane Johnson and Susan Graham, John Denver, Joe Ely, Jimmy Dale Gilmore, Butch Hancock, Terry Allen, Sonny Curtis, Ralna English, Natalie Maines of the Dixie Chicks, Pat Green, and others have all spent time in Lubbock. In 2005 and 2006, singer Natalie Maines, who expressed embarrassment and shame that George W. Bush was from Texas, paid a price in her hometown. With their music boycotted on local radio and in stores, the Chicks' popularity and sales plummeted in West Texas. In other parts of the country, the popularity of their music soared.

Musicians and artists of every stripe have at one time or the other called the Llano Estacado home. Those creative types, especially those artists who become well known, leave town to do so, settling in places like Austin, Nashville, or Santa Fe, with Lubbock soon a fading mirage in their rearview mirrors, like the line of a song by Mac Davis. To be fair, many of them come back—which is the follow-up to Davis's more famous lyrics in the song—to re-ignite the creative fires that led to their journeys years before. Buddy Holly was not accorded in his hometown the fame generated by fans in England and elsewhere until he was long dead and buried. City fathers noticed reluctantly and late that Holly's popularity might generate tourist dollars.

Long before Holly's rockabilly rocked Lubbock's Hi-D-Ho drive-in, ninety miles to the north, Georgia O'Keeffe spent a good portion of the 1920s wandering out from Canyon City to observe the sensual shapes and colors emanating from nearby Palo Duro Canyon. Even earlier, landscape pastel artist Frank Reaugh took many a sojourn from his studio in Dallas to capture on canvas the colorful skies and sunsets of the High Plains and beyond. More recently, Glenna Goodacre, a graduate of Lubbock High School and the sculptor of the Women's Vietnam War Memorial in Washington, has called Lubbock home, as has Paul Milosevich, the Santa Fe artist and bon vivant who rendered the uncanny portraits of premier athletes and singers. Contrasting sharply with the work of musician and artist Terry Allen, another Lubbock expatriate now living in Santa Fe, Goodacre's and Milosevich's styles appear conventional and safe, much the way Lubbock appears on the surface. Allen's go-ahead, rebellious, international appeal reflects the creative underbelly of Lubbock and the Texas High Plains. Waylon Jennings once commented that playing music was a hell of a lot better than picking cotton all day. Then again, perhaps like the sunsets and sensuality represented by hoodoos and textured canyon walls, artists find in the staid cultural conventionality and geographic similarities of the Llano a backdrop from which they can stand out, from which they can rebel, as Ivins put it.

Someone once said that appearance is everything, and so it is on the Llano. A land of fundamentalist religion, Lubbock in particular, and the rest of the Southern High Plains communities to some degree, pride themselves on the appearance of respectability. It was not always so, but the image of wild times and the preeminence of rowdy cowboys faded fast in Lubbock. In 1891, when the village of Lubbock came into existence, cowboys posed for photographs while disdainfully reclining on a shipment of lumber meant for the town's first buildings. Cowboy disdain notwithstanding, Lubbock grew quickly into a supply town for ranchers and farmers in the area, with a reputation for sobriety, entrepreneurial spirit, and law and order.

Actually, there were two towns, each sponsored by a different promoter. In the fall of 1890, each group agreed to abandon their respective townsites, Old Lubbock and Monterey, and combine into a single settlement. This required the moving and reassembly of a fairly large hotel and other buildings across Yellowhouse Canyon.

Not long after the combined town began, city fathers approached the purveyor of the only saloon in town and convinced him that his business pursuits could be better served elsewhere. From the beginning, Lubbock was promoted as a sober, clean, industrious town. During the decade of the 1930s, Lubbock won state awards every year for being the cleanest town in Texas.

During the previous decade of the 1920s, Lubbock citizens used the city's image as a forthright temperate place to live as a reason for the state legislature to locate a new college in the town. Against thirty-six competing towns including Amarillo and Sweetwater, proponents for locating the new school in Lubbock pointed to soil conditions, an "inexhaustible supply of purest underground water," an invigorating climate, "religious institutions necessary to care for . . . a great student body," and "the favorable influence of a 100 percent White American Citizenship that is wholeheartedly hospitable, optimistic and imbued with the Spirit of Western Progressiveness."

Such rhetoric was not limited to Lubbock. During the late nineteenth century and into the twentieth, the issue of prohibition dominated state politics. With few exceptions, the towns on the Llano Estacado professed an undying belief in the merits of "dryness" and the evils of drink. Preachers from towns small and smaller used rhetoric tinged with nativism and anti-Catholic bias in denouncing saloons, their patrons, and demon rum.

Ironically, beginning with Prohibition and continuing well into mid-century and beyond, the denunciation of drink coincided with a lucrative network of moonshiners and alcohol runners distributing the evil liquids far and wide across the Texas High Plains. Students attending " the Tech," as Texas Technological College was called in the 1920s, split their time between selling the milk from dairy cows, and ferrying moonshine in the rumble seats of Henry Ford's Model A's.

Pioneer Hank Smith's granddaughter related the story of how she paid her way through Texas Tech by selling prescriptions (provided her by her family doctor) to her fellow students for "medicinal" alcohol. Some bootleggers, like the infamous "Pinky" Roden, parlayed illegal activities into legal moneymaking bonanzas after wet precincts arrived in the 1960s. No longer would thirsty fraternity boys have to drive to the New Mexico state line for refreshment. Soon the likes of the Bloated Goat, a very popular bar and liquor-selling establishment in New Mexico across from Bledsoe, or the Border Bar across the state line from Bronco, faded from collective memory. So, too, did Lubbock's Cotton Club, the most notorious honky-tonk in West Texas, where Elvis Presley once raised the ire of local country boys by hitting on their dates. Reminiscent of the Comancheros who ferried Taos Lightning (*aguardiente*) and other firewater to the Comanche in a trade system which flourished for two hundred years, comparatively modern-day honky-tonks and liquor runners with souped-up cars made good money conducting business on the High Plains into the 1960s.

The irony of packed church houses on Sunday mornings and the prevalence and mass consumption of alcohol on Saturday night were probably not lost on many, including ministers, liquor runners, and dirt farmers trying to get by,

Surveying crew, West Texas, circa 1900.

Southwest Collection, Texas Tech University, SWCPC 326-E39

Well beyond the Prohibition era shown in this photograph, bootlegging enjoyed a long and illustrious history in West Texas.

Southwest Collection, Texas Tech University, SWCPC 313-E1-25

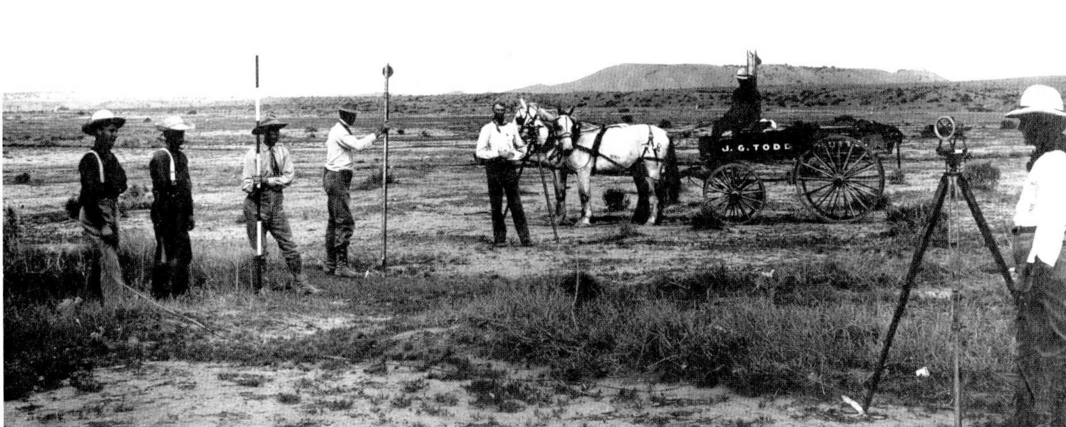

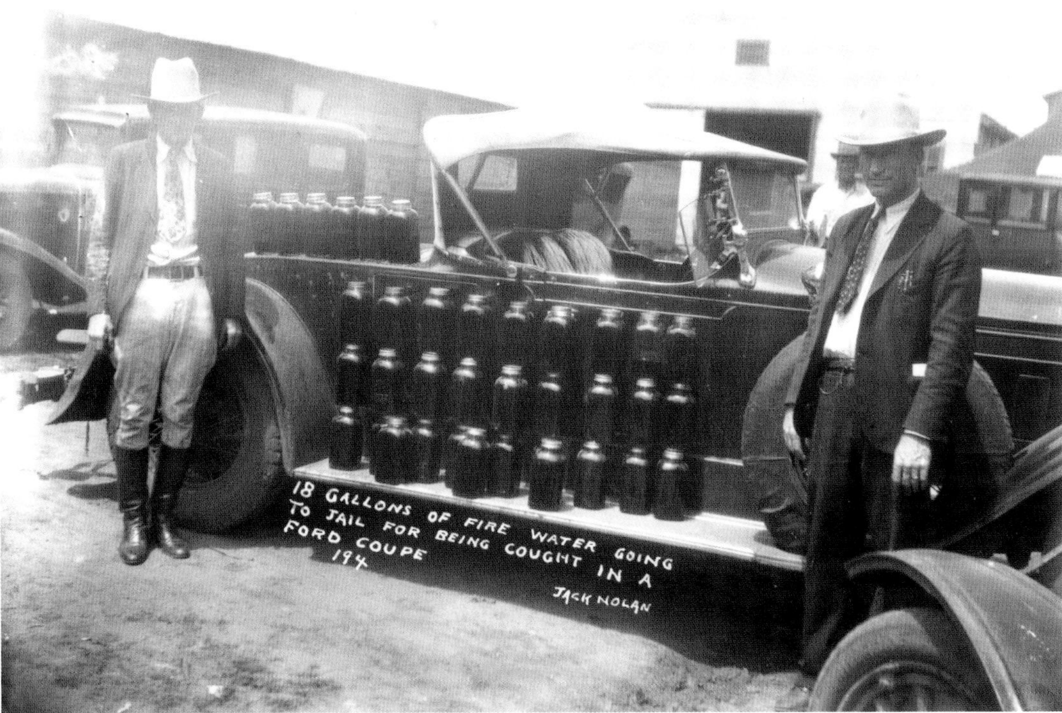

but the veneer of respectability masked the contradictions on the High Plains. Most counties on the Texas portion of the Llano Estacado remain partially dry to this day, allowing only certain precincts to sell beer or liquor. In Amarillo, half the town lies in a wet county and half in a dry county, causing the city to shift a good portion of its population on Friday and Saturday nights.

In Lubbock, the most prosperous area of the wet precinct on the southeastern outskirts of town is called "the strip," until recently part of the only legal area to buy package liquor and beer—and it was not even within the city limits until 2006 when the city annexed the area. City sales tax receipts from the strip were appreciable. The strip resembled on a tiny scale the old neon strip of Las Vegas, Nevada. In 1971, the city of Lubbock finally allowed liquor by the drink. At this writing, the drinking age in Texas is twenty-one; never mind that on any given day or night, underage students from Texas Tech, Lubbock Christian University, and Wayland Baptist University, spurred on by liquor ads in student newspapers, seek out ways to secure their favorite beverages.

Until Lubbock reached the official population of 200,000 in 2000, the various grassroots attempts to spread the wealth of moneymaking from the strip to other Lubbock precincts met with little success. One of the stranger occurrences in Lubbock has been to watch the purveyors of the strip team up with the more conservative elements of the local clergy whenever the notion of another wet precinct arises. Allowing or disallowing the sale of beer and wine in grocery stores is truly an issue of dollars and cents cloaked in the long-running crusade against the evils of drink. In 2008, for the first time in history, the Lubbock Chamber of Commerce came out in favor of allowing Lubbock citizens to decide for themselves whether the city at large should go wet, and in 2009, Lubbock voters, after 110 years, approved alcohol sales within the city. Owners of businesses on the strip and others immediately launched a suit alleging an illegal election, which prompted a court injunction to keep Lubbock dry a bit longer. In September 2009 the Texas Alcoholic Beverage Commission dismissed protests against alcohol sales, and local supennarkets and convenience stores sold beer and wine for the first time.

To the west of Lubbock lies the oil and agriculture town of Levelland, a community of thirteen thousand in Hockley County. Only recently has the town allowed alcohol in restaurants. In the early 1980s, a Hockley County judge figured out a way to create his own "strip." To do so, he started his own town. Opdyke (pronounced "Opie-dike," for some reason) West lies four miles east of Levelland and was incorporated in 1984. With a population of 188, the town's main attraction—besides the trailer park on this otherwise empty spot on Highway 114—is WayneBo's, a full-service liquor store with convenient drive-through bays to accommodate the customer's every need.

The land of the Llano is often seen by outsiders to be a dull, monotonous stretch of earth and sky. Road maps of the area show much the same picture, a continuous land of square counties and small towns few have heard of. But natives revel in the wide-open spaces where they can see what is coming across the horizon. Emily Nash, a native of the Llano, embraces the wide view. In one of her photographs, a wide-angle shot of a lonely farm-to-market crossroads, where the intersection of asphalt, grass, and sky suggests emptiness, even abandonment, there is a curious billboard in the middle distance down one axis of the highway. Looking closely, one discovers, superimposed on the billboard, a picture of a handful of humans lying face up in the middle of a similar intersection, staring into the sky. The image is a snapshot of Nash and her family, taken years before.

Nash's photographic journey began in an antique shop, with the discovery of love letters stashed away in an old radio.

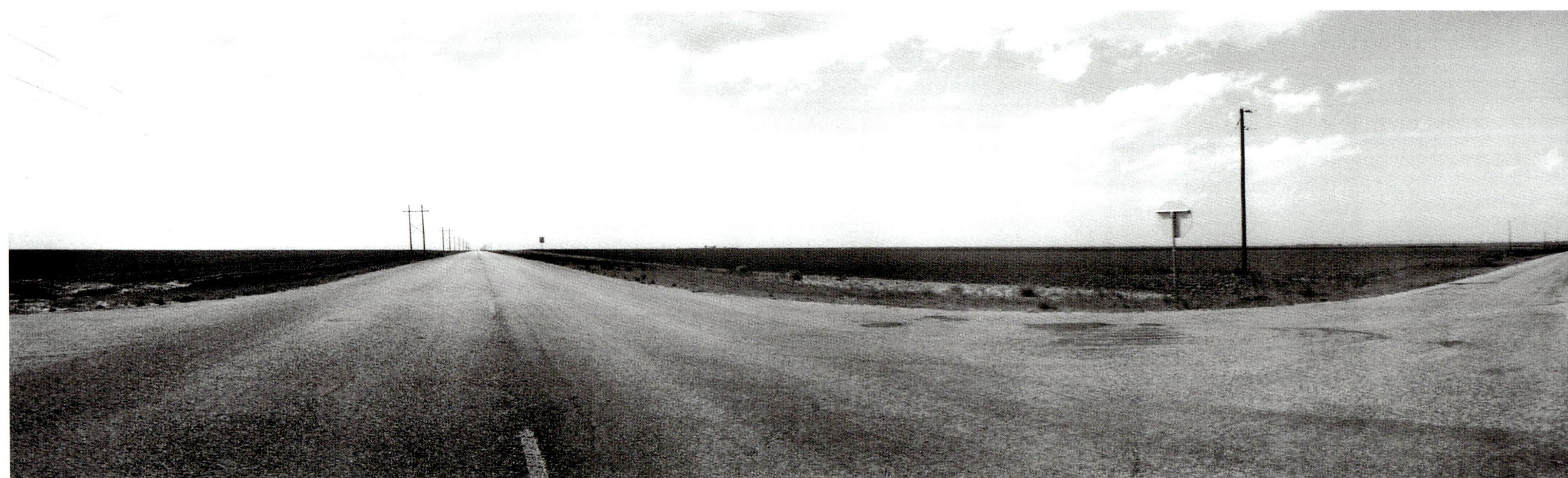

An ensuing discussion about a popular, now defunct Lubbock barbecue joint, a popular hangout for artists and musicians called Stubb's, led her to realize that Stubb's was as much about camaraderie, family, and community as it was about barbecue. That realization led her to consider the importance of her own family and, by extension, to an understanding that we are all connected to one another—even amidst the vastness of an open plain.

In the sixteenth century, Spanish chroniclers noted these wide-open spaces and a peculiar phenomenon. They noticed that the bright light and the long stretches of open land allowed them to see for miles. Objects such as horsemen or buffalo, miles distant, appeared gigantic and clearly in focus due to bending of the sun's rays. Today, the phenomenon has largely disappeared with the destruction of the grassland, but the earliest settlers and cowboys used to tell stories of huge horses galloping in the distance.

Another locally famous optical phenomenon occurred in 1951. Four years earlier, a number of people believe, space aliens had visited Roswell, New Mexico. Beginning on August 25, 1951, and for several nights thereafter, folks in Lubbock and surrounding communities reported seeing dots of light flying in U- and V-shaped patterns traveling from northeast to southwest. The color, number, and pattern of the lights varied from one story to another, but they were not attributed to aircraft in the area. Professors at Texas Tech estimated the objects were flying at an elevation of 2000 to 3000 feet above the Llano at approximately 750 miles per hour. The so-called "Lubbock Lights" have remained a mystery, though some retain the belief that they were somehow connected with the earlier alien visit.

Beyond the surreal and the unexplainable are the names given to the land itself. They reflect a continually changing and integrating cultural pattern on the Llano Estacado.

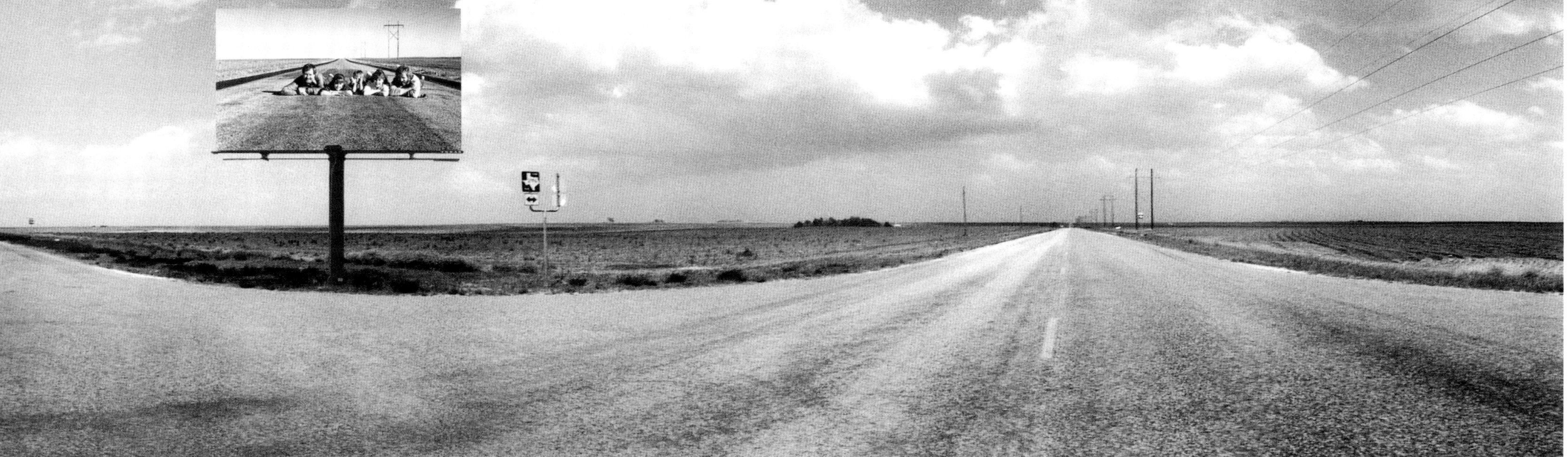

A Highway with No One On It, Spring 2004.

Southwest Collection, Texas Tech University, Millennial Collection 468, © Emily Nash Long

Plainview, *Levelland*, and *Sundown* reflect the imprint of more recent arrivals to the Llano and what they saw in the land. But names like *Tahoka* and *Mobeetie* reflect an earlier cultural imprint made by Native Americans, and *Tule*, *Palo Duro*, and *Blanco* reflect a Spanish presence as well.

In spite of appearances, the Llano Estacado is not really flat, either in its topography or in its own brand of history. Rather, it is a land of fabulous vistas where the sky makes up about 85 percent of what you see, where life is viewed in various shades of black and white, where the wind blows, the people are God-fearing, and the roads all stretch at right angles to the four cardinal directions. The traditional wisdom is that folks in Lubbock and across the Llano like to think of themselves as straight shooters. They like to look a man in the eye, shake his hand, and believe what he is saying. Perhaps that explains the elder George Bush's response several years ago when asked about his stand on the issues of the day. Bush wanted to see "how it played in Lubbock" first. Almost two decades later, the President's eldest son urged Congress to craft a bill in words "the boys in Lubbock [could] understand." The irony is that the widely accepted political notion that Lubbock represents only conservative values and black-and-white decision-making on key issues of the day belies the complexity and contradictions of a burgeoning political culture on the island called El Llano Estacado.

Lubbock and the Llano Estacado—this vast island in the sky—make up a land of opportunity, a wide-open place of sun, grass, canyon and sky, a land of paradox where one can find rain, wind, heat, cold, sunshine, lightning, and rainbows, almost all in the same place at the same time.

THE PHOTOGRAPHERS

PETER BROWN

Peter Brown has photographed the open landscape and small towns of the Great Plains for the past twenty years. He is the author of *Seasons of Light*, *On The Plains*, and the recently published *West of Last Chance*, a collaboration with the novelist Kent Haruf that won the Dorothea Lange-Paul Taylor Prize. His work has been collected by the Menil Collection, the Museum of Fine Arts in Houston, MoMA New York, the Los Angeles County Museum, the Getty Museum, and the San Francisco Museum of Modern Art, among others. Brown's work can be seen at the Stephen L. Clark Gallery, Austin; Harris Gallery, Houston; Stephen Cohen Gallery, Los Angeles; PDNB Gallery, Dallas; Stephen Bulger Gallery, Toronto; and the Highland Gallery in Marfa, Texas.

Brown has received a National Endowment for the Arts Fellowship, the Alfred Eisenstaedt Award, the Imogen Cunningham Award, and grants from the Graham Foundation and the Cultural Arts Council of Houston. His work has appeared in *Harper's*, *DoubleTake*, *Life*, *The New Yorker*, *Aperture*, *American Photographer*, *Texas Monthly*, and other magazines. He has degrees in English and art from Stanford University and currently teaches at the Glasscock School of Continuing Studies at Rice, where he recently won their inaugural teaching prize. He was named Photographer/Educator of the Year by the Houston Center for Photography in 2004. He lives in Houston with his wife Jill and daughter Caitlin.

RICK DINGUS

Since the late 1970s, Rick Dingus's photographs have been widely exhibited, published, and included in many public and private collections such as the San Francisco Museum of Modern Art, the Getty Museum, the Amon Carter Museum, the Metropolitan Museum, the Museum of Modern Art, le Bibliothèque Nationale, the Australian National Gallery of Art, the Library of Congress, and the Smithsonian American Art Museum. He is the author of *The Photographic Artifacts of Timothy O'Sullivan* (Univ. of New Mexico Press, 1982), has worked on a variety of collaborative projects that include the Rephotographic Survey Project; Marks in Place:

Contemporary Responses to Rock Art; and Dine'tah-Hajiinei: Place of Emergence. He helped establish the Millennial Collection archive at the Southwest Collection/Special Collections Library at Texas Tech University, where he is professor of photography in the School of Art. (For more information, or to contact him, visit his web site, rickdingus.com.)

STEVE FITCH

After graduating from the University of California at Berkeley in 1971 with a bachelor's degree in anthropology, Steve Fitch began work on a project photographing the vernacular roadside of the American highway. He received two National Endowment for the Arts fellowships to aid in the completion of this project, in 1973 and 1975. Eventually, the photographs were published in the monograph *Diesels and Dinosaurs* in 1976.

After receiving a master's degree in fine arts from the University of New Mexico in Albuquerque in 1978, Fitch accepted a teaching position at the University of Colorado in Boulder. In 1981, as a member of the Marks and Measures project, he began photographing prehistoric Native American pictograph and petroglyph sites. This project was partly funded by the last National Endowment for the Arts survey grant awarded in 1981. His work on the project, along with that of the other four project members, was published in a monograph titled *Marks in Place* by the University of New Mexico Press in 1988. He received several purchase awards in various exhibitions for photographs made during this period.

In 1990, after teaching at Princeton University for four years in the Visual Arts Program, Fitch moved to New Mexico, where he currently lives and taught at the College of Santa Fe until its closing. In 1991, he began photographing the ongoing abandonment of the Great Plains and received the Eliot Porter Fellowship from the New Mexico Council for Photography in 1999 to aid in the completion of this project. In 2003, a book of these photographs titled *Gone: Photographs of Abandonment on the High Plains* was published by the University of New Mexico Press, and a traveling exhibition of the photographs was organized by University of New Mexico Art Museum. In 2008, the Smithsonian American Art Museum purchased the entire exhibition of forty photographs and will be organizing an exhibition of them.

MIGUEL GANDERT

Miguel Gandert, a native of Española, New Mexico, is a fine arts and documentary photographer and professor of communication and journalism at the University of New Mexico. His recent work explores the contrast between Hispanic life in Spain and in colonial America, including Bolivia, Old Mexico, and New Mexico. He is also working on projects on women and agriculture, the Llano Estacado, the High Plains of West Texas and eastern New Mexico and a book, *Center Place, Plaza Square: The Cultural Space of New Mexico*.

Gandert's photographs are in numerous publications and have been shown in galleries and museums throughout the world including the Museum of Fine Arts in Boston, the National Museum of American History at the Smithsonian, the Center for Creative Photography in Tucson, the Beinecke Rare Book and Manuscript Collection at Yale, and the Museum of Fine Arts in Santa Fe. His series *Nuevo Mexico Profundo, Rituals of an Indo-Hispano Homeland*, was the subject of a book and a one-person exhibition for the National Hispanic Culture Center, in 2000, and his work was selected for the 1993 Biennial at Whitney Museum of American Art. In 1990 his series *VSJ: Scenes from an Urban Chicano Experience* was the subject of a one-person exhibition at the Smithsonian. His most recent book with Enrique Lamadrid, *Hermanitos Comanchitos: Indo-Hispano Rituals of Captivity and Redemption,* was awarded the Southwest Book Award as well as the Chicago Book Prize from the American Folklore Society.

TONY GLEATON

Tony Gleaton has exhibited work at galleries throughout the United States and Mexico, including the National Museum of American Art and the Los Angeles County Museum of Art. His Smithsonian exhibit, *Tengo Casí 500 Años,* traveled extensively throughout the United States. Gleaton, who has traversed the American West, has also lived and traveled extensively in Mexico and South America chronicling *mestizaje*, the assimilation of Asians, Africans, and Europeans with indigenous Americans. Gleaton's recent work has taken him throughout the United States, where he is at work chronicling the Black route west.

ANDREW JOHN LICCARDO

Andrew John Liccardo received his B.A. from Loyola University of Chicago and his M.F.A. from Texas Tech University in Lubbock, Texas. He is currently assistant professor of photography at Northern Illinois University.

Liccardo's current photographic work looks at the cultural and geographic landscape with a specific interest in how the built environment can act as a barometer of our cultural evolution. He understands landscape in broad terms as a uniquely human construct, and seeks to understand it as a dynamic system that both absorbs and reflects us.

Recently, Liccardo has exhibited work in Iceland, Illinois, Massachusetts, Georgia, Michigan, Florida, New York, Wisconsin, and Texas. He has received numerous grants, awards, fellowships, and residencies. He has work in the permanent collection at the Museum of Fine Arts Houston, and was a 2002 National Graduate Seminar Fellow of the Photography Institute at Columbia University.

THE ESSAYISTS

RICK BASS

Rick Bass was born in Fort Worth, grew up in Houston, and attended college at Utah State University, where he studied wildlife science and geology. He is the author of 25 books of fiction and nonfiction, including most recently a novel, *Nashville Chrome* (Houghton Mifflin Harcourt). He is the recipient of grants from the National Endowment for the Arts, the Guggenheim Foundation, the Lyndhurst Foundation, the Mississippi Institute of Arts and Letters, and the Texas Institute of Letters. A memoir, *Why I Came West*, was a finalist for the National Book Critics Circle Award. He divides his time between Missoula and Yaak, Montana, where he is a board member of the Yaak Valley Forest Council (www.yaakvalley.org), a community service organization working to help protect as wilderness the last roadless lands in the Kootenai National Forest.

STEPHEN BOGENER

Steve Bogener is currently assistant professor of history at West Texas A&M University in Canyon, where he coordinates the public history program and teaches courses on environmental history, the Llano Estacado, and the American West. Prior to serving at WT, Bogener worked for Bemidji State University in the North Woods of Minnesota for two years. While serving as assistant archivist and coordinator of exhibits and outreach at the Southwest Collection/Special Collections Library at Texas Tech University, Bogener served as chief grant-writer for the Archive while also teaching American and Texas history courses as assistant professor of history. A resident of West Texas for two decades, he has taught at the secondary, community college and university levels.

As outreach coordinator of the Archive, he facilitated numerous interdisciplinary projects including publications, symposia, lectures, workshops, conferences, photographic and other exhibits across the University and West Texas/Southwest communities, and was contributing editor of the

Southwest Chronicle. Working with the writer Barry Lopez, whose papers and those of other natural history writers are located at Texas Tech, he coordinated efforts to produce *The Working Life of a Writer*, a multi-panel exhibit focused on the writer and the process of writing.

Bogener has published numerous articles and two books, *Ditches across the Desert: Irrigation in the Lower Pecos Valley*, and *Lubbock: Gem of the South Plains*. Most of his work focuses on social interaction including violence, and water in the American West. Currently he is examining the confluence of environment, history, and culture on the Llano Estacado, the southernmost extension of the High Plains. An inveterate traveler, Bogener is partial to following the blue trails and highways of the American West.

STEPHEN GRAHAM JONES

Stephen Graham Jones grew up in Greenwood, between Midland and Stanton in West Texas. After earning degrees in English and philosophy from Texas Tech, he got a Ph.D. from Florida State University, and now teaches in the MFA program at the University of Colorado at Boulder, where he's a full professor. His seven books have been set everywhere from Clovis, New Mexico, to the moon. His latest novels are *Ledfeather* and *The Long Trial of Nolan Dugatti*. Next up will be the horror story collection *The Ones That Almost Got Away*. Jones has been an NEA fellow, a Texas Writer's League Fellow, a recipient of the Texas Institute of Letters Jesse Jones Award for Fiction and the Independent Publishers Award for Multicultural Fiction, and has more than a hundred stories published, from journals to e-zines, anthologies to textbooks, and two or three essays.

WILLIAM KITTREDGE

William Kittredge grew up on a cattle ranch in southeastern Oregon and taught at the University of Montana for 29 years, retiring as Regents Professor of English and Creative Writing in 1997. Kittredge's books include a memoir, *Hole in the Sky*; and two collections of essays, *Owning It All* and *Who Owns the West* along with *Balancing Water: Restoring the Klamath Basin*, *The Best Stories of William Kittredge*; and *The Willow Field*, a novel published in 2006. *The Last Rodeo: Best Essays of William Kittredge* was published by Graywolf Press in 2007.

Kittredge and Annick Smith edited *The Last Best Place: A Montana Anthology* and were co-producers of *A River Runs Through It*. Kittredge received the Montana Governor's Award for the Arts, was co-winner of the Montana Governor's Award for Humanities and co-winner of the National Endowment for the Humanities' Charles Frankel Award for service to the humanities, awarded by President Clinton. In 2006 he was given the Chiles Award for Service to the Great Basin, in 2007 the Robert Kirsch Lifetime Achievement Award from the Los Angeles Times and in 2008 he received a Lifetime Achievement award from the Western Literature Association.

BARRY LOPEZ

Barry Lopez was born in 1945 in Port Chester, New York. He grew up in southern California and New York City and attended college in the Midwest before moving to Oregon, where he has lived since 1968. He is an essayist, author, and short-story writer, and has traveled extensively in remote and populated parts of the world.

Lopez is the author of *Arctic Dreams*, for which he received the National Book Award; *Of Wolves and Men*, a National Book Award finalist for which he received the John

Burroughs and Christopher medals; and eight works of fiction, including *Light Action in the Caribbean*, *Field Notes*, and *Resistance*. His essays are collected in two books, *Crossing Open Ground* and *About This Life*. He contributes regularly to *Granta*, *The Georgia Review*, *Orion*, *Outside*, *The Paris Review*, *Manoa*, and other publications in the United States and abroad. His work has appeared in dozens of anthologies, including *Best American Essays*, *Best Spiritual Writing*, and the "best" collections from *National Geographic*, *Outside*, *The Georgia Review*, *The Paris Review*, and other periodicals.

Lopez's most recent book is *Home Ground: Language for an American Landscape*, a dictionary of regional landscape terms, which he edited with Debra Gwartney.

JESSICA SCOFIELD

Jessica Scofield is an artist. She is a graduate of the Pennsylvania Academy of Fine Arts and the University of Pennsylvania. She lives in Portland, Oregon, with her baby daughter.

SANDRA SCOFIELD

Texas native Sandra Scofield is the author of seven novels and a memoir of her Texas childhood, *Occasions of Sin*. She received the Texas Institute of Letters Best Fiction Award in 1997, and was a National Endowment for the Arts Fellow and a finalist for the National Book Award. She lives in Montana and is an ardent landscape painter, with a particular affection for West Texas vistas.

ANNICK SMITH

Annick Smith is the author of the memoir *Homestead*, a collection of essays, *In This We Are Native*, and a history of the tallgrass prairies, *Big Bluestem*. She was co-editor with William Kittredge of the Montana anthology, *The Last Best Place*, and co-editor with Susan O'Connor of *The Wide Open—Prose, Poems and Photographs of the Prairie*. Her short stories and essays have appeared in many magazines and journals including *Story*, *Outside*, *Orion*, *Audubon*, *Travel & Leisure*, and the *New York Times Traveler*.

Smith's film credits include being executive producer of the feature, *Heartland*, and co-producer of *A River Runs Through It*. Her documentary credits include a public television series about seven tribes in the Inland Northwest, *The Real People*, as well as a portrait of poet Richard Hugo, *Kicking the Loose Gravel Home*.

Smith has taught creative writing at the University of Montana as well as numerous writing workshops and conferences. She is currently completing a dog/memoir/travel book entitled *Crossing the Plains with Bruno*. She has lived in Montana's Blackfoot Valley for many years.

WILLIAM E. TYDEMAN

William E. Tydeman currently serves as Archivist at the Southwest Collection of Texas Tech University. He completed his doctoral work at the University of New Mexico under the direction of the late historian of photography Beaumont Newhall.

FURTHER GLIMPSES OF THE LLANO

The literature on the Llano Estacado covers a wide range of diffuse material. The books listed below are only a small sample of the scattered information on the Staked Plains. They are doors that expand our perception, stimulate our imagination, and lead, we hope, to greater understanding of a misunderstood region. A quick glance at this list shows the traditional emphasis on and biases of the Anglo and settler communities of the region. There is a paucity of books on the ethnic and multicultural Llano Estacado. Much work remains.

Bogener, Steve. *Ditches in the Desert: Irrigation in the Lower Pecos Valley.* Lubbock: Texas Tech University Press, 2003.

Burnett, Georgellen. *We Just Toughed It Out: Women in the Llano Estacado.* El Paso: University of Texas at El Paso, 1990.

Brooks, Connie. *The Last Cowboys: Closing the Opening Range in Southeastern New Mexico, 1890s–1920s.* Albuquerque: University of New Mexico Press, 1993.

Carlson, Paul H. *The Centennial History of Lubbock: Hub City of the Plains.* Virginia Beach, VA: Donning Co. Publishers, 2008.

Carlson, Paul H. *Deep Time and the Texas High Plains: History and Geology.* Lubbock: Texas Tech University Press, 2005.

Carlson, Paul H. and Tom Crum. *Myth, Memory, and Massacre: The Pease River Capture of Cynthia Ann Parker.* Lubbock: Texas Tech University Press, 2010.

Cunfer, Geoff. *On the Great Plains: Agriculture and Environment.* College Station: Texas A&M University Press, 2005.

Erickson, John R. *Prairie Gothic: The Story of a West Texas Family.* Denton: University of North Texas Press, 2005.

Fields, Helen Mangum. *Walking Backward in the Wind.* Fort Worth: Texas Christian University Press, 1995.

Flores, Dan Louie. *Caprock Canyonlands: Journeys into the Heart of the Southern Plains.* Austin: University of Texas Press, 1990.

Gwynne, Samuel C. *Empire of the Summer Moon: Quanah Parker and the Rise and Fall of the Comanches, the Most Powerful Indian Tribe in American History.* New York: Scribner, 2010.

Hämäläinen, Pekka. *The Comanche Empire.* New Haven: Yale University Press, 2008.

Flint, Richard and Shirley Cushing Flint, eds. *The Coronado Expedition: From the Distance of 460 Years.* Albuquerque: University of New Mexico Press, 2003.

Johnsgard, Paul A. *Prairie Dog Empire: A Saga of the Shortgrass Prairie.* Lincoln: University of Nebraska Press, 2005.

McDonald, Walt. *Great Lonely Places of the Texas Plains.* Photographs by Wyman Meinzer. Lubbock: Texas Tech University Press, 2003.

Morris, John Miller. *El Llano Estacado: Exploration and Imagination of the High Plains of Texas and New Mexico, 1536–1860.* Austin: Texas State Historical Association, 1997.

Opie, John. *Ogallala: Water for a Dry Land.* Lincoln: University of Nebraska Press, 2000.

Smith, Loren M. *Playas of the Great Plains.* Austin: University of Texas Press, 2003.

Smith, Sherry L., ed. *The Future of the Southern Plains.* Norman: University of Oklahoma Press, 2003.

Spikes, Nellie Witt. *As a Farm Woman Thinks: Life and Land on the Texas High Plains, 1890–1960.* Edited by Geoff Cunfer. Lubbock: Texas Tech University, 2010.

Steiert, Jim. *Playas: Jewels of the Plains.* Photographs by Wyman Meinzer. Lubbock: Texas Tech University, 1994.

Worster, Donald. *Dust Bowl: The Southern Plains in the 1930s.* Oxford: Oxford University Press, 2004.

INDEX

The editors, contributors, Southwest Collection, and Texas Tech University Press are deeply grateful to The CH Foundation, whose generous support has made this book possible.

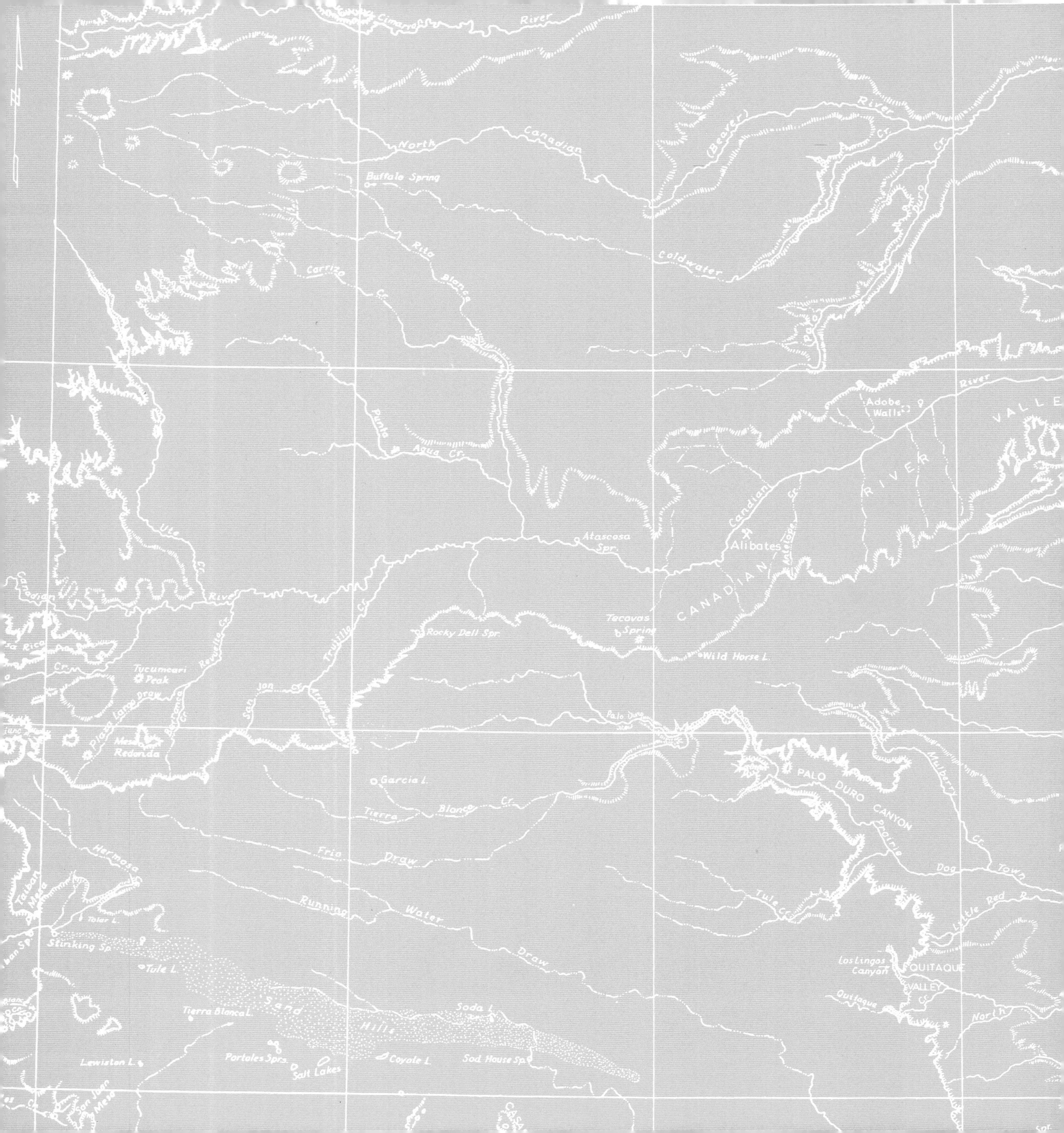

Cimarron
River
North
Canadian
(Beaver)
River
Cr.
Palo Duro Cr.
Buffalo Spring
Coldwater
Carrizo
Cr.
Rita
Blanca
Punta
Agua Cr.
Adobe Walls
River
VALLE
RIVER
Canadian
Cr.
Alibates
Antelope
Atascosa Spr.
Ute
Cr.
Canadian
River
CANADIAN
Tecovas Spring
Rocky Dell Spr.
Trujillo
Cr.
Wild Horse L.
Revuelto Cr.
Tucumcari Peak
Plaza Larga Draw
San Jon Cr.
Mesa Redonda
Palo Duro
PALO DURO CANYON
Mulberry
Cr.
Garcia L.
Tierra
Blanco
Cr.
Fria
Draw
Prairie
Dog
Town
Hermosa
Taiban Mesa
Running
Water
Draw
Tule Cr.
Little Red R.
Toler L.
Stinking Sp.
Tule L.
Los Lingos Canyon
QUITAQUE
VALLEY
Quitaque
Cr.
Sand
Hills
Soda L.
Tierra Blanca L.
North
Lewiston L.
Portales Sprs.
Salt Lakes
Coyote L.
Sod House Sp.
San Jon Mesa